Pre-Col

Influenced the History of the World

Carl L. Johannessen, Professor Emeritus

Biogeographer

Jerrid M. Wolflick, Editor
Kathleen Wheeler, Editor
Paul McCartney, Editor

First Edition 2016

ISBN: 1522732667
ISBN-13: 978-1522732662

DEDICATION

I would like to dedicate this book to John L. Sorenson, Professor Emeritus in Anthropology, and the late Carl O. Sauer, Geographer, whose invaluable research contributed to the early field of Diffusion.

TABLE OF CONTENTS

TABLE OF FIGURES

ACKNOWLEDGMENTS

I would like to thank all of the people who have supported the process under which this book came to fruition. First and foremost, I would like to thank my wife Doris. She has stood beside me through the 67 years of research, travel, and frustration that has accompanied the creation of these new ideas and the proper paradigm for the history of human civilizations. I would also like to thank my friend, Prof. Ronald Wixman; my editor, Jerrid Wolflick; my second editor and travel companion, Kathleen Wheeler; my third editor who also helps me keep the benches warm at the local coffee house, Paul McCartney; my foil, Dan Davis; my friend of many years, Jeneen Beckett; and the many others who have tirelessly helped me refine my ideas and writing so as to easily communicate with the public readership rather than the rarified readership in the academic world of geography. I would also like to thank Prof. John L. Sorenson for the many years' partnership spent in writing our more scholarly, *World Trade and Biological Exchanges Before 1492, published in 2009, and World Trade and Biological Exchanges Before 1492, Revised and Expanded Edition,* published in 2013. We have come a long way since we first began our conversation and yet the research is just beginning

.

PREFACE

The prevailing paradigm in Cultural Geography and Anthropology has been that there had been no significant interaction between the tropical and subtropical cultures of the Old World and the Americas prior to the European voyages starting in the late 15ᵗʰ Century C.E. This idea has been maintained, in my opinion, because the authorities in archaeology and anthropology have not generally been willing to hire young Ph.D.'s who believed otherwise. This behavior tended to stifle research which would have created a different paradigm. There also seemed to have been a refusal to acknowledge any research that might indicate such a paradigm shift, by claiming that the data must simply be wrong because they "thought that is was." This stance was also taken, in my opinion, because to change would have meant that the textbooks and lecture notes would have to be rewritten, and no one seemed to want to do that. In addition, by accepting the idea that a lot of earlier interaction had taken place among the non-European cultures of the world, they would have had to re-examine the cultural bias inherent in how the history of human culture and civilization was viewed and taught. They would have had to acknowledge that many ideas and processes that had been traditionally accepted to be of European invention may well have been spread by diffusion from non-European cultural hearths perhaps by a method so simple as a sailor from one tropical culture showing someone across the ocean how to perform a given process. This is what we purport to show happened in this book, and in so doing, hope to effect sufficient doubt about so called truths that have been held for centuries, that a major paradigm shift could begin to take place in academia.

Now, if you are going to be an agent of change, I understand that you will need a brilliant mentor who is willing to buck the tide even if it is rising. For me that early mentor was my professor at the University of California-Berkeley. Carl O. Sauer. Nevertheless, it seems all boats have risen on the tide of environmental determinism early in this century and we were somehow trying to assist all those craft even if they were stuck in the mud of the past. As this book will show, that has now changed. But first some background notes.

Carl Sauer began his career as a student at Northwestern University studying Geology. He became interested in the wider study of Geography and finally earned his Ph.D. in Geography from the University of Chicago. Sauer went on from there to teach at the University of Michigan and taught the traditional theory of geography known as environmental determinism. In 1923, while studying the loss of pine forests in lower Michigan, Sauer became dissatisfied with environmental determinism and started studying how humans and cultures might have influenced the environment. This was in direct opposition to the teachings of the environmental determinists. In 1925, Sauer left the geography strongholds east of the Mississippi (geography was not really taught west of the river at that time) and took a position at the University of California-Berkeley. He was influential in making geography an important subject in the West as well. He created the Berkeley School of Geography, which taught that human culture, and societies impacted the environment rather than that they were at the mercy of the environment. This idea became the foundation for the field of Cultural Geography. Sauer's students have been an important influence in Geography ever since. Sauer retired in 1957 and died in 1975. He spent his life as a dedicated researcher and fierce questioner. He had seen enough evidence of early movements of cultures that he taught us to read the landscape and its people "directly."

Later, when I met up with John L. Sorenson, a specialist in Anthropology/Archaeology who had already written an annotated bibliography on the diffusion of cultural traits (some 5,000 of them), I had already joined the fight and we forged ahead irrespective of the "torpedoes" that were coming our way. We wrote a book entitled *World Trade and Biological Exchanges Before 1492*. In that book we presented our data in charts and graphs with scientific explanations for our findings. We did this in order to show the rest of the academic world that there was a new paradigm rising out of our evidence. Of course, we had already made most of it available to scholars by publishing the data in many peer-review journals, which is the "gold standard of academic research." This academic book collated the available evidence for all the plants, animals, and diseases that we could find that had been transported to another tropical landscape across the southern oceans, and to other areas by raft or boat along the glacial ice, all prior to the sailing of Columbus We spent years poring over peer-reviewed journals for published information about species recorded to have appeared before 1492 C.E on a continent where they did not originate. These data show that the listed species of plants, animals, diseases, and parasites had to have got to the South and North American continents via a method other than the traditionally accepted one of European transport after 1492.

In that research we searched through published studies in English, German,

Spanish, French, Dutch and Russian. If we could not read the material in the original language, then we acquired the help of a professional translator to do so and what we found was more than abundant evidence for early trade and interaction between the Eastern and Western Hemispheres.

We then turned to articles written in Sanskrit, a language that is generally considered to be the religious/ceremonial language of Hinduism. We also sought cultural names and names of organisms being talked about by the people of India, who were talking in their own languages, and who were inclined to share with us. Now, while this research might be considered to be extensive, it was by no means exhaustive of all that is available. It is believed that at best we were only able to access about 20% of what is out there. This means that well over eighty percent of the historical literature on earth is still waiting to be mined for data which would show these kinds of movements. We have begun the search and now it will be up to someone else to continue it. Since there are peer-reviewed journals and magazine articles that have been and are being written in many other languages, we are sure that there is a wealth of information still to be found by anyone who would take up the cause. To this end, John and I included additional tables in the book, listing some of the species that had some, but unfortunately inadequate proof of early presence. These tables in the back of the book will give future students a strong base from which to work when they start looking for other likely species. In addition, we also included tables of plants, animals, parasites and diseases that John and I had encountered over the years while living in the tropics that did not show signs of transference, but which we figured will probably be found to have been brought across the oceans millennia ago.

In summary, for your convenience, I have included a condensed version of the tables found in *World Trade and Biological Exchanges Before 1492* in this book as well. Tables A1, A4, and A6 in the back of this book, are lists of the plant, disease/parasite, and animal species we found with definitive evidence of trans-oceanic diffusion before Columbus. Tables A2 and A5 are lists of the species for which there is some evidence for transfer but not enough to be called definitive. Tables A3 and A7 are lists of species that we believe were transferred but for which we do not yet have the evidence.

SECTION 1: HISTORY OF SAILING AND SAILING RUDIMENTS

CHAPTER 1: SAILORS AND SAILING - BUILDING THE HYPOTHESIS

THE FIRST SAILING ADVENTURES

Sailing has been a way of life for people throughout the world during all of history and long into the dim recesses of our Pre- history. We cannot say, with any certainty, when people began to sail. We can be fairly sure that soon after people settled near water they figured out a way to build rafts and float on them in order to more effectively get fish, shellfish, and other aquatic animals which they needed for food, fur, tools, ornaments and clothing. Since it is well established that early people, in fact people throughout history even to this day, settle near water sources, it would not be too much to infer that people very quickly discovered ways to utilize the water's vast and rich resources. Rivers, lakes, streams, ponds – all the variety of freshwater sources – would have been known to and utilized by early tribal peoples long before they settled in towns or villages.

When they first began harvesting the riches that existed in the water habitats, they would likely have used both logs and other floating debris to get to the deeper water and richer fishing areas. Since we humans always seem to tinker and improve on any tool we use, even if that timeline took a hundred thousand years, changes would occur and it would not have been too long before we began improving the floating logs, either by lashing them together or by hollowing them out. We can witness this creative thinking yet today while watching groups of children playing near a lake or pond. It takes only a short time to discover the usefulness of a log floating near the shore. Within a short time, most kids will be removing waterlogged boards or logs to improve their floatation and steering. If they have the tools and time, children will invariably create some form of raft from things they find floating on the water. This kind of children's summer play likely

1

mirrors what our ancestors did as they became masters of water as well as land.

Rivers, lakes, and ocean shorelines developed as important means of support and ways of life for people. It was important to develop river crossings and improve our ability to navigate coastal water both so we could effectively cross to the other shore and so we could harvest water plants and aquatic animals that we needed for sustenance or that grew near to or on the opposite shores from our villages. Just as with the modern children playing in the water, it seems obvious that these earliest of human attempts to travel on and across the water were done with bamboo or wooden logs lashed together or logs that could be mounted for short experiences on water. Soon after they settled in the area, people would have developed larger rafts of woody material that was bound together in order to transport themselves or food and other products across the water. Once they started, these innovators naturally improved the watercraft to make them watertight, large enough to transport cargo, and easier to propel and steer.

Let us take a step back in time. Imagine that you are a member of a tribe that lives by the sea. It is 100,000 years ago and your people have been gathering shellfish, hunting sea mammals, and fishing off the coast for many generations. Your people have designed boats or rafts that are safe and seaworthy. You have figured out how to use the winds and waves, and you can navigate around both during the day and at night, using celestial objects that people 100,000 years later will call stars. In the caves and on cliff faces near your community your elders have painted pictures that remind the tribe of this knowledge: how to kill the large mammals, how to find your way home from the seas, how to build your houses, etc. There can be no doubt that the people in your group are consummate mariners, at least in the shallower waters within sight of land. Although it is likely that members of your group have sailed farther out. Humans are nothing if not curious about what is over the next hill, or in this case, the next wave.

Let us say you live on the coast of what is now Southern California, and after hunting on a nearby hill, you notice, over the water, a mountain off in the distance across the ocean that you haven't noticed before. It does not seem to be connected to your land. Running down to your tribe's camp, you ask the elders how the hunting is over in that land. They don't know. After walking up and down the coast for several days trying to find a way to get over there, you decide that there just isn't any way to get across on foot. So you grab a few of your friends and paddle out onto the water under the guise of going fishing. You aim your boat in the direction of the land you saw.

Now let's pretend for a moment that we're talking about Catalina Island, which is about 22 miles off the coast of Southern California and would have been easily visible to villagers living on the coast. Of course there are many other islands just off the coast of California, but this one suits our purposes just fine. It would take two men paddling a canoe about 12 to 13 hours to get to this new land. But it is doubtful that anyone would undertake such a trip in a canoe, even back then, so let's assume they also had a sail. This would speed you up a bit, provided the wind was blowing offshore. So you arrive on Catalina. Once there you would discover that it has fresh water and animals, but does not connect at all to the land where your tribe lives. You sail back after a day or two of exploring and tell your tribe what you've found. Some of the tribe wants to move to the island. There are other tribes living in the area, with whom you have traded and into which your tribal members sometimes marry. Together a group of people, younger men and women take plant starts and other necessities and sail across the strait and set up a new village on the coast of Catalina Island. This move will now become a story in your tribe, which will be told around campfires for centuries. This story, in a few more generations, may inspire another young person to wonder if there is more land beyond the edge of the world. Sailing craft have improved and eventually someone will try to find out. You have the sun and stars for navigation (of which all oceanic fishing tribes had knowledge). Traditional social science and religious writ-

Figure 1 - Dugout Canoe Construction.
Dugout canoe construction example on the Costa Rican frontier.
Photo taken by Carl Johannessen.

3

ers of the last 500 years have been saying that this scenario is impossible, that your mariners would not have sailed your "advanced, seaworthy boats or rafts" that we know were built in your time and sail them across the oceans to explore. In fact, most of world history is currently taught with this as a truism: "No peoples prior to the Europeans of the 15th Century C.E. were able to sail outside the sight of land because they did not have a way to navigate." Remember, however, that your people have been navigating on the oceans using the sun, stars, winds, and currents for generations. We know that the early tribes had vast knowledge of the night skies simply by looking at their writings and paintings and listening to their stories. We also know that Australia, far beyond even the sight of other islands, was colonized at least 50,000 years ago, and that the colonizers likely moved there intentionally. In fact, the various islands and island chains across the Pacific were all colonized long before Columbus set sail. Furthermore, recent evidence suggests that Homo erectus, another line of the human family tree who became extinct around 143,000 years ago, sailed to islands that are 200 miles East of New Guinea.

KNOWLEDGE OF BOATS AND SAILING

In the modern world scores of people have sailed across both the Atlantic and Pacific Oceans in one-person craft, some even built specifically to ancient specifications, and without the aid of any modern technology, including the compass. These people have repeatedly successfully crossed these mighty expanses of ocean with similar technology to that of early tribes. Remember that these modern mariners would be far less competent sailors than any adult in these early tribes would have been. They sail for fun and adventure, as a hobby, while the early tribes sailed for food and other necessities of life.

The Indians, Chinese, Phoenicians, Arabs, Africans, Incas, and Mayas all had extensive knowledge of sailing as well as intimate knowledge of the fixed stars and locations of and pattern of the moving stars (planets) in the night skies. We know this from the extensive records that exist from all of these cultures. Observers in early ships would have easily recognized that the Earth was, at least curved, if not a sphere. We know that the Greek sailors accepted that the Earth was a sphere. Many early Greek writers and philosophers discussed this in books, copies of which are still available to be read. It is likely that the early Greeks got the idea of the Earth as a sphere from the past research done by the Persians and likely from the earlier empires. There is some evidence that the Chinese, by the Han Dynasty (206 B.C.E. to 220 C.E.), had a good idea that the Earth was a sphere as well. It is likely that our earlier ancestors had a pretty good idea that the Earth was a sphere, as there are telling references in many important religious and mythological works, including the Christian Bible, that give us clues to the earlier oral traditions of tribes.

Our ancestors process for creating a canoe started by assembling of a few large logs in one place so they could create several canoes at once. Since it is also likely that the first canoes were built long before the smelting of ore and creation of metal tools, we can be fairly certain that the first canoes were created by carefully building fires along the center axis of the chosen logs. The fires were carefully tended and watched while they burnt out the center of the log to create the opening where people could sit and cargo would be carried. After the fire was out and the log is cooled people could scratch out the charcoal left in the opening using either sharpened sticks that were fire-hardened or shaped stone tools. Our early ancestors would have also, not at first but as improvements happened, used the shaped stones to shape the exterior of the canoe to make it more balanced or sleek. See Figure 1 for an example.

So, why have we, the current Western World and, by extension, the former colonies of the Western powers, accepted the false hypothesis that until 500 years ago everyone believed that the world was flat and that until the advent of measuring longitude we could not sail out of sight of land. Oddly enough, the idea of the Earth being flat does not originate from ancient religious doctrine written hundreds if not thousands of years ago. It originates from a story written by the American storyteller Washington Irving when he wrote, in 1828, a highly romanticized and fictionalized biography of Christopher Columbus that included naysayers proclaiming that

Figure 2 - Dugout Canoe on the River
Traditional dugout canoe floating on a local river. Costa Rica frontier. Photo taken by Carl L. Johannessen.

the Earth was flat according to scripture. This was a common fiction writing device to increase tension in the story, nothing more. Because of Irving's stature and presence in American education and literary circles, the biography was mistakenly taken as scholarly and became part of the required education of young people across the United States and eventually most of the world. The literary device became so believed and so prevalent that after Darwin wrote Origin of the Species in 1859 several scholarly and academic defenses of the work included the "Flat Earth" concept as fact. So stubborn was this myth that in 1945 Members of the Historical Association stated that: "The idea that educated men at the time of Columbus believed that the earth was flat, and that this belief was one of the obstacles to be overcome by Columbus before he could get his project sanctioned, remains one of the hardiest errors in teaching (pp. 4-5)." Marshall Payne in the meeting of ISAC in Columbus, Georgia, U.S.A. expounded on the processes that primitive sailors could have known and been able to approximate longitude from their own celestial observations. Recently, this rigid acceptance has begun to change as modern writers and historians, for the most part amateurs, have begun to bring to light evidence of earlier visits to the Americas by Old World civilizations as well as evidence of travels from the Americas to the Old World. This evidence comes in many, many forms, some of which we will explore in this book.

The idea of transpacific or transatlantic contact between the Americas and the Old World is not only a logical idea, given the current available evidence, but it is also subversive to the, earlier, current belief systems still perpetuated by most academic and religious teachers. From the beginning of the occupation of America, the Catholic priesthood travelled with the conquistadors of Spain and Portugal described the cultural characteristics of the people that were being conquered as well as documenting and describing plants and animals that were in the area in their personal and professional journals. The priests recognized the beauty of the Native Americans' buildings, cities, and monuments (especially those in Mesoamerica), but they felt that the Christian European culture was definitively superior to the various American cultures. That sense of superiority and the philosophical mindset, later called Manifest Destiny in the United States or Catholic Dominance in Europe, of the European-descended peoples as the superior culture continues even to the present day in some educational curricula and social constructions. This institutional Eurocentrism forced all earlier academic and scholarly writers and researchers of history, historic geography, sociology, and anthropology to repeat and uphold the dominant Catholic hypotheses, if they wanted continuing employment and funding and/or secure the next grant from the granting agencies or if they wanted to be published through the peer-review process and advance their academic careers up to and including tenure. This has led to a Eurocentric Worldview, even among the many non-European countries who were once European colonies (most of the world). It is actually fascinating to note that some of our most powerful evidence of transoceanic diffusion of plants and animals is from the meticulous notebooks of the literate priests, especially from the scholarly Society of Jesus (Jesuits), traveling with the conquistadors.

As with any overarching and dominant view, there are visionary researchers who, in the face of every obstacle, push forward through the cobwebs of old and accepted ideas to move humanity into the future. It is, after all, the duty of scientific researchers to continue to ask questions and seek answers. Every prevailing theory or dominant idea leaves much unknown and yet to be discovered areas of fruitful research. In the field of the history of civilization, Archaeologist Dr. Betty Meggers' and Geographer Carl O. Sauer were two amazing visionaries, whose view that human cultures and civilizations had to have interacted across both oceans long before the 15th Century C.E. directly opposed the leading theories and ideas of their day. Many of the old or traditional theories are still prevalent in both education and in the research community to this day. The study of the maritime interaction between civilizations that arose across the oceans from one another is a vast study covering branches of science as diverse as Zoology and Linguistics, Botany and Art History, Semiotics and Geography. (Semiotics is an important field of study for this book as it is the study of how humans create meaning from the input streaming into our brains from our senses. This includes sign, symbols, language, and gestures just to name a few.) As with any scientific endeavor that spans so many different areas of science, there are actually quite a number of peer-reviewed articles already published that demonstrate evidence for a robust interaction between civilizations and cultures across the oceans long before the European Expansion beginning in the 15th Century C.E. These scientists recorded their observations of the world around them based on the evidence that they found in the field rather than what they had learned in the books. These observations contradicted the established 'truth'. These researchers included people like Carl O. Sauer, Thor Heyerdahl, David Kelley, Jim Parsons, Gunnar Thompson, John L. Sorenson, Steve Jett, Svetlana Balabanova, Alice Kehoe, and Bill Woods. The search has also included several notable amateur researchers such as Gavin Menzies, S. A. Wells, and Demetrio Charalambous.

After I looked at 150 years of already published evidence as well as going to India, China, Columbia, Mexico, Guatemala, and Honduras among other locales to re-verify the older published articles and discover new evidence, it seemed indisputable that a great deal of sailing between the hemispheres had occurred prior to 1492 C.E. Only researching cultural traits that may have been passed across the oceans allows the traditional researchers to claim something called "parallel evolution," the idea that humans trying to fix the same or a similar problem will likely come up with the same or similar solutions. We decided to look at whether or not their plants and animals had existed in common between civilizations across the tropical and subtropical oceans. If there was evidence that species were present before 1492 C.E., then we had to look at just exactly how the species got across the oceans. Mapping and researching the dispersal of plants and animals across intervening ocean expanses from one hemisphere to another – including possible occupation of islands in between – is the most effective method of identifying and confirming that transoceanic sailing was much easier than has been believed by academics in the West. We chose this method because most world-renowned evolutionary biologists agree that a species can only arise in one location on the planet, and that this will happen only once for a given species. If a species is found in some other part of the world, then it had to have been transported there somehow. Did they walk? Were they herded? Were they carried? How did they get moved? In the case of species being found on the same landmass, we can assume that they very likely were transported overland, although this may not be true in every case. But how did they get moved across the tropical oceans? If the only explanation is that people took them across the oceans on rafts or in boats, then the old ideas and paradigms, which said "nay" to this, must fall in the face of this new revolutionary, if circumstantial, evidence to the contrary.

In a recent dramatic discovery in Crete, Dr. Thomas Strasser, archaeologist from Providence College, discovered irrefutable evidence of open sea sailing on the Mediterranean Sea over 175,000 years ago. This evidence was in the form of hand axes which are very similar in style to old Acheulean stone technology originating with pre-humans in Africa. The stone tools date back to at least 130,000 years ago and since Crete has been an island for more than 5 million years, it would be safe to postulate that the people who sailed there either brought the tools with them on their rafts or created them on the island, or some combination of the above. Although all the researchers agree that more study needs to be done to establish the exact dating of the sites and the tools, it is reasonable to state that we have been sailing for a very, very long time. One of our early ancestors sailed out into the Mediterranean Sea and came upon an island. This mariner was able to get back to where his or her tribe was located and tell them about it, but was also able to navigate back to the island. This shows a very sophisticated knowledge of the stars, the ocean currents, nautical distances, and understanding of the principles of navigation.

With these discoveries and thoughts starting to generate new possibilities and ideas we can begin to consider how current research and evidence can influence the development of these ideas. For instance, there is nothing in biological science more complex than the structure of the DNA of living creatures with the millions of chemical bonds in the chromosomes of each organism. Using the powerful tool of DNA chemical testing and gene sequencing, we can strengthen the evidence for early transoceanic diffusion by tropical mariners by doing the genetic testing on available samples from the various archaeological sites around the world. Granted, DNA analysis is costly, but in order to change the paradigm and create a more inclusive theory, it seems that the money would be well-spent. We absolutely establish the reality of early diffusion when an organism has been found on both hemispheres dating to before 1492 C.E., and which have the same genetic makeup. If the dated tissue and its DNA from the archaeological remains indicate that the species had been domesticated (plants or animals that have been altered by people to make them more useful to us) then it is even more valuable for showing intentional transfer. Domesticated species began from a wild ancestor and the wild ancestor can only have evolved originally on one continent, as has been repeatedly stated and shown by renowned evolutionary biologists worldwide.

THE ARRIVAL OF COLUMBUS

According to eyewitness accounts recorded in written diaries, logbooks, and letters home from the seas, the earliest contacts with Columbus's sailors and the aboriginal Arawak tribes of the Caribbean were friendly and cooperative. The sailors, it seems, were especially enamored with the idea that the local women were their own bosses when it came to intimate sexual relations. The female was in control in these matriarchal and matrilineal people. That was a type of human society that the Catholic Spaniards were not acquainted with, and found fascinating. Anacaona, the chieftain of the part of Hispaniola where Columbus first made contact was apparently attracted to Columbus, and he to her, although there is no evidence that their relationship went any further than attraction.

Columbus decided to return to Spain from the Greater Antilles (Puerto Rico, Cuba, and Hispaniola) to engage in some much needed politicking with the King and Queen of Spain, hoping he could amass more funds for future sailors and soldiers to fuel his exploits. He left one of his ships and the crew on the north shore of Hispaniola to continue exploring the area. Unfortunately, the people he left soon realized that they could become fabulously wealthy from the seeming abundance of gold and people who they could enslave, both on Hispaniola and in the rest of the New World. They apparently began to mistreat the Arawak Natives. The cooperative, friendly relationship between the Spaniards and Arawak disintegrated and by the time Columbus returned from Europe the Arawak tribes rose up and killed the Spanish crew. Until a few years ago, it was accepted throughout the Western educational establishment, except by a few, who were termed, fringe theory radicals, that the Columbus contact was the first contact between the Eastern Hemisphere and the Western Hemisphere. No reputable "establishment" researcher accepted that there was any possibility that earlier cultures, except possibly a minor interaction by the Norse in Northern Canada or possibly in the Great Lakes region, had ever crossed the vast Atlantic or Pacific Oceans and interacted with the peoples of the Americas or vice versa. Researchers in the last 150 years who brought up evidence showing at least some form of contact between the tropical peoples of the Eastern Hemisphere and the Western Hemisphere had occurred were marginalized, ignored, and informed that such contact was impossible because no culture prior to the 15th Century Europeans had ever created the necessary technology to make these voyages across the open oceans. The "establishment" researchers continued to say this in the face of mounting evidence to the contrary, including numerous voyages by modern explorers in small ocean crafts – often far less sophisticated than those used by the ancient Phoenicians, Indians, Arabs, and Chinese, as well as the Maya and Inca – sailing across these vast oceans without relying on any technology beyond ancient Greek or Incan technologies was indeed possible.

CUTTING EDGE RESEARCH

We are on the cusp of a revolution in understanding the history of the ancient world, even the history of civilization itself, and the extent to which we owe early sailors and explorers from tropical cultures around the world for our modern civilizations. There is now overwhelming evidence that long prior to the Spanish entry into the New World, cultural aspects, such as religious, technological and philosophical traits had been exchanged between various Eastern and Western Hemisphere tropical and sub-tropical cultures. There are currently a number of researchers working in this budding and important field. A few of them are introduced below.

John L. Sorenson is an influential anthropologist, archaeologist, and researcher in this controversial field. From the beginnings of his academic career Professor Sorenson was interested in creating an accurate chronology of Mesoamerican culture based solely on the archaeological record and evidence from ancient sites. John pursued this goal throughout his entire academic career and continues to explore it after his retirement. One aspect of his research included gathering every article he could find which referred to any evidence of early interaction between the Eastern and Western hemispheres. Working with Doctor Martin Raish (a librarian at the David O. McKay Library at BYU), Professor Sorenson collected these peer-reviewed and published articles and books, created an indexing system, and wrote detailed abstracts showing how the article related to early transoceanic diffusion. In 1990 he and Raish collated their notes and published them as Pre-Columbian Contact with the Americas across the Oceans: An Annotated Bibliography. This two-volume work details 5000+ articles that include many types of cultural characteristics and physical evidence of cultural traits as well as plant, animal, parasite, and disease diffusion between the Eastern and Western Hemispheres beginning over 8,000 years ago. These articles both supported and detailed this diffusion prior to the 15th Century C.E. and rebutted those which defended the status quo and argued against early diffusion. John and Martin were careful to illustrate both sides of the debate. In 1996, Sorenson and Raish revisited their monumental work and reviewed every article from the original text. They added many other articles found in the subsequent years and removed articles that did not meet their new and stricter criteria. They then published a second and revised edition. The annotated bibliography includes an index that has every subject that has ever been suggested as a diffusion topic anywhere in the world so researchers using the books can quickly locate the articles of interest to their research. Since 1996, many more articles and a number of books have been published in this field, accessible through Google Scholar or other online search engines, and they can be perused for more and new insights in early transoceanic diffusion.

The relatively new journal <u>Pre-Columbiana</u>, edited by Steve Jett, should also be searched. Other journals that are also influential in publishing in this area are: NEARA Journal (New England Anthropological Research Association), ESOPS (Epigraphic Society, Occasional Papers), and the Midwestern Epigraphic Society, Occasional Papers, Migrations and Diffusion, etc. All of these explore and publish new discoveries about diffusion across the oceans before 1492 C.E. The first two look at research from around the world, and the last one focuses on the Americas. We should not leave out the mainstream magazines such as National Geographic Magazine, The Smithsonian, The Atlantic, Ancient American Magazine, and Scientific American which have begun to publish these types of often previously rejected discoveries in long established journals. The recent change of attitude about the old and broken paradigm allows these more popular scientific magazines to accept the modern changes. This change of attitude makes it easier for the public to begin to accept Professor Sorenson and my book, <u>World Trade and Biological Exchanges Before 1492, Revised and Expanded Edition</u> (2013), which shows that diffusion occurred through the use of biological evidence. In this book, we bring together research evidence from both academic professionals and gifted amateur researchers showing that plants and animals (including the important domesticated ones) have been transferred from the tropical and subtropical cultures of the world across the oceans. We found 128 species of organisms that had previously been definitively documented in the literature, which had simply been ignored by the scientists who had claimed that there was no proof of travel across the oceans by tropical and subtropical mariners!

The initial evidence for the diffusion of these domesticated entities, along with several wild varieties of weeds and other perhaps accidental transfers, is found in the multitude of archaeological sites across the Old World and the Americas. It is true that the case for the domesticated organisms will go back around 15,000 years, which started in Southeast Asia with vegetatively reproduced plants like the banana or sugarcane. Fifteen thousand years ago is currently the accepted date for the beginning of the domestication process, since dogs were among the earliest of domesticated species. Remember that the plants and animals that were taken by sail from tropical lands were not previously present on the other continental hemisphere. The eminent Harvard evolutionary biologist Stephen Jay Gould (1941- 2002) said that the likelihood of a species of wild plants independently evolving in two separate locations on the earth was so astronomically small as to be considered impossible. This sequence of diffusion events is also true for wild species that are now considered weeds. The date for early domestication may be pushed back further as researchers continue to expand their archaeological searches to South and Southeast Asia and Central Africa.

Carbon 14 (^{14}C) dating by archaeologists who have recorded their discoveries or by botanical information from sculptures, bas-reliefs, or paintings, written literature, and artwork that have been discovered in temples and burials of the artifacts have shown that all of these species were present in the hemisphere not of their origin prior to 1492 C.E. The most likely explanation that includes all the evidence we have discovered is that there was intentional and repeated contact between the tropical civilizations of the world long before 1492 C.E., and that this contact was by sailors, mariners, and ocean- going traders. This interaction is what carried the organisms and cultural traits across the oceans.

Historical literature from the various civilizations and cultures has detailed descriptions of plants and animals present in these new locations. This literature includes religious texts, flora and fauna catalogs, literary texts, and other writings of the time. Another valuable source of historical literary evidence was the records, notebooks, diaries, and letters written by the very first European explorers and priests soon after they made contact with new locations in the tropical world. These were locations where Europeans claimed they had not had contact before 1492 C.E. (by Columbus's crew) in the Americas and 1498 by Vasco de Gama in Calcutta, India.

Sanskrit, the Hindu's holy and religious language, has not added nouns (other than loan words) to its vocabulary since around 1.000 C.E. Moreover, since Sanskrit is a religious language, nouns that are in its vocabulary were added when the object became part of the religious life of the subcontinent Indians. A plant that just arrived with the Europeans would not warrant such treatment, as Hinduism is a very conservative religion when it comes to adding new elements. When the name of plants in Sanskrit is found to be similar to American names for the same plants, it is likely to mean that the names of the plants and animals of old are still being carried to the present. This is especially important in the case of the 50 plants that originated in the Americas and were also found in India. That these plants have been enfolded into Hindu religious life by 1000 C.E. means that the plant was introduced to the region far earlier. This allowed for the time necessary for the plant to gain religious significance in this new land. A search for names in the common regional languages of the time would likely turn up similar words. These names would have been transmitted by the very early traders and explorers upon interaction with the receiving culture whenever that exchange occurred.

One of the alternate ideas proposed by researchers opposed to the idea of early transoceanic contact between the tropical and subtropical cultures is that the species were transferred when the peoples first migrated across the ice/land bridge connecting Asia with the Americas over the Bering Strait. However, very few of these useful plants show any trace of ever being located in the temperate and arctic regions of the Americas. There is no evidence whatsoever that these plants were ever in any lands outside the tropical and subtropical regions where they are found in current archaeological sites. This indicates that the plants were not transported across the "Ice Bridge" or "Land Bridge" during the earlier migrations of people into and back from the Americas. Moreover, the earliest dates of transfer that we have thus far discovered is about 9,200 years ago from certain parasites that could not have survived in the population (due to the lifecycle requirements of the parasite) during a migration across a long defunct Ice/Land Bridge. These species crossed the oceans by boat from one tropical or subtropical culture to another in the other hemisphere. The farmers of India and Latin America were in contact with the mariners who knew the habitats and cultivation requirements of the transferred plants. American plants in India, for instance, are found in the same and proper ecological habitat that they are found in Mexico or Peru, which was their original location, and vice versa.

Although cultural traits are considered by many researchers to be less conclusive evidence for early diffusion due to the idea of parallel evolution; in conjunction with the overwhelming physical evidence in the form of various wild and domesticated species along with certain diseases and parasites we can begin to see how cultures interacted and what they gave to each other. Many important religious traits were imported from the Middle East and helped formulate similar characteristics in the Mexican cultures that existed as far south as Honduras. For instance, in a 2009 paper, John Sorenson provides 300 different traits that indicate past contact between the Middle East and Mesoamerica. These exchanges produced significant similarities in the cultures of both peoples that can only be explained by direct contact over significant time periods in the millennia before the coming of the Spaniards. Much contact over a long period was necessary for these multiple traits to have successfully become established within these cultures.

No matter what sailing route was used to take the plants to the Old World and ultimately for them to arrive in India, the mariners and traders, as well as the local populations, recognized the organisms needed to be planted in the appropriate ecological niche, one similar to the one from which it was taken. Therefore, the plants were cultivated in those locations by the local farmers, also possibly the returning mariners, as they made their way back to their homes throughout India. For plants moving from the Indian Ocean area to the Americas, the same held true. These tropical mariners and traders on both sides of the oceans were the explorers and risk takers in the international trade of the time and we in the modern age ought to give them the credit they deserve for their innovative thinking and risk-taking.

The literature of the ancient Greeks, Minoans, Egyptians, Indians and Chinese substantiate these contacts out of the East without including specific information as to travel routes across the seas. No ship's captain wanted anyone else gaining knowledge of their routes, ports of call, cargoes, or trading destinations. Keeping the actual trade routes and trade port locations secret was likely the modus operandi in the marine world trade 1,000 - 8,000 years ago. It gave the pilot and/or captain a certain advantage over those trying to break into the business. This is a reasonable assumption to make given that we still do not possess many actual pilots' log books even though it is well-documented that most   pilots and/or captains surely had one or more of these books (rutters or books of rhumb charts, or charts and books showing the safe navigation routes between ports.). We do not even have many examples of these charts from the post-1492 era of European sailing. Moreover, as trade was very competitive, we also know that maps were purposefully drawn with minor inaccuracies to throw off competitors. This extreme secrecy was true throughout not only early European trading powers and activities, but likely also during other maritime powers and activities. These types of records exist in tiny numbers among many of the early tropical marine trading powers or known sailing societies (Minoan, Greek, Arabic, Indian, Chinese, Polynesian, Incan, and Mayan, among others). From the dearth of information and lack of these documents, we only have secondary sources for some of this information; we can conclude that routes and passages to trading partners anywhere in the world were carefully guarded secrets.

We can postulate from what we now know of the patterns of currents and winds what the probable trade routes that the rafts and ships would have used during their transoceanic travels. Sailing before the wind was the only logical way to cross the oceans in sailing craft before Columbus. The modern atlases and charts of these patterns make it possible to predict what those routes were. The Trade Winds had to have been followed in the early days from east to west across the oceans. The only rational way to sail from west to east across the Pacific and Atlantic Oceans was to sail in higher latitudes and follow the ocean currents or to sail north or south to the Roaring Forties. The stronger westerly winds found in the southern hemisphere between latitudes 40° and 50° would have been the easiest route to take. Many sailors doubt the use of the Roaring Forties by early sailors as these winds are considered to be too violent for safe travel. Nevertheless, these wind patterns tend to set ecological limits to possible routes for sailors. This holds true except in the Tropical Monsoon regions of the world where the winds change direction every six months. No matter, it is still more rational to sail with the winds at your back.

John Erlandson, Professor of Anthropology and Director of the Anthropology Museum at the University of Oregon, hypothesizes that the human occupation of North Western America was done by paddling in small craft. He postulates they traveled on the south edge of the Pacific Coast margin of the ice, at the edge of the continental ice sheet out over the Pacific margin during the glacial expansion of the Pleistocene Era. Professor Erlandson thinks that this is the most logical way for immigration to occur, as there would be abundant sea mammals and fish in the forest of algae attached to the bottom of the ocean in front of the ice. They could move on either the water or the snow and ice across the Bering Strait on any winter's day throughout the cold times of the Pleistocene Era. During the post-Pleistocene Era the Bering Strait was frozen every winter so it does not matter what the sea level was, high or low, whether it was covering the exposed land or not. Even to this day, the Bering Sea freezes over every year. In fact, the newer thoughts

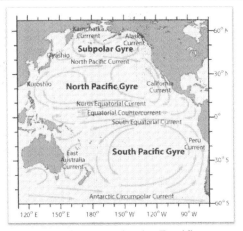

Figure 3 - Currents in the Pacific Ocean.
This picture shows the major ocean currents of the Pacific Ocean. These currents are crucial to successful sailing between the continents.

15

suggesting that these maritime explorers from Southern Asia may well have sailed with the wind, blowing their crafts in the 'Roaring 40s'. The wind at their back would have allowed them to pass the Aleutian Islands and Alaska and then Northwestern North America to Central America. This hypothesis is likely correct.

From Mexico, South to Peru, the sailors surely sailed, tacking as needed, as far as Peru. But they surely sailed with the Trade Winds at their back to East Asia (China) and South Asia (India) when they left the Americas. If this route was in fact used regularly it would have allowed the discovery of the islands in the Pacific on the way, just as Thor Heyerdahl suggested. The Pacific Islands were likely originally occupied from the east with the currents and the winds pushing the sailors across the Mid-Pacific Ocean, even if they missed most of the islands that later became known as Micronesia and Polynesia. The education of the sailors as to the location of the islands would have been made in this way, which is much more logical than tacking into the trade winds to discover everything in the Pacific when they first began to hunt for ways of obtaining plants and animals to replace supplies on their sailing routes back to Asia. See Figure 3.

It is hard to know much about the actual sailing technologies and routes of the ancient peoples. Trade, then as now, likely was a very secretive and secured profession. One would not want the competition to get its hands on his maps, routes, trade lists, and the like. We know that the European sailing pilots had coded books filled with their routes, notes, current information, maps, and stops. This level of secrecy probably existed through most of the early history of transoceanic trade as well, especially when the trade dealt with very rare or valuable items. However, since trade and travel between the tropical societies of both hemispheres began long before the current paradigm indicates, it follows that some of these documents may have survived. The fact that the Mayan equivalent of a university library at Merida, Mexico was burned by the Spanish conquerors, specifically on Bishop Pedraza's orders and possibly for the same reason that the famed Library at Alexandria in Egypt was burned, creates a tremendous gap in our understanding of the history of world knowledge, including possible references to transoceanic trade between the Mayan Empire and the Old World. We are left with trying to find the bits of evidence that may still be available to piece together the tropical history of the world.

CHAPTER 2: ANCIENT GLOBAL OCEAN ROUTES

Was it possible for a meaningful flow of ideas and cultural traits to cross the oceans in ancient times? The belief among many scholars that humans did not have the capability of navigating and sailing across the major oceans before the present era has been a major block to the acceptance of the large amount of cultural data that has accumulated indicating that they not only had the capability but did in fact sail across the oceans. Furthermore, there is evidence that ancient humans have carried the new developments of existing high civilizations in both directions across the oceans. The rejection of this data, because of the belief that people could not possibly have come in sufficient numbers and with a specific intent to establish expansions of a new cultural base, has greatly confined thinking about Amerindian and European as well as Asian and African cultural origins and exchanges.

The belief that transoceanic voyages could not have been managed prior to the development of sophisticated sailing vessels around the time of Columbus in Europe first came under question many years ago. In the early 1800s Alexander von Humboldt suggested that there was trade between the hemispheres. Orator F. Cook, in his monumental work The Origin and Distribution of the Cocoa Palm, showed that both the sweet potato and two kinds of hibiscus (*Hibiscus tiliaceous* and *Hibiscus rosasinensis*, known as the Rose of China) had been carried out of the Americas into the Pacific Ocean still bearing their American names. These domestic plants, whose seeds are incapable of floating across salt seas, were present in early times on both sides of the Pacific. Furthermore, to survive in a new homeland such plants would have required humans with the knowledge of how to propagate, cultivate, harvest, and prepare them for use. Any domestic plant, whether used for technology, as with cotton, or for food, as with maize, had to have been introduced by human's familiar with its characteristics.

Throughout his career as a botanist, entomologist, and agronomist for the US Department of Agriculture (eventually the Principal Botanist) O.F. Cook discovered and listed several domestic plants that have been present both in the Old World and in the Americas since long before Columbus. He specifically stated that, "the existence of these two seedless plants [sweet potato and banana] on both sides of the Pacific in prehistoric times goes far to demonstrate former human communication by means of more extensive land masses, or through greater nautical skills, across seas commonly deemed impassible to primitive man" (Cook, 1901, p. 273). Cook further noted that these plants, among others, allowed researchers to strongly infer that the plant exchange occurred entirely in the tropical and warmer subtropical regions. This realization led him to the following insight:

For the present purposes, it suffices to remember that the actual introduction of plants by human agency discounts in advance all objections on the grounds of distance and difficulties of communication, and justifies the fullest use of biological or other data in tracing the origin and dissemination of agricultural civilization in the tropics of both hemispheres. (Cook, 1917, p. 437)

We could simply accept this statement and then go on to other research questions related to diffusion without discussing the direct issues this theory raises. However, the problem of how such voyages may have been made would still remain. This chapter focuses on the evidence and issues of early voyaging by prehistoric and earlier historic mariners. We will first briefly discuss the ocean winds and currents that exist across the Pacific and Atlantic Ocean so everyone can understand the actual conditions through which our early mariners would be voyaging. After this, we will discuss the various nautical issues, such as hull types, sail types, navigational aids and requirements, and supplies. Lastly, we will discuss the five navigable maritime routes to and from the Americas.

THE OCEANS, THEIR CURRENTS AND WINDS

If voyages were being made across the oceans in early times, the first requirement in understanding how this travel could have been done is to know something about the oceans, their currents, winds, and their influence on the routes and the technology of the time.

CURRENTS. The unequal heating of the equatorial areas relative to the arctic regions provides the power for the winds and waters in motion. Once started on a poleward or any path, they become subject to the Coriolis Effect. The Coriolis Effect is a complex physical occurrence involving motion, rotation speed, and flow, but can be fairly easily explained as follows: The water and air on Earth flow around the planet in currents. The speed of the planet's rotation is faster at the equator than at the poles. This difference in speed creates a situation where the currents in the air and water curve away from the equator (to the right in the Northern Hemisphere and to the left in the Southern Hemisphere) causing the familiar air and water currents we see when we are watching the weather on the TV news. Of course land masses and temperature play a part in creating these currents as well, but the Coriolis Effect is important to the creation of an ocean environment on which early humans could successfully travel long distances. In the Northern Hemisphere, all ocean and air currents, once started, will flow in a clockwise direction, while in the Southern Hemisphere will flow in a counter-clockwise direction. Various parts of this continuous circulation have local names: The Gulf Stream, the California Current, the Kuroshio Current, the Humboldt Current, and the Benguela Current for water, and the Jet Stream, the tropical Prevailing Westerlies, the Polar Easterlies or

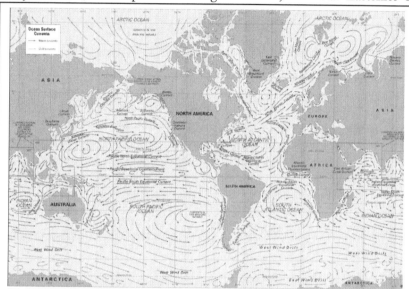

Figure 4 - All Major Ocean Currents on Earth.
Red Arrows indicate warm water currents while Blue arrows indicate cold water currents. Map used with permission.

Polar Hadley Cells, and the Roaring Forties for wind.

One minor exception to this rule that has led to major misunderstandings is the so-called Equatorial Counter Current. When a strong wind from one hemisphere blows across the equator, it sets in motion a series of events that leads to a temporary current running counter to the prevailing trade wind- powered current in the equatorial regions. In older atlases, this current was often portrayed as a broad continuous current running west to east just north of the equator. Modern atlases also show it as a narrow current running intermittently from west to east. It originates in Indonesia and flows towards the Americas in the Pacific Ocean. However, even this modern depiction is misleading, for the crossing of the equator by a strong air mass is episodic. The resulting current is discontinuous both in place and in time, and it is limited to a relatively small area and with slow speeds at any given time. Thus, it cannot be relied upon for continuous travel. Its average rate is one mile per hour, and the latitude in which it occurs is that of the equatorial side within the Trade Winds, whose average rate of flow is between 15 and 25 miles per hour. Any ship attempting to sail eastward by using this current would be overwhelmed in its effort by the much stronger Trade Winds. Currents averaging only one mile per hour are weak forces compared to the vigorous winds.

WINDS. For some purposes, a very simple diagram of wind circulation over the oceans would probably be sufficient, but for considering issues of early voyaging, a more in depth analysis is desirable. At a minimum, one must consult the January and July maps for winds and currents. For more detailed study the United States Navy charts of the Oceans are available. They give wind and   currents and sailing conditions month by month with the data presented by ten-degree squares as these movements shift with the change of maximum heat from the sun, as the vertical sun at noon shifts north and south. The observations and conclusions given here are based on such study.

The winds are subject to the same laws of physics as the currents, but being more fluid and moving more rapidly they show more extreme differences in response to seasonal changes. Large high and low pressure cells are the dominating forces in each ocean, and these shift greatly from January to July. Most scholarly atlases show these winds and currents well, giving the major shifts in the great high and low pressure centers and their accompanying winds as they change with the seasons.

In the northern Atlantic in winter, an intense normally low pressure at the Earth's surface lies just below the southern tip of Greenland and dictates the wind pattern of that area. The Westerlies are intensified and dominate in the northern Atlantic down to 35 degrees north latitude off the North section United States coast, slanting northeastward toward the North Atlantic over on the English Channel. In January, a greatly reduced high-pressure cell lies to the southeast, opposite the Strait of Gibraltar in mid ocean. Of particular interest is the fact that the winter pattern increases the flow of westerly winds from the vicinity of the hump of Africa towards northern South America, and the Northeast Trades then extend south to the vicinity of the mouth of the Amazon River. In July, the winds change so that the low of the North Atlantic is greatly reduced, and the Westerlies are weaker, shifting north to about 40 degrees north latitude. In summer, the high cell strengthens and moves north. The winds from North Africa then barely reach northernmost South America but flow strongly into the Caribbean.

In the North Pacific, similar shifts occur. In January, a low develops near Siberia, and a weak high lies near the latitude of California in mid ocean. The Pacific low is weaker than the North Atlantic low, and the seasonal shifts are less. The dominating factor in the Pacific in July is the great high-pressure system that moves north carrying the Westerlies to the latitude of the state of Washington. The start Trades then have moved north to the latitude of northern Baja California.

In the southern hemisphere there is far more ocean than land masses, and at all times the high pressure cells dominate the weather in the mid ocean, shifting primarily north and south with the seasons. The changes in location of the winds are correspondingly smaller, and the winds are more reliable, and fiercer in the Southern Roaring Forties, than they are in the northern hemisphere. During all seasons, there is a steady flow of wind from the tip of South America toward the Cape of Good Hope. North of that, in July, the Southeast Trades over the Atlantic are strong and reach south to the mouth of the Amazon River. Thus, the North Atlantic and South Atlantic Trade Winds, in alternate seasons, flow towards the vicinity of the mouth of the Amazon River or to the north to the Lesser Antilles.

The Indian Ocean is somewhat different. The northern quarter is north of the equator, the rest south of it. In January, the Indian Ocean winds are influenced by the enormous cold in Siberia and the Himalayan Mountains, and the resulting high pressure causes strong out-flowing winds. At the same time, strong winds also flow from south of Arabia towards Madagascar. In summer, the intense heat that extends from Arabia across northern India and into the area south and east of the Caspian Sea area creates a huge heated low-pressure system with the rising air and strong winds. This low draws strong winds across the Indian Ocean from the latitude of Madagascar into the interior of the Indian subcontinent in a great eastward curving sweep that keeps south and west of the high Himalayas and finally ends in Siberia. This system with its annual reverses provides the monsoon winds and precipitation six months later. It should be obvious then that winter offers the most favorable winds for sailing southwest out of the Indian Ocean and toward the Cape of Good Hope. Summer is the best season for sailing eastward in the Indian Ocean to India and on to Indonesia from Madagascar.

Before discussing the specific ocean routes that existed in ancient (and modern) times, we will explore the issues involved in navigating through the winds and currents of the world's oceans. Different types of and complexities of sailing crafts have been used throughout the ages to travel across bodies of water. Different types of craft had different advantages and disadvantages in the process. Rafts, without sails, are totally at the mercy of currents and winds and may only go where these currents take them with the mariners being able to make slight corrections and changes with centerboards as well as pole oars. With the addition of sails, more speed is gained, but more maneuverability is not achieved until centerboards, rudders, and eventually keels are added. The ancient square-rigged sailing vessels allowed mainly downwind sailing, and the simple square sails changed little over a long expanse of time. This type of sail restricted long distance sailors to only what could be accomplished following the winds and currents around the oceans.

TYPES OF SAILING CRAFT

RAFTS. Most probably, the first watercraft was the reed-bundle raft. The only materials required to construct such a craft are reeds or similar light materials that can be bundled up and tightly tied together with vines. The significance of the reported presence of humans on Flores Island, located in Indonesia half way between Java and Australia, 800,000 years ago is relevant here. It has long been thought that in Indonesia mammals were not able to pass the deep channels separating the islands beyond Java from the

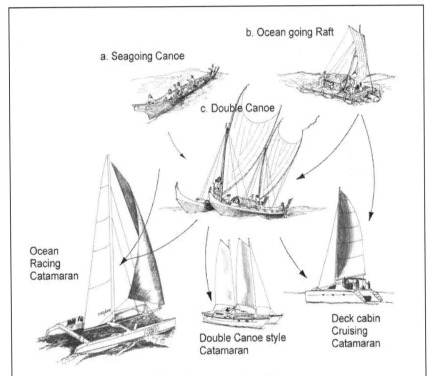

b. Ocean going Raft

a. Seagoing Canoe

c. Double Canoe

Ocean
Racing
Catamaran

Double Canoe style
Catamaran

Deck cabin
Cruising
Catamaran

Figure 5 - Evolution of the Ocean-going Canoe.
This picture shows how the canoe evolved from its basic design to one that was ocean-worthy and able to sail long distances across the oceans. Used with permission.

Sunda Shelf, which was dry land during periods of glacially lowered sea levels. During the periods of extensive global glaciation, mammals were able to occupy the Shelf, but the deep channels remained impassable to the higher mammals. Alfred Russell Wallace (1859) first recognized the significance of this line, and made its significance known in his book. However, it is now known that humans did cross several of these deep-water passages. To do so requires a craft of some kind. The most likely candidate is a reed-bundle or perhaps the bamboo raft. These craft were and are widely distributed around the world still today. Simple forms of such craft are still in use by the Tasmanians, for example, to travel as far as 5 miles offshore in order to reach islands they wish to visit. They are also still in use by an Amerind group in the Gulf of Baja California, the Seri, and by yet other groups on the Santa Barbara Islands, on Lake Titicaca by a Bolivian group, and on the Pacific by the indigenous people of Chile. The evidence for humans on the Indonesian island of Flores, which dates back 800,000 years makes it clear that these Lower Paleolithic people (Homo erectus), among other Homo species, were capable of crossing sizeable expanses of water. The reed or bamboo bundle raft, or perhaps balsa log rafts most probably provided the means.

Heyerdahl's reed ship, the Ra II, with which he crossed the Atlantic in 1971, was simply an improved version of this type of primitive raft. Bamboo rafts, used originally by the Asians, are related to log rafts, but bamboo logs are smaller and lighter than the green balsa logs used earlier by Heyerdahl when he caught the world's imagination with his Kon Tiki raft.

Today, bamboo logs that approach the diameter of small telephone poles can be obtained. A raft constructed of poles of such girth would be a light, seaworthy craft and it would not lose buoyancy. Heyerdahl's ponderous balsa raft was inhibited in its inability to maneuver easily by its size. It made only two miles per hour with one mile per hour credited to the ocean current and only one mile per hour due to the sail. Against a one mile per hour ocean current, no progress would have been made. Bamboo rafts are credited with speeds of three miles per hour, but while rafts with square sails were clearly limited to going with the currents and the winds, with the addition of dagger boards these rafts could tack a few degrees into the wind. We will discuss dagger boards in a later section of this chapter.

DISPLACEMENT HULLS. Displacement hull craft gain buoyancy by displacing water with the shape of the craft. They can be described as a watertight hole in the water, and their buoyancy factor is related to the mass of water displaced. Unlike rafts, they are more easily sinkable, but they are also relatively light and faster. The hull as it passes through the water makes waves in thrusting water out of its way. The boat is subjected to the square root law, which states that the limit of speed for a displacement hull is equal to the square root of its length times 1.3. The underlying limiting factor is that, wave making friction, increases as speed increases. This effect can continue until the wavelength from crest to crest matches the waterline length of the craft. Then the craft just sits in the trough of the wave and further speed is not attained.

This relationship assumes a perfect hull shape, minimum friction, and sails of perfect design. Since the state of perfection is never realized, the simplest strategy for design of a primitive craft is to apply the square root rule and ignore the potential for added speed. Thus a thirty-six-foot ship has a potential speed of 6 miles per hour. A one-hundred-foot ship's potential speed is ten miles per hour. Even modern 60-foot yachts do not attain their potential speed, except under ideal conditions and for short distances. Long distance voyages by modern yachts with the latest fore and aft rigs only average about 5 miles per hour on long trips. This is because the usual wind variations that are met over any considerable length of time during which winds can vary from strong to weak to calm; or even shift into a headwind. One cannot use the square root law to project the length of a voyage over any great distance.

Hull shapes have been derived from experience and adjusted for the uses to which their crafts were intended. For safety, a bowl- shaped bow ensures that the craft will rise on meeting a wave, thereby minimizing the amount of water coming aboard. For speed, a sharp bow is advantageous, but when meeting a wave, the tendency of a sharp bow is to dive into the wave, thereby taking on large amounts of water over the bow. The Norse and the Greeks used sharp-bowed war vessels, where speed was desired, and broad-bowed merchant vessels for greater safety and carrying capacity.

Chinese displacement hulls developed by following a different path from western displacement hulls and their study supplies one of the best examples of either stimulus or independent invention. The Chinese developed their displacement-hulled craft from rafts, which were the earliest type of sailing vessel in both China and Japan. Building up the sides and ends of a raft created a vessel with blunt ends. Solid bulwarks replaced the framing used in western displacement hulls. The word 'junk' carries the wrong connotation when applied to these Chinese craft, for they displayed many innovations in design, such as watertight bulkheads in the hull, freestanding masts, plural masts, adjustable depth rudders, ingenious methods for furling sails, with through-going battens. The Chinese junk is an efficient and seaworthy vessel.

Joseph Needham is tightly bound to the printed page, and this limits his discussion to relatively late time periods. However, referring to linguistic sources, he finds that the junk was fully developed by the Shang Dynasty (1500 B.C.E.). The actual time of appearance of the junk is unknown, but the Japanese were reaching the Americas by 3000 B.C.E. using sailing rafts, so we may conservatively estimate the appearance of the junk at between

3000 and 1500 B.C.E. The development of hulled craft progressed from a dugout, to which planks were added. As planks were added, the need for bracing was met by inserting frames after the hull was completely formed. Shipwrights only belatedly developed the custom of first framing up the hull and then adding the outside planks for the bulkheads. Egypt and Sumer both possessed large displacement vessels by 3000 B.C.E. The Chinese, the Mediterranean peoples, and the sub-continental Indians each held to their own way of building complex hulls.

KEELS, DAGGERBOARDS, ETC. A square-rigger sailing downwind has little problem with side thrust, for all thrusts come from behind the craft. However, when sailing somewhat upwind, wind on the sail is only part of the complex of forces that drive the ship into the wind and create side thrust. Side thrust on the sails is transferred to the hull from the mast. In fore and aft rigged ships, these side forces increase as the angle of attack into the wind becomes sharper, and they tend to drive the hull down wind, thus offsetting some of the up wind gain. The resulting departure from the desired course due to this effect is called the leeway and it results in less than the steered course being achieved.

Obviously, it is advantageous to limit this loss of potential up wind gain. The solution can vary, depending only on the hull to resist the side thrust, to resorting to a number of more efficient devices. Seemingly, the earliest of these was the use of a steering oar. Increasing the area of the steering oar would increase the resistance to the side thrust. This discovery led in some places to the use of greatly enlarged steering oars that were subject to increased breakage. The Polynesians sailing craft apparently never got beyond that technology.

On sailing rafts, it is possible to thrust a long thin board down through the spaces between logs or the cut bamboos used for planking. Technically, boards used in this manner are called 'dagger boards'. Many are found in graves on the coast in Peru. A dagger board may be a single board, as on the three-log raft such as the jangadas, a traditional fishing boat used on the open ocean in isolated areas of Northern Brazil that consists of an improved raft design with a single mast using a lateen sail. This type of vessel is still in use in the open ocean off Brazil and India. It is unlikely that these craft originated in Brazil. One school of thought places them originally in Greece as the ship on which Ulysses sailed in Homer's Odyssey. Another group feels that it likely came from India along with the parasites and trade goods we will look at throughout the rest of this book.

For the great sailing rafts four dagger boards were used, two toward the bow and two near the stern. With this multiple dagger board system there is no need for a rudder, for, by balancing the forces acting on the sailing raft, any course can be established and adjusted by moving the dagger boards up or down in the bow or in the stern. With appropriate use of these boards, such rafts can be tacked and sailed upwind if also equipped with fore and aft sails. Later, other devices were introduced: centerboards, great-hinged leeboards, and finally the modern deep keels. But these devices all developed too late to be significant for our problem of getting chickens to the Americas and coca to China.

THE CAPABILITIES OF SAILS

Sailing is not as simple as merely tying a cloth to an upright pole and letting the wind push the craft forward. There must be a means of controlling the direction of the craft. Men had to learn how to erect a mast and brace it by tying it with ropes to withstand the force of the wind on the sail. For all reed-bundle craft, erecting a mast was a large problem often solved by using a bipod mast. Finding the best position for the mast—central, aft, or forward—and many other problems had to be solved.

Seeking a solution to the challenge of sailing upwind gave rise to many kinds of fore- and aft-sailing rigs, all of which allowed for pivoting the sail to present its surface at an angle to the wind. The differences in efficiency of different types of sail in sailing upwind are diagrammed in Figures 5 and 6. The ability of the later full-rigged square-sail ships to sail upwind was

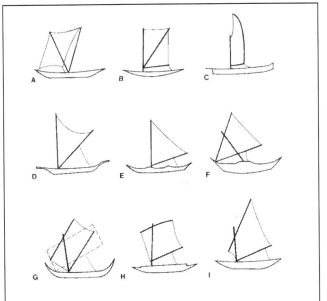

Figure 6 – Principal Austronesian sail types
A, Double Sprit from Sri Lanka; *B*, Common Sprit or Boom from the Philippines; *C*, Oceanic Sprit from Tahiti;
D, Oceanic Sprit from the Marquesas; *E*, Oceanic Sprit from Sulu; *F*, Crane Sprit from the Marshall Islands;
G, Rectangular Boom Lug from the Moluccas; *H*, Square Boom Lug from the Gulf of Thailand; and *I*, Trapezoidal Boom Lug from Vietnam.
Used with permission

due to their using jibs, staysails, and gaff rigs attached to the forward or aft mast. These adjunct sails gave the 'square riggers' modest upwind capability. The time of the first sails is unknown, but there is no doubt that the simple square sail was the earliest. The ancient square- rigged sailing vessel allowed only downwind sailing, and this type of rigging changed little over a long expanse of time. The spars that carried the sails laterally could be hauled to an angle to the wind to a very limited degree, and this limitation affected the sailors' ability

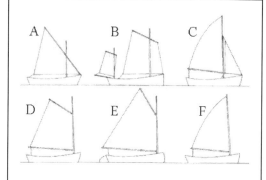

Figure 7 - Western Rigging Sail Types
A, Lateen Rig; B, Lug Rig, Dipping Lug Mainsail, Standing Lug Mizzen; C, Sliding Gunter Rig;
D, Gaff Rig; E, Gaff Rig with High Peaked Gaff; F, Bermudan Rig, Marconi Rig, Jib Headed Rig, Leg of Mutton Rig Used with permission.

to vary the course while sailing downwind. This type of sail limited long distance sailors to follow the winds and currents around the oceans.

The lateen sail and its relatives all carry part of the sail before the mast and the rest aft of the mast. These arrangements are all relatively inefficient, allowing the boat only to point 18 degrees toward the wind. To gain one mile upwind requires five miles of lateral tacking. Although the lateen rig is only halfway along the route to the fore and aft rig, it does give a craft vastly improved ability in lateral sailing. Lateen sails were important for exploring the Central Pacific but are believed to have contributed little to the development of Amerind culture directly. This, however, may be an inadequate judgment on our part.

The average Atlantic Ocean crossing is 3000 miles; the average Indian Ocean crossing is 6000 miles; and the Pacific Ocean crossing from San Francisco to Japan on the great circle route is 6000 miles. A great circle route is the shortest route between two points on the earth's oceans. A Great Circle route is a route that allows sailors to travel the least distance from one port to another.

If one were to draw it on a flat map, it might look longer but that is because the Earth is a slightly flattened projection of a sphere. Notice that the route does not go over the bulge of the planet, rather it goes around it. This means that no long voyage ever follows a single straight line or a single compass bearing, but deviates from a fixed course to adjust to the continuous variation of the winds and relative location on the Great Circle.

Table A - Sailing Rates

Log raft	2 mi./hr.	48 mi./day	1,440 mi./mo.	2 month s
Bamboo raft	3 mi./hr.	72 mi./day	2,232 mi./mo.	1.33 month s
Displace ment hull	5 mi./hr.	200 mi./day	6,000 mi./mo.	.5 month s

The craft available and the sails capable of reaching the Americas prove not to be a problem, but they do define the routes that could and could not be taken by whatever kind of craft with whatever type of sail. Also important would have been the time of year when the voyage occurred.

NAVIGATION AIDS AND TECHNOLOGIES

Although traditional scholars have insisted that no significant sailing outside the sight of land could have been done by people until the advent of a method of measuring time accurately enough the determine Longitude (the imaginary lines running from the North to South Pole on the globe), there is a great deal of evidence that tends to undermine this belief. We know that humans populated many islands that are out of sight of land as long ago as 60,000 years for Australia. As far back as 200,000 years ago Homo erectus another and earlier species of humans crossed the Pacific Ocean at least as far as two islands beyond New Guinea. New Guinea is already far beyond the sight of the mainland and these islands are far beyond the sight of New Guinea. Homo sapiens were only just evolving into a separate group in Africa at this time. Early humans living near the ocean would have been master sailors since they would have had to learn the skills in order to successfully harvest the ocean's bounty. We have a lot of evidence that our ancestors were quite knowledgeable about the stars and the motion of the planets in the form of highly complex beliefs and practices that required extremely accurate measurements of the moving stars (planets) and fixed stars. In order to cast a natal chart for astrology (an important and precise practice that led to modern astronomy) the practitioner was expected to be able to accurately measure where the planet would be in a zodiac sign to half a degree (an accuracy few people today could accomplish by looking at the sky without modern instruments). This accuracy and the importance of astrology to most ancient ocean-going tropical and subtropical societies around the world shows that the ancient peoples had very sophisticated techniques for looking at the sky. These techniques would easily transfer to complex and advanced celestial navigation processes that would allow sailors to not only sail outside of the view of land, but to navigate very accurately from one location on the globe to another. Remember that the Flat Earth idea was a fantasy dreamed up by Nathaniel Hawthorne two centuries ago.

SEA ROUTES TO THE AMERICAS

There are only five routes to the Americas: the North Pacific (followed by both Chinese and Japanese and sometime the Indians from the subcontinent; the North Atlantic (followed by the Norse, Celts, Basques and probably the Red Paint People); the tropical North Atlantic (followed by Columbus and all other Mediterranean peoples using the Trade Winds, early and late); the Cape of Good Hope (followed by the Sumerians, East Africans and peoples from India and Indonesia); and the later Central Pacific (followed by Polynesians) using a lot of tacking.

NORTH PACIFIC ROUTE The North Pacific route has long been known by the Asians. This sea route, as it crosses the ocean from Japan or China to the West Coast of North America, lies along the coast line, which was also close to the great circle route by an accident of geography. It then continues on down along the Pacific coast of the United States, Central America, and as far south as Ecuador. Near the latitude of Acapulco, there is a gyre that provides a route further south on its outside, and, on its inside, a route back from Ecuador to Mexico. Also at this latitude, the winds and currents swing west to form the Trade Winds, thus providing a route back across the ocean towards Asia. This route is well known to archaeologists and has often been referred to by scholars with knowledge of sailing.

On the voyage towards the eastward, the route runs for a great part of its distance in the stormy Westerlies. The Manila Galleons' difficulties with it are reflected by the difference in time required for the return crossing from the Philippines via the Northern Westerlies and the easy voyage out to the Philippines sailing before the Trades. The voyages to America were frequently attended by delays so lengthy that the crews faced starvation. In one such voyage, the whole crew was lost, and the ship came sailing down the American coast without a living soul aboard (Schurtz 1959). Perhaps the ship had been caught in the Doldrums on the way to the Americas.

NORTH ATLANTIC ROUTE Despite its high latitude – Greenland's tip is at 60 degrees north and Iceland is only a little to the south – the North Atlantic route also lies in the domain of the Westerlies flowing from North America to Europe. These winds create problems for Europeans sailing for North America. Nevertheless, Europeans did navigate (seemingly by paddling) those stormy seas in both directions. There are frequent shifts in wind direction from southwest to east, and during summers to strong northwesters. It is not unusual to experience all three winds within a ten-day period. These wind shifts require that a ship shorten sail in adverse winds and set sails in favorable winds and paddled or rowed in between. However, these winds play a small role in the tropical Atlantic areas of particular interest to our study.

In the Atlantic, the Trade Winds blow on both sides of the equator steadily towards America from Europe and Africa, depending on the season. The distance is relatively short: 3000 miles. For sailors coming from the eastern Mediterranean, an additional 3000 miles would have to be added. In ancient times, sailors from anywhere on the Mediterranean shore could have taken the winter Trades from the Strait of Gibraltar to the Americas, for, at that season, the North Atlantic High shifts from a more northerly zone in the North Atlantic towards the southeast. The only objection to this possibility is that Mediterranean sailors in that era were not accustomed to sail in the winter. But in summer, Mediterranean sailors could have used the more northerly belt of the Trades and have returned to Europe by the northern Westerlies. Columbus did it this way on his first voyage, so he must have known about the route from earlier sailors. He certainly did not return the way he had arrived.

SOUTH ATLANTIC ROUTE "It is surprising that this South Atlantic route to South America has not been generally noted by navigators before, although Carl Johannessen first brought to my attention the potential for a sea route between the Indian Ocean and the Americas via the Cape of Good Hope," according to George Carter. Sufficient recent knowledge of cultural relationships between these widely separated regions has appeared to compel a serious analysis of this route.

The northern Indian Ocean is in the area of the annual storms known as the monsoons. The seasonal reversal of winds associated with the monsoon is suggested on Map 1 by the arrows pointing in both directions in the northern Indian Ocean. During the winter monsoon, the winds will carry a ship from anywhere in the northern Indian Ocean westward to the latitude of Madagascar, where the Mozambique current flows towards the Cape of Good Hope at the tip of Africa. Here, the Agulhas gyre, a local counterclockwise circulation, can aid the navigator who stays inshore going west and offshore returning east. From the southwestern tip of Africa, the north-flowing Benguela current, located to the west of Africa, eventually feeds into the westward-flowing Southern Trades once you are in the tropics. These winds would land a voyager on the coast of Brazil. A branch of the Southern Trades swings north along the eastern coast of South America and provides entry into the Caribbean Sea, still with favorable winds and currents depending on the season. The return route to the Cape of Good Hope could have been made by running with the Southern Westerlies, which can be picked up at the latitude of Rio de la Plata in Argentina. The navigator would have had to stay north of the main stream of the South

Atlantic Westerlies in order to avoid the full blast of the Roaring Forties and Howling Fifties. In summer, the monsoon winds along the eastern coast of Africa could have been ridden northward and eastward back into or across the Indian Ocean from the Cape of Good Hope. Or from the tip of Africa, a ship could have sailed toward Australia in order to pick up winds for the completion of the return.

This route to the Americas could have successfully been used by any people living along the coasts of the Indian Ocean, or any people having access to the Indian Ocean from Arabia, Mesopotamia, or Southeast Asia. Sailing westwards from India to take advantage of the winter monsoon, the winds would be favorable all the way except at the Cape of Good Hope, and the temperatures would be moderate in the mid-latitudes.

From the Sunda Straits (between Sumatra and Java), the distance to the Cape of Good Hope is 5000 miles. From there to the hump of Africa is 3000 miles, and the Atlantic leg to South America brings the distance from the Cape to the Americas to 8000 miles. To go from Recife, Brazil, on to Mesoamerica adds another 2,000 miles, for a total voyage after leaving the Cape of Good Hope of about 10,000 miles. This distance corresponds to the distance to Mesoamerica from Japan.

SOUTH PACIFIC ROUTE This new hypothesis does not change the significance of the North Pacific route, but it does present an entirely new and interesting set of possibilities. On the American side of the tropical region of the Pacific, on both sides of the equator the dominant winds are the Trade Winds, blowing towards Asia. They are notable for steady direction and a force of 15 to 25 miles per hour. They extend at least 20 degrees both north and south latitude depending a little on the sun and season. A craft sailing east from Indonesia or Polynesia heads directly into these strong, steady Trade winds. The restriction imposed by the prevailing winds resulted in the islands of the central and south Pacific remaining inaccessible to Asian sailors until the Polynesians developed the lateen sail and could sail upwind through a maneuver called tacking. Proof of the islands' isolation from human contact lies in the fact that when Polynesian sailors finally did reach them the islands were inhabited by several species of flightless birds which generally only evolve indisputably in the absence of humans.

The equatorial counter current, which has been discussed above, is no help to a voyager trying to evade the Trade Winds. With the relatively weak ability of the lateen rig to sail up wind, it is difficult to understand how the Lapita (Polynesians) people with their early sailing managed even to reach the islands of the central tropical Pacific. Perhaps, as Finney suggested in his 1985 article, Anomalous Westerlies, El Niño, and the Colonization of Polynesia published in the journal American Anthropologist, they used the occasional El Niño's to penetrate into the central Pacific, but even in El Nino years, it would have been impossible to reach farther east than the central Pacific. Once a central location, such as Samoa or the Tuamotos, had been reached, lateral sailing would have made adjacent islands reachable. But the winds opposing eastward sailing are truly formidable, and even modern yachtsmen, after sailing in the Tuamotos and enjoying Tahiti, dread the long sail back to the Americas against these winds. They often look for a buyer for their yacht, and fly home instead.

There is a considerable amount of literature on efforts—mostly unsuccessful—to use the wind and current systems to cross the southern Pacific heading east. As referenced earlier, the finest treatment of this subject is found in Heyerdahl (1980). He catalogues the successes and failures of some recent voyagers who have attempted this route. However, Heyerdahl thought that the Southern Westerlies route was too dangerous for ancient voyagers to have used successfully most of the time.

It may be instructive, however, to consider in more detail the prospect of getting out into the Pacific. To navigate eastward through the islands of Indonesia, broadly speaking, is difficult. A route into the western Pacific and then on to the Americas could have been navigated from the Indian Ocean only if the voyagers had sailing rigs adequate to slip between the islets and islands to Australia. From there, holding close to the eastern coast of Australia, sailors would have had to head south until they reached the latitude of the South Island of New Zealand. Then, they could have sailed east, riding the equatorward side of the Westerlies toward South America. But this route runs through a narrow corridor all the way. Traveling too far north would take a ship into the Doldrums where, with little consistent airflow, it could have been becalmed for long periods. Traveling too far south would take a ship into the aptly named Roaring Forties, which blow uninterrupted past the continents from the Indian Ocean, across the Pacific, and on to the Atlantic Ocean.

INDIAN OCEAN ROUTE In the Indian ocean travel to and from India, Malaysia, Indonesia and Australia would be the major concerns. Much of what we discuss in this book has to do with travel to and from these important places. The two major currents which would dominate travel in the Indian Ocean are the Northern Equatorial Current, which flows from the Persian Gulf area past India to Indonesia and the Southern Equatorial Current, which flows from Indonesia to the southern edge of the African continent. As we have discussed earlier, the prevailing winds change every six months with the arrival and departure of the monsoon season, but further discussion of those winds is perhaps warranted here.

There are two major wind patterns that dominate in the Indian Ocean and one who might wish to sail across this ocean must be mindful of them. They are the Northeast Monsoon Winds and the Southwest Monsoon Winds.

The NE Monsoon winds are prevalent during winter in the northern hemisphere, or from about November to March. They usually maintain a wind force on the Beaufort scale of 4-5 (13- 28mph) and are considered to be moderate to light winds or breezes. These winds are mostly cool and dry, so a perfect time to sail from Northern Africa to India or Indonesia and beyond would be in the early part of the year when the Northern Equatorial current is at its slowest (1-2 mph) but compliments the prevailing winds.

The SW Monsoon winds, on the other hand, are hot and humid and generally bring torrential rains with them. They are also stronger winds ranging from 7 to 8 on the Beaufort scale, or 30 to 48 mph. These winds

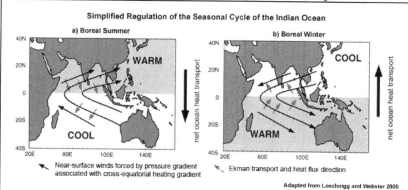

Figure 8 - Monsoon Cycles in the Indian Ocean
These two charts show the summer and winter directions of the near ocean surface winds in the Indian Ocean. Used with permission.

blow from about May to September or October. These winds blow in the same general direction as the NE Monsoon winds, i.e. from North Africa to SE Asia.

If one had sailed this route in ancient times and wished to return to North Africa he would have to take advantage of the Southern Equatorial current and wind, which cross from Indonesia to Madagascar and South Africa. Sailing from Australia via Chagos to East Africa or Madagascar would best be undertaken in the period of the Southeast Trade Winds, which blow from about April to November. This route would also take advantage of the mild Southern Equatorial current which flows in the same direction. From Madagascar one could take advantage of the Madagascar current which flows south along the coast of East Africa in the direction of South Africa.

One could also sail from Northern Australia via Christmas Island, Cocos Keeling thence via Mauritius and Reunion and end up in East Africa. This route is fairly safe during April to June and mid- November before the Cyclone and rainy monsoon season begins. This is still a well-known sailing route and any ancient mariner would have been aware of it.

SEAFARING AND TRADING

Approximately 5,000 years ago the developing civilizations of Mesopotamia and Egypt engaged in considerable seafaring and trading, first with India, and then a millennium later, following up leads resulting from the Indian trade, with China. An additional 500 years later, the high civilizations of the Americas reached full development after a slow and gradual beginning. However, as we will see in a later chapter, Southeast Asians with four specific parasites visited South America as far back as 9-10,000 years ago. We have discovered evidence of all four parasites in the same sites in interior Brazil. The remains in these sites, at least of Ascaris parasites, date to at least 9,800 years ago. Writings and depictions in the tombs, temples, and pyramids of these cultures, which have not been thoroughly researched so far, should entice young scholars to begin the study of them and the languages in which they are recorded. Deciphering these ancient languages and scripts will produce valuable evidence when specialists undertake comparative studies designed to show how each culture derived from and influenced the other. For instance, as we will discuss in a later chapter, there is epigraphic evidence of Chinese writing on boulders in the deserts of the United States Southwest. These glyphs are sentences, not single word characters, according to John Rushcamp. There is also evidence of Chinese writing on sculpted figures found in South America.

Ocean travelers always carried with them much of the world's knowledge. Trading vessels, as well as overland caravans, traveled across the then known world and thus rapidly and exponentially expanded man's knowledge of other cultures and ideas across the globe as it continues to do today. Trade developed between the Middle East and Asia, Africa, and even the Azores, a tiny speck in the middle of the Atlantic Ocean, and all the way to the Americas. The isolated location of the Azores, suggests that sea traders, at least from Europe, had already traveled extensively and had the necessary knowledge of navigation to land on a tiny island in the middle of the Atlantic Ocean long before Columbus and certainly before recorded history.

The famed Phoenicians extended their contacts to the entire Mediterranean Sea and around Africa early. They began the trade of metals such as gold, copper, bronze, and brass, as well as weapons to supply their maritime needs. During the height of the Chinese, Indian, and Roman civilizations, ocean trade continued to expand. The Indonesians, for example, developed extensive trade networks and extended colonization at least as far as Madagascar, whose language is closely linked to Javanese. The Indian Ocean became known as "a traders' sea," as people from western India sailed to southern Africa by the tens of thousands to work in the gold mines found there. The notion that the Polynesian and Malay peoples, who spread north to Japan and the intervening islands as well as east to Hawaii, the Marquesas, and Easter Island, could not have reached the Americas is almost humorous. However, that has been the hypothesis believed as dogma by United States academia in Anthropology, Archaeology, and History. The arrival 7,000 to 10,000 years ago in South America by Southeast Asian mariners may have occurred before Polynesia had become known.

It is important to recognize that the discovery process was a multilateral development. Mainly American crops (and their weeds) were taken across the oceans of the world to locations where those plants and animals would grow and thrive. However, the Spaniards, for example, when they arrived with ships in the Pacific Ocean did not discover Easter Island until the Inca priesthood had given them precise sailing directions. Even then, the Spanish mariners had trouble finding that tiny speck of rock, named Easter Island by the Spanish, in the Pacific Ocean. At the earlier times, the Polynesians were sailing with huge wooden ships carrying families, warriors, pigs, chickens, dogs, food, and trade goods for colonization of new-found lands, or simply for visits to known islands. Rats were commonly present in these cargoes and they were eaten as protein on the trips. In a later chapter we will discuss the possible diffusion of rats and other fauna in more detail.

In modern times, Thor Heyerdahl, a respected archaeologist and anthropologist, created rafts in an indigenous style from sketches and plans as recorded in illustrations by Spanish conquistadores. He proved that balsa logs or reed rafts could be used to cross any ocean and to carry chemicals, plants, and animals in those crossings. If Heyerdahl could travel such distances on rafts, surely the sleek, fast Polynesian ships could have made the trip to the Americas and back even more easily. The abundance of American crop plants and weeds found in the eastern islands of the Pacific (also discussed later in this book) indicates that maritime folk had traversed these eastern stretches of the Pacific Ocean many times.

Currently, developing evidence strongly suggests that the Olmec civilization on the Gulf coast of Mexico derived from the Shang People of Chinese origin who entered Mexico on the Pacific coast near Oaxaca and migrated to the Atlantic coast within a century or two. The Olmec culture was in full bloom roughly during Roman times and as it spread south, other Central American cultural elements fused with it. The exchange of crop plants with the Mediterranean region, which we will discuss in the next section of this book, may also have resulted in the Egyptian influences that are still evident in the so-called Indian languages such as the Mixe and Zoque of the Gulf region of Mexico today. The colossal Olmec stone heads that attest to the presence of Negroid facial features in the leaders of that region are good evidence for early cultural contact as is the agave fiber from Mexico found in the Mediterranean Sea area. Prickly pear cactus and annona (custard apple) from Mexico – both rich sources of vitamin C – were carried in ships to the Old World by sailors who probably recognized them as substances that would prevent scurvy and its deadly consequences. It is possible that mariners even raised crops, such as pineapples, in pots on board their ships for the same reason. Documentation of the presence of these plants on the other side of the ocean from early times can be used as evidence of early contact even though the mariners who carried them may have had minimal or no letter writing abilities. But I digress and all of this will be discussed in detail in later chapters of this book.

CONCLUSIONS

Looking at the above data regarding prevailing winds and currents as well as established sailing routes, we can say definitively that it is unlikely that any major cultural influences were carried from Asia across the Pacific via the "Central" Pacific. It is obvious that the early peoples living around the Indian Ocean could not effectively have reached the Americas by trying to take a route over the central Pacific. All traffic, both eastwards and westwards between the present-day nations of Indonesia, Vietnam, Cambodia, Burma, India, and ancient Mesopotamia on their way to the Americas, sailed before the wind on rafts and boats via the Cape of Good Hope, the North Pacific, or South Pacific Routes. All the earlier assumed trans-Pacific voyaging, by which, as we shall see, blowguns, bark-paper making, and great varieties of art and architecture typical of India and India's colonies in Cambodia, Java, and Bali—as well as plants and chickens—reached the Americas, now appears much more likely to have gone via the Cape of Good Hope or the North Pacific Route. It is up to those who still think otherwise to document the nautical equipment that could have been used to overwhelm the winds that blow so relentlessly away from the Central Americas into the tropical Pacific as do the Trade winds. The Cape must have seen a lot of traffic and it would be reasonable to look for more traces of this travel. Given the wealth of evidence that we will discuss in upcoming chapters about plants, animals. diseases, and parasites being transported across the oceans in early times, it would be absurd to believe that these same travelers did not also bring with them their cultural norms. Moreover, if they saw something that they thought would be useful or interesting to their society back home, it makes no sense to believe that they didn't ask about it and learn it. When people of different cultures interact, there is much information and knowledge shared. Since it is reasonable to accept that these voyages were fairly regular and that traders likely repeated the trips on more than one occasion, it seems reasonable to believe that friendships and trust would be built up over time. People like to communicate with others and we are very curious about the world around us. Isn't it possible that the aboriginal American peoples initially treated the European sailors with kindness and welcomed them because they were used to travelers arriving from across the oceans. The story that these early contacted tribes did not even see the European ships has no real basis in scholarship. It is far more likely that they were simply confused because the European ships looked significantly different than the rafts that they were used to seeing. However, where the Spanish and Portuguese mistreated the local inhabitants in selfish and greedy ways, they had their welcome removed.

SECTION 2: FLORAL EVIDENCE FORTRANSOCE-ANIC DIFFUSION BEFORE 1492 C.E.

CHAPTER 3: AGRICULTURE AND THE PROCESS OF DOMESTICATION

It is likely that the practice of saving some piece of the root that had been dug up for food by putting some of it back in the ground to show their deity what they would like next year has been common to most tribal people for the last 50,000 years. We can infer this from the Australian aborigines, who are still at this level of modifying plants. They are an extremely traditional culture and it is unlikely that they will change their lifestyle rapidly, so long as they remain isolated. All the tuberous food plants probably fit into this method of harvest and vegetative replanting.

We have found manioc starch grains on the grinding stones of the early hearth sites in the tropical region of the Amazon. Although he modern technology of starch identification on stone tools is in its infancy, we have begun creating a detailed database of plant starches to use for identifying starches on more stone surfaces, such as the starches of corn found on grinding stones in French Guinea and St. Thomas. The early development of grinding and extracting starch from the tuber of manioc is the logical place to look for the first of the domestication process in America. If the harvesters put a piece of the plant in the ground, it grows and reproduces the maternal tissue; so the technology has come down to us today. This is the first step to becoming farmers. Plants that reproduce by out-crossing, pollen that is traded between plants of the same species, are very difficult to reproduce and obtain the same quality of plant every time. A popcorn plant with large and tasty kernels, for example, might get pollen from another type of corn plant with small and soft kernels and the new seed produces a corn ear with large and soft kernels, not the popcorn you were trying to reproduce. Therefore, early farmers would have likely used another method of planting and reproducing plants that they wanted to continue growing from that type of plant. This other, previous method is called vegetative reproduction; branches being able to develop root systems when put into the soils and tended. In this method a piece of the plant, such as a piece of the root or a cutting of sufficient size, is actually just pushed into the ground where it will root. Because this cutting is the same as the plant from which it was taken, it will grow into exactly the same type of plant. For example, a tribe finds that it likes the olives on a certain tree in the valley where they are living. Instead of planting the olives seeds (which, as we have already mentioned, may or may not produce exactly the same fruit), the farmers cut several branches from the tree and plant them. These branches will root and the resulting trees will mature far faster than if they had planted seeds and also will produce fruit that is exactly the same size, shape, and taste as the tree from which the branches were taken. Many early cultivars, plants or groups of plants that were chosen for cultivation because of desirable traits, are plants that easily vegetatively reproduce. They include grapes, olives, some fruit trees, sweet potato, sugar cane, figs, banana, potato, pineapple, and Bixa (red-dye producing plant) among many others.

As the farmers became more sophisticated in their observations of the plants that produce consistent fruits over generations, they were able to plant a larger variety of plants and get a better or at least similar harvest from year after year. Although the farmers were not yet aware that these plants reproduced by self-pollination (the process where a plant pollenates its own flowers thus passingon the same genetic material generation after generation), they were aware that they continued to produce a similar type of fruit in each succeeding seed planting. This observation and advancement was very important in the development of human civilization as it allowed tribes to quit wandering either as hunter/gatherers or as pastoralists and settle down in one place. The process of human settling allows for the rise of more complex and advanced forms of civilization to come into being.

Only two to five percent of all plants are monoecious (are capable of self-fertilization without a vector such as wind or insects). These plants have an advantage for the farmer who wishes to reproduce hybridized plants in that these plants are most likely to maintain any improvements that have been made. Because it pollinates itself the plant will reproduce the desired fruit variety for which it was planted in the first place, barring random mutations, of course. Since some of the grains that would have been important for human settlement are self-pollinating – including wheat, barley, and rice – early man's discovery of this fact allowed domestication and can therefore be said to be among the most important discoveries in human history. For the first time humans had plants that produced consistent fruits and gave bountiful harvests with characteristics that they wanted from seeds. Moreover, we discovered that by selecting the grain plants from the best parts of the field's production was how the farmers made their selection of the next year's seeds. This activity insured them a good harvest, the weather deities willing of course. Other than grains there are several other old food plants that are self-pollinating, such as: tomatoes, lima beans, kidney beans, peanuts, and chili peppers.

Oddly enough, the two grains most important to Northern European survival, oats and rye, are not self-pollinators. As wheat and barley were moved out of the Fertile Crescent and into Europe, farmers discovered, much to their dismay, that these grains did not grow well in the colder climates that make up the climate north of Mediterranean Europe. Interestingly, the two weed grains, oats and rye, thrived in the moist, colder climates and began to dominate the harvested grain crops. Both rye and oats were annoying weeds in the Fertile Crescent and warm countries of Iran, Iraq, Egypt, Turkey, and the Levant. They were weeds that the farmers were trying to get rid of. Yet in the cold north countries of Europe, where the traditional staple grains could not grow well, they became the staple of the people. These two grains are both wind-pollinated, but responded to the horticultural seed plantings even with the wind-blown pollen.

In the aboriginal Americas, the process of using the vegetatively reproduced plants first set the stage for planting in the horticultural style of handling the reproductive material, be it a seed or vegetative crop. From the beginning, when maize, a wind-borne pollinated plant, arrived as a potential seed crop it was planted from the best few ears harvested the prior year. It was planted one group of seeds at a time by poking a hole in the prepared earth with a stick and dropping three, four, or five seeds into the hole. After a time, the technology and understanding of controlling the mixing of the wind-borne pollen occurred along with mastering the techniques of seed handling. This allowed farmers to select for color, kernel shape, starch type, and ear shape, among other maize traits. Many religious and cultural beliefs and rituals became associated with the process. All of this activity and understanding allowed for a faster and vast improvement of the maize crop in the Americas. In the end, this institution allowed for the growing of monstrous ears that filled the corn stalk with more and larger ears per stalk than the ancestors of wild popcorn had. In Asia the farmers did not recognize that wind brought about pollination in maize so they did not select maize seeds effectively for?

A very common method of controlling the uncontrolled spread of wind-borne pollen involved the people of your village who selectively cleared patches of the forest in which to plant the corn. This reduces the likelihood that the corn will be pollinated by a different variety of the crop. If corn is planted in the clearing surrounded by trees, then it is far less likely that pollen from the more distant community's, possibly different cornfields, would blow into the field and pollinate your corn. The villages in the immediate vicinity of your village likely had very close variants of the same corn types, therefore cross-pollination between them was not a disaster. Each region likely had slightly different variations of the corn plant, one that they had created through careful selection. This not only created regional variations in corn seed, but also gave the villages in an area something to trade with more distant villages. For example, let's say that your village grew a very large- eared yellow corn and red popcorn, and the village across the lake grew a smaller-eared black-kernelled corn among other varieties. Since your village group wants to maintain the integrity of your corn varieties, it would be unlikely that you would ever plant the black- kernelled corn or the other varieties from the other village group in their fields. However, since your village likes the variety of kernel color and flavor offered by the black-kernelled corn the other village grows, you now had a perfect trade product between the two groups of villages.

Figure 9 – Detail of Corn
Detail of Corn ear held in the Hand of a Goddess on a Temple in Karnataka, India. Photo By Carl L. Johannessen

In the Americas, the farmers discovered that corn was a wind cross-pollinator and improved the size of the ear and output of the plants. It seems that the Asian farmers never discovered or learned about corn being a wind-borne, cross-pollinator. They treated it then, as the small local farmers in China and India still do, as a self- pollinator similar to rice, wheat and barley. Therefore, the only large and many-eared stalk corn plants in Asia were those introduced from the Americas. As a result, the maize they grew across Asia remained relatively small. In a later chapter we will go into detail as to how we know that larger eared corn was introduced to India long before 1492, but for right now let's simply say that the temples of the Hoysala Dynasty, in what is now Karnataka Pradesh, date from between the 10th and 13th Century C.E. and there are many images of corn carved into the walls of their stone temples. There are other temples in the same region dating as far back as the 5th Century C.E. that also have recurring images of corn carved as statues. It is generally and erroneously currently hypothesized that the larger corn ear was first introduced to Asia from the Americas about 1500 years ago. There is some evidence, which I observed during several research trips, that maize may have been introduced several times to Asia, the first being about 9,500 years ago as the tiny Sikkim Primitive (SP) popcorn and then at least one reintroduction of the larger soft-kernelled corn more recently.

Although the general ideas of economic botanists regarding the domestication of crops may not have been completely accurate, we can use it to look at a general timeline of domestication of plants around the world. In tropical Asia domestication likely got its start with species that were planted from root stocks -- the root was planted directly into the ground and it formed a new plant -- yams, taros, sugar cane, and bananas were of this type. In the Americas, similar tuberous roots were the manioc, the sweet potato, and the maranta (arrowroot). Soon after the root crops (crops planted this way) were established, other plants would have been added to the farming knowledge and stores. In the Americas, these plants would likely have included all the fruits (such as the guavas), the trees that produced various fish poisons, dyes, and food coloring (achiote or Bixa) as well as trees that were used as hedgerows. All of these are vegetatively reproducing plants and are, therefore, likely to have been among the earliest domesticated plants.

Each research group and every independent researcher has his own favorite plant to use for the story of the origin of domestication and no-one has firmly established which species was actually first. George Carter, a highly respected geographer, suggested that we ought to think about the problem of origins and that no a priori assumption should be taken as fact. In other words, anyone studying domestication should set aside any preconceived notions they have of how or where it might have occurred and simply look at the available facts. Although the idea of looking at every phenomenon with fresh eyes, without a priori beliefs and ideas, is a central tenet of science. Scientists, like most other people are prone to look at new situations from the perspective of their previous knowledge. This is truer in the social sciences where data is interpretable and more complex than it is in the cut and dried world of physics or mathematics. Therefore, it is important to remind researchers regularly that *a priori* assumptions, especially those based on our own previous work, can blind us to innovative discoveries and new ideas. George Carter, who died in 2004, was a highly innovative thinker who was far ahead of his time in his ideas and conclusions about diffusion. Given that there are plants shared by early farmers on both sides of the Pacific and Atlantic Oceans, maize being but one example, it is likely that American farmers and tillers were in contact with the Asians and became knowledgeable in some aspects of agriculture as a way of life from the Southeast Asian farmers and tillers. George Carter was convinced that both groups of farmers were tillers and that the ideas came from the same source of knowledge, whichever hemisphere developed the domestication technology first. For the moment, we will leave undetermined exactly which region of the world's tropical people began to cultivate vegetatively soft, nondurable root crops of foods first.

Although the vegetatively reproduced form of cultivation was the earliest, there was a lot more to cultivation and domestication that we needed to develop before becoming masters of agriculture. Tribal people would have to learn how to cultivate crops using a variety of more complex tools, select crop plants from weeds that sometimes looked very similar, and control a wide variety of pests: insects, birds, mammals, and even other humans. Once our ancestors understood plant care (weed and pest control) and that they were not going to lose their entire crop, they then would have begun planting large patches of ground with out-crossing seed crops. Remember that in the Middle East the settled tribes developed wheat and barley, which are both self-pollinating grains, while in the East Asian tropics the settled tribes developed rice, another self-pollinating grain, and in the Americas the settled tribes developed maize which is a wind-pollinated grain. These grains became the staple of the region, thus allowing the fledgling societies to have storable and durable food goods. This surplus and the ability to store food for the future allowed these groups to advance and become great civilizations we know and study, such as Mesopotamia, Akkadia, Norte Chico, Olmec, Xai Dynasty, and the Jaihu culture. The development of agriculture took a very long time, from the discovery that man could plant cuttings and thus reproduce a crop to the plowing of fields and the warding off complex threats such as pests and raiders as well as unwanted pollens.

POTTERY'S ROLE IN PLANT CULTIVATION

When researchers are looking for the oldest regions of cultivation, one of the important things that they look for is pottery in household debris. Pottery is considered to be an important element of the agricultural society for several reasons: including the safe storage of seeds and more innovative cooking techniques which allowed people to live in greater numbers in small areas. Finding pottery and shards, therefore, implies that there was likely an agricultural community in the region at least that long ago. For instance, Wilhelm G. Solheim II, an archaeologist specializing in Southeast Asian history, found pottery dating from 9,000 B.C.E. in Thailand near the Myanmar (Burma) border. Oddly, given that the earliest agricultural signs in the Americas are from roughly 7,000 to 10,000 years ago, roughly the same time as agriculture was being developed in the rest of the world, pottery did not show up until about 5,000 years ago in Valdivia, Ecuador. The late Betty Meggers, a respected archaeologist from the Smithsonian Institution, discovered that some of the earliest pottery in the Americas has many similarities to pottery from the Jomon culture dominant in Japan at the time. However, the archaeologist Henning Bischof reported finding very primitive technique pottery in Puerto Hormiga, Colombia that dates to around 7,000 years ago. He claims it does not have decorations similar to the Valdivia, Ecuador pottery so it is similar to Asia in general.

Even though clay and ceramic pottery do assist cultures in the development of agricultural advances and a more settled life style, it is likely that in the Americas the lack of pottery did not severely limit it. This was, in part, likely due to the horticultural planting method used in the Americas. The grinding stones in northern South America have shown grains of starch from manioc that were smashed with a grinding stone possibly as long as 10,000 years ago. The roots are objects that could have been easily roasted in the coals, just as were all the various kinds of bananas that were present before active tilling began and spread in East Asia. All varieties of bananas and plantains may have been planted by hand very early as well.

The cultures in northern Mexico developed advanced basket weaving skills by 6,000 B.C.E. These skills were tremendously useful to gatherers and early cultivators of food crops in the Americas. It is likely that the basket weaving techniques spill over into making fiber sandals, mats and various nets to be used as lightweight containers and fish nets. Learning to waterproof the baskets added another level of sophistication in the social system. Waterproofing the baskets allowed the food preparers to cook more effectively and for more people, in a way similar to that of pottery for other cultures. Water held in the basket could be boiled by dropping fiery hot stones into it without compromising the integrity of the basket. Weaving technology developed with very similar looms in both Asia and America. The back-strap or belt-loom is still in use around the world and you can find them when you leave the main roads and tourist centers most anywhere on both continents where weaving occurs.

Once the knowledge of horticulture and agriculture were recognized by the various local populations then the process of introducing plants and animals from one location to another location across the oceans were more easily carried out. In our more academically targeted book, <u>World Trade and Biological Exchanges Before 1492 C.E.</u> published in 2009 and the Revised and Expanded Edition published in 2013, my co-author John L. Sorenson and I present an overwhelming amount of evidence for regular and sustained interaction between the warm climatic regions of the Old World and the Americas prior to 1492. Few other scientists have ever suggested this sort of American plant introduction into the Old World (East Asia, South and Southeast Asia, Middle East, Australia, New Zealand, Africa and Europe including the Mediterranean and all the islands more than a couple thousand miles from the Americas). In this book, like in the academic book, I will not use the standard terms Old World and New World, as these terms were created by anthropologist under the mistaken assumption that these were totally isolated and separate hemispheres until the Christian European sailing of Columbus; instead I will use Old World and the Americas to denote the two major land masses on the Earth. The Pacific Islands (except for those closest to the shores of the Americas), the Azores, Greenland, the farthest west Aleutian Islands, and the Canary Islands will be part of the Old World for convenience. The Caribbean Islands, Catalina, the San Juan del Fuego Islands, and the Eastern Aleutian Islands are all part of the Americas. We are ignoring Antarctica because it was not settled until the Twentieth Century by crazed researchers that love the cold and mountain climbers chasing the goal of climbing the highest mountain on each continent, the Vinson Massif being the highest one in Antarctica.

CHAPTER 4: DISPERSAL OF CIVILIZATION

About ten thousand years ago, before the rise of kings in Northwest Europe, tropical sailors of Southeast Asia departed from home on sailing rafts and, risking everything, went to sea to explore the oceanic world. Researchers, among them Chris Stringer of the Human Origins Research Group, Department of Paleontology, Natural History Museum in England, agree that Australia was colonized at least 60,000 years ago, perhaps even up to 100,000 years ago, and the rest of the Pacific Islands followed from the colonization of Australia or the colonization of Japan and Taiwan. However, no standard textbook anywhere in our education system, from kindergarten through graduate school, talks about these sailors traveling just a little farther and arriving at tropical and subtropical areas of the Americas. It seems that, according to accepted ideas in American academia, our ancient ancestors could sail across the vast open oceans to Australia and to the many large and small islands scattered across the enormous space of the Pacific Ocean, but that our more recent ancestors, who would have had much improved sailing technology, could not make the longer journey to or from the Americas across the very same oceans. There is actually a lot of powerful evidence that sailors did, in fact, cross the Pacific in watercraft long before 1492 C.E., sailing before the winds to the northern Pacific Ocean. The evidence of who sailed in these regions and of what, in fact, was possible seems lost in the focused attempt to preserve the myth of European Christian Exceptionalism. This is the mistaken idea that until the Western European Christians were able to master a skill that no one in the 'pagan' world beyond their borders could possibly master. This myth is perpetrated by the story of Columbus discovering the "New World" in 1492 C.E. Current researchers are more likely to question elements of the Columbus story, often accepting that the Norse, according to the ruins and artifacts being found in Canada and the northern United States, at least visited the Americas prior to Columbus. They are still, however, unwilling to accept that tropical cultures from Southeast Asia, India, the Middle East, and Africa as well as cultures in the Americas sailed back and forth across the Pacific and Atlantic Oceans for millennia prior to Columbus' voyage. American Academics have come to believe that the historic Eurocentric attitude brought about through the European Colonization of the rest of the world generates a very strong need for traditional scientists to maintain the fiction of the accuracy of the Columbus story.

When contact between civilizations and peoples in the Old World took place, there was a natural sharing of cultural traits between the societies, as well as the sharing of plants, animals, parasites, and diseases. The evidence of the contacts across vast mountain ranges, deserts, plains, and tundra is accepted by anthropologists, archaeologists, historians, and geographers. The accepted conclusions are often based on little more than the discovery of a collection of similar cultural traits and linguistic traits alone, rather than solid evidence of shared crop plants and useful animals, as well as weeds, diseases, and parasites. Even if researchers do not immediately accept the data, they may see it as reason to dig further into the areas to find better evidence for contact. When it comes to looking at evidence of contact across the oceans researchers simply deny the validity of anything that undermines their Eurocentric ideas, not feeling that it is worth looking further for more or better evidence. They summon the explanation of 'parallel evolution' to ward off the idea that these cultures may have interacted. Most arguments given against transoceanic interaction by early sailors boil down to, 'it didn't happen because they couldn't sail across the oceans' or 'it didn't happen because they couldn't'. Then the traditional researchers reset that evidence bar, making it higher and harder to jump. If someone jumps it, the establishment simply raises it higher. This is not the behavior we need from research professionals when dealing with the evidence of intracontinental interaction by sailors.

There is now very compelling evidence that there was significant contact, not only among various societies and cultures living in either the Old World or in the Americas, but also between societies in the Americas and the Old World. The evidence clearly demonstrates that people in the Americas were interacting with people in Eurasia, Africa and perhaps some of the Pacific Islands much earlier than has been generally accepted. Even though the evidence that is available to show this interaction across the oceans, is exactly what the researchers requested after ignoring previous data as unlikely, these academic experts, especially in the United States, have remained opposed to changing the paradigm from "there was no significant or purposeful contact across the oceans before the Christian Europeans" to "there was regular and purposeful contact between tropical and subtropical cultures across the oceans for at least 9,000 years." When we diffusionist researchers offered them a plethora of examples and evidence of plants, animals, and diseases traveling in both directions across both the Atlantic and Pacific Oceans, they demanded DNA evidence before being willing to accept the idea. When we offered them DNA evidence, they demanded more. There is a point at which, careful skepticism becomes intentional obstructionism and in this field of research, the mainstream researchers have long since crossed over that line.

In a Chinese museum there is displayed a terra cotta image of a dove which was created by pressing clay around a corncob from which all the kernels had been removed. The image of a dove was used as a representation of food for eternity and was found in the casket of a deceased nobleman in northern Henan, China. The dove figure was baked which burned the cob away leaving only the telltale impressions of a corncob without kernels. The set of impressions in the hardened clay inside the bird show all the telltale signs of a corncob, including the spiraling pattern of corn cupules that were left after the seed was removed from the cob. The dove was certainly created using the cob as an armature, and then baked to harden the clay into a ceramic. Later at the gravesite, the head and tail of the dove were broken off exposing the clear image of the corncob inside the "bird". This piece is definitely an important part of the archaeological evidence showing that maize was in China long before the Europeans got there. Other evidence for annona was found in Chinese literature and artwork dated to long before 1492 C.E.

Over the next several chapters, we will look at the evidence for various specific examples of the diffusion of plants, animals, and diseases. In

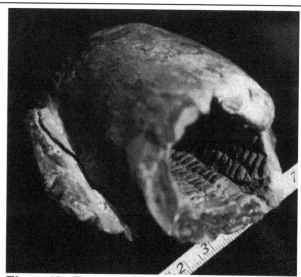

Figure 10 - Funerary Sculpture
This funerary sculpture of a bird shows the markings of a corn cob which was used as a central mold around which the bird was molded. Photo by Carl L. Johannessen.

this chapter, we will look at an overview of the evidence. Later in this book, we will look at the corollary evidence in the form of cultural traits that were also likely transferred as a result of these sailing voyages. Cultural traits are corollary evidence because it is harder to prove that the separate societies did "not" come up with the traits on their own in a manner known as parallel evolution of traits. Parallel evolution is absurd, as we have already discussed. Evolutionary biologists, perhaps the most famous of which being the late Steven Jay Gould of Harvard University, agree that the process of evolution is so precise that a specific animal, plant, or living microorganism could only have arisen in one place in the world. If it is found elsewhere, then it had to have been transferred to that locale by some other method.

For example, if a group of people on one continent should happen to die of a disease that originated on another continent then there had to have been contact between the peoples of those two continents. We see this today in the spread of the common cold or in the annual flu epidemics. The disease begins in Southeast Asia and spreads around the world via contact among the people who travel back and forth among the various regions of the world. That is why the flu spreads generally from China through the Americas and then across Europe, because this is the more common pattern of travel, although recently, with more flights moving people between Europe and Asia that cycle is increasing in intensity.

The great majority of the plants that were diffused across the oceans evolved or were domesticated in the Americas, and then were taken to the Old World. Fifty percent of these plants ended up in India, either by way of other Southeast Asian countries where evidence of the plant has not yet been discovered, or through direct interaction between cultures in India, China and the Americas. The larger animals for which we have decisive evidence seem to split with about 15% traveling to the Americas from the Old World, both Europe and Asia, and 85% traveling from the Americas to the Old World, both Europe and Asia. In addition, there are numerous cultural traits that exist in both hemispheres, which further indicate some fairly significant level of interaction.

Solid archaeological data is generally more readily accepted by social science researchers than almost any other kind of evidence, so we focused on the flora and fauna for which we have archaeological evidence. Remember those sailors at the beginning of the chapter that left Southeast Asia 9,000 years ago or more? According to the archaeological remains in South America, they likely left Southeast Asia and encountered one of the coasts of North or South America one thousand years earlier. Nine thousand years ago an intrepid band of adventurers sailed away from a port in Southeast Asia and headed out to sea. As would normally be the case with people from Southeast Asia, some of them were infected with one or both of two parasites of a variety known as a hookworm, either *Necator americanus* or

Ancyclostoma duodenale. It is generally accepted in medicine and biology that both of these parasites originated and evolved in Southeast Asia. We believe these infected people got all the way to the coast of South America where they interacted with the local people and then perhaps left. We don't know if they ever returned to Southeast Asia or if they continued on their way, but we do know that they were in South America. We know this because we have found the archaeological remains of *A. lumbricoides*, *N. americanus*, and *Ancyclostoma duodenale* in a very famous archaeological site in interior Brazil, and the *Ascaris* dates back 9,800 years according to a 2008 article by Daniela Leles and her associates. These artifacts were found at *Sitio do Meio* in the southern region of Piaui State, Brazil. This site is the second major rock cave settlement to be found and is very similar to its more famous cousin, Pedra Furada which is located in the northern area of the same state. Moreover, the remains of *A. duodenale* have been discovered in human mummies and coprolites (fossilized feces) in Peru as well, and those remains date back to 4,700 years ago.

The Pedra Furada Caves are located 500 miles inland, so anyone arriving by sea would likely have only interacted with, and infected, coastal cultures, it would have taken some time for the infection to have spread that deeply into the forests. It is important to note that the lifecycle for both species of the hookworm is quite specific so the parasites could not have come across from Asia via any of the Bering Strait theories of migration to the Americas (land bridge, ice bridge, ice sailing). An infected person must excrete the egg of the hookworm (either species) into warm, moist soil through defecation. The egg then goes through several life stages in the soil (which must remain warm and moist) before it is able to burrow upwards out of the soil and through the skin of the barefooted human walking by, thus infecting them and creating an environment in which its eggs can be produced again. In addition, researchers have not found any evidence of hookworms in any ancient pre-Columbian North American population or archaeological site, indicating that this parasitic infestation did not exist in the Northern regions of the Americas. These parasites had to have arrived in infected sailors very early. Generally, hookworms are not deadly so can be transmitted over a long period. They are also pretty easy to catch. Often, especially after repeat infections, the infected people do not even show symptoms other than loose bowels. In the next chapters we will explore the evidence showing that people sailed across the tropical oceans long before the European Conquest.

CHAPTER 5: THE DIFFUSION OF PINEAPPLE, AN-NONA, AND MAIZE BEFORE 1492 C.E.

In this chapter, we are going to look at the extent to which the artists of roughly 2,000 years ago sculpted or illustrated the pineapple, annona, maize, and other crops from America in the frescos, murals, bas-reliefs, and paintings around the Middle East and the Mediterranean Basin. It is helpful to understand, and it is something we will discuss in a later chapter, that maize, annona, and sunflower are all amply demonstrated to be present in India before they were present in the Mediterranean Basin. In 1996 Dr. Shakti Gupta, an ethnobiologist from India, published a comprehensive work showing plants in the temples of India. She shows the sculptural evidence of the following plants both on the exterior walls and on the interior walls of pre-15th Century Hindu, Jain, and Buddhist temples: pineapple, annona, maize, sunflower, chili pepper, cashew, kapok, the houseplant monstera, the magnolia, and perhaps species of bamboo. There may be even more species of American plants in India. I simply do not know all the species from the New World biota so I cannot compare the multitude of species of plants for which she has found evidence in the Indian temples with the master list of American plants. Her research increases the menu of plants from the New World proven to be in the Old World long before the Europeans arrived in the early 15th Century C.E. Although some people would argue that identifying plants from sculptures is uncertain, there is very little chance for error when looking at a sculpture of the cashew fruit: its aril and curved seed case/fruit look nothing like any other plant. The curve of the chili pepper fruit and its calyx and the 'J' curl of the silk on a maize ear cannot be misinterpreted either. All of these little details are present in her survey.

We could explore the evidence for transoceanic transfer of plant and animal species for many more plants. In this chapter we will look at three different domesticated plants that originate in the Americas and were present in the Middle East prior to the Columbian voyages: the pineapple (*Ananas comosus*), annona (*Annona squamosa*), and maize (*Zea mays mays*). All three of these crops were first cultivated and domesticated in the tropical areas of the Americas. Their wild ancestors originated in the soils of the Americas. Over the next few chapters, we will look at plants, such as the sunflower (*Helianthus annuus*) and annona which originated in the Americas and made their way to India, Southeast Asia, and the Pacific Islands. We will also look at two specific specialty plants – coca (*Erythroxylon novagranatense*) and tobacco (*Nicotiana tabacum*) – that were transported specifically to Egypt from the Americas and one specialty plant that was transported from Egypt to the Americas – marijuana (*Cannabis sativa*) – long prior to the voyages of Columbus.

As we have already stated, if the early dispersal of crops and cultures occurred before the voyages of Columbus then we have to rethink all of ancient history and the development of civilization around the world. Our evidence shows that tropical mariners from various cultures and civilizations around the world sailed across the oceans and made contact with cultures and civilizations on the other sides of those oceans. These mariners and traders left their calling cards on the contacted cultures with the introduction of new crop plants, hundreds of technological innovations, a multitude of cultural beliefs, and even new and exotic diseases and parasites. Domesticated crops are one of the best footprints for us to use to track human cultural dispersion with seed contact around the world prior to 1492 C.E.

PINEAPPLE AND ANNONA

E.D. Merrill, a researcher well-known to be completely opposed to the idea of any contact between the Americas and the Old World prior to Columbus, did a detailed analysis of the ethnobiology (the study of how plants and animals were treated and used in specific cultures) in Pompeii in 79 C.E. In this analysis of that data he referred to the presence of both the pineapple and the annona in Pompeii, Italy. He admitted that the presence of pineapple, a domesticated plant of American origin, in Italy at that time had to imply that the people of the region had also seen pineapples. This shows that some form of contact between the Americas and the Mediterranean Basin had occurred. He further allowed that there was a possibility of illustrations of annona in the murals at the Pompeii ruins. Even with the presence of the pineapple already shown, he was unwilling to accept the presence of the annona unequivocally. He postulated that someone might have much later touched up the murals just to look like annona, even though Mount Vesuvius destroyed Pompeii in 79 C.E. and the city was

Figure 11 – Austen Henry Layard Drawing
This is drawing of an Assyrian Priest/Deity holding a Pineapple by the panel discoverer Austen Henry Layard. Used with permission.

never to be rebuilt or repopulated. The city was not even rediscovered until 1599 C.E. with excavation of the site beginning in 1748 C.E. It was his contention that if murals in Pompeii had annona painted on them then the crop would be grown all over the Middle East and Asia, and he was not aware of it growing in Europe or the Middle East. So, rather than accept the possibility of trade across the Atlantic Ocean, Merrill postulated that sometime after 1748 C.E. someone purposely retouched the murals of Pompeii to show an annona fruit. He claimed this even after acknowledging that the pineapple representations in Pompeii implied some level of contact between the two hemispheres prior to this time.

In Senacherib's Palace in Nineveh, Assyria (present-day Iraq), bas-relief carvings covered the walls of the main palace. Researchers spent years carefully sketching these bas-reliefs as this was in an age prior to photography. Since the early discoveries of these bas-reliefs, many have disappeared, likely into the private collections of wealthy aficionados, but the detailed and careful drawings remain. I have looked across the world to find the original bas-relief that shows a clear image of pineapple but, alas, it has been swallowed up into the hands of collectors. These collectors are not likely to come forward as owning any of these treasures because it is illegal and worthy of hefty fines and confiscation of the artifact. This particular bas-relief is about 2,700 years old and shows a person bearing the most esteemed fruit, the pineapple, striding toward the King and leading the other people bearing trays of food. The bearer holds the pineapple by a stem that protrudes below his hand by almost the width of the bearer's hand. The fruit itself has the typical overall pineapple shape along with the crisscross patterning that we recognize from the covering on fruit. It also has a protruding top-knot of leaves sticking out from the top that are very like the leaves of the most common form of pineapple. The size of the fruit when compared to the bearer's hand and face for scale indicates that it is definitely of the right size and shape to be a pineapple. The other items on the banquet trays, carried by others behind the pineapple bearer, included grapes/raisins, figs, dates, grain in heads, pome fruits, rabbit, poultry/game, etc., although the fruit is not named in the sources I have read. As we did not read Assyrian script, I suggest that others look for literature citations to crops that include pineapple.

Since most of the other marble panels in this palace were taken to England and are now housed in the British Museum, it is most likely that someone will be able to discover the illustrated panel in some private museum or art-fancier's den. It is also possible that the panel is sitting in storage at the Museum but is miscataloged or the catalogue listing has been lost. For the moment, we have only the sketch and this description from Austen Henry Layard who was on the second expedition to Nineveh when the slab was discovered:

The earth had been completely removed from the sides of the long gallery on the walls of which were sculptured the transport of the large stone and of the winged bulls. An outlet was discovered near its western end opening into a narrow descending passage an entrance it would appear into the palace from the river side. Its length was ninety-six feet its breadth not more than thirteen. The walls were paneled with sculptured slabs about six feet high. Those to the right in descending (sic) represented a procession of servants carrying fruit, flowers, game, and supplies for a banquet preceded by mace bearers. The first servant bore an object, which I should identify with the pineapple unless there were every reason to believe that the Assyrians were unacquainted with that fruit. The leaves sprouting from the top proved that it was not the cone of a pine or fir tree (p. 163)."

We hope that when and if this panel is found, the discoverer will take a photo of the carving and publish it even if the current possessor does not wish to contribute the giant slab of carved marble over his fireplace to a museum for the advancement of science. Under the topic of maize, we will discuss several other bas-relief panels.

Sir Austen Henry Layard indicated in his initial description of the panel after his discovery of it, that it was impossible for the bas- relief to show a pinecone. Even though Layard rejected this idea, many scholars still put forth the pinecone idea as an alternative hypothesis to this being a pineapple. As Layard pointed out, pinecones rarely have a 10 cm long stem, straight out of their base, nor are they at the end of a long, straight stem. In addition, pinecones do not have bromeliad leaves extending out of their tops nor would they be mixed with food crops in a banquet line of food servers. Very few, if any, pinecones in the Middle East forests are as large as pineapples, nor would they have been carried into a banquet as a separate item.

Many scientists have argued for the giant art museums to return art objects collected by European colonials during the 19th Century. Unfortunately for the history of art, some of these irreplaceable pieces now housed in Middle Eastern and African museum collections have been destroyed by certain extremist Muslim groups in a mistaken belief that all representational images are against the teachings of the Qur'an. These fanatics, ISIL foremost, have intentionally destroyed artworks and statuary that are a cultural legacy to everyone in the world and have made it more difficult for researchers and historians to piece together a coherent narrative about human history and human interconnection. Moreover, these actions are making it more difficult for museums and collections in Europe and the United States to consider returning the artwork that is the cultural heritage of these societies. In Egypt, radical clerics and ISIL have argued for the need to destroy the millennia old art created by the Ancient Egyptians; the Sphinx and the Great Pyramids at Giza and others around the country. In 2001 in Afghanistan, the Taliban destroyed numerous irreplaceable statues of Buddha, including the world- famous Buddhas of Bamiyan. In light of these tragic acts of destruction, it may not be in the world's best interest to return these priceless artifacts to their homelands at this time.

In Turkey, there is also reasonable evidence of pineapples, in the form of marble sculptures in the round, dating from the 2nd Century C.E., the Roman Age. We should not be surprised to see Roman sculptors using the pineapple as a motif in their artwork in Turkey. These statues date to a period only a century or so after Pompeii was covered in volcanic ash. Since we have already shown that there were pineapples in preserved murals at Pompeii, this evidence in Turkey simply strengthens the case. There is a statue of Tyche, the Greek/Roman goddess of fertility, at the National Archaeological Museum in Istanbul that I consider to be the best example I have seen of the sculptor's art illustrating pineapple. The statue, like most statues of Tyche, shows the goddess holding a cornucopia overflowing with abundance and fertility. The pineapple is sculpted as a part of the bounty flowing out of the cornucopia. Looking at the photograph on this page, you can see it best from the front. If you put yourself in the mind of a sculptor who does not want to have the sculpture damaged over time, as they knew often occurred, then putting the leaf tips in line with the fruit near the back of the arrangement makes the best sense. We see that arrangement on this

and many other stat-
ues of Tyche from
around Turkey. The
pear, peach, apple,
grape, quince, and
pomegranate share the
top exposure on the
cornucopia. The pine-
apple is by far the
largest fruit on the
arrangement, as it
should be. Although
the pineapple looks a
little unusual on the
statue, and some argue
that it does not fit be-
cause it is not multi-
seeded (one element
of many fertility sym-
bols), it should be
noted that all the oth-
er items in the cornu-
copia are fruits and
that not all of these
fruits are multi-seeded,
therefore the pineap-
ple again makes more
sense than does a pinecone.

Figure 12 - Statue of Tyche
This famous statue of Tyche is in the Ankara,
Turkey Museum of Anthropology. It is carved
with a Pineapple in the Cornucopia beside her.
Photo taken by Carl L. Johannessen.

In the Archaeological Museum in Bursa, Turkey is another 2nd Century
C.E. sculpture of the Goddess Tyche, also holding a similar cornucopia.
Although part of the pineapple is broken off along with the lower part of
the Tyche statue, the leaves for the pineapple are still visible in the back-
surround of the cornucopia. In Ankara, the Tyche statue in the National
Archaeological Museum is also holding a cornucopia with a pineapple at the
top, although this pineapple does not have top leaves and is much smaller.
It is possible that the statue in Ankara actually does have a pinecone on it,
instead of a pineapple, but this would make it unique among the Tyche
statues found in the region. It is still not likely that a pinecone would be
placed in a cornucopia and deity symbology does not often or easily change.
At Izmir's archaeological museum the 2nd century C.E. Roman sculpture of
the God of the Sea, Kaistros, holds a cornucopia with part of the pineapple
broken off. Enough of this pineapple remains however, for definitive identification. The sculpture of Kaistros was found in the nearby Ruin of Ephe-

sus.

In many cultures, plants with many large and prominent seeds become fertility symbols and are often found among the symbology of the fertility deities. These plants include plants like the pomegranate, the maize ear, the lotus, and the sunflower. Like these plants, the annona (*Annona squamosa*) also has many significantly large seeds that would also make it a reasonable fertility symbol. Many years ago, on a research trip to Turkey my research companions and I found that many Roman sculptures of the Artemis of Ephesus, a Goddess of Fertility, had a belt of bull testicles around her chest and above these a row of ten fruits hanging in little niches, likely a necklace. The lumpy fruits are very distinctive and look very much like the actual annona fruit from the Americas. The fruit on many of these statues are carved in three dimensions, making the identification of them as annona much easier. We were told that the four statues on display at museum in Selçuk (Seljuk), Turkey, the city just outside of the ruins of the ancient Greek city of Ephesus, were only small representatives of the original, giant sculpture of Artemis that was located in Ephesus while it was still inhabited. The practices of the adherents to the worship of this Fertility Goddess (among the many others in the region) were a dramatic challenge to early followers of Jesus, especially to Paul of Tarsus. Because of the temptation from the physical and sensual nature of these practices, Paul wrote strongly worded letters to the followers of Jesus in Ephesus. Due to Paul's interpretation of the words of Jesus, which he learned from his followers in Asia Minor, not from Jesus himself, he felt that it was his duty to attempt to change their

Figure 13 - Kraitos Statue
This statue of hte god Kraitos shows a Pineapple on carved column. This statue was found at Izmar, Turkey where it is now displayed in the Archaeological Museum. Photo taken by Carl L. Johannessen.

unbecoming behaviors and activities and return them to the bosom of Jesus's teachings as he interpreted them in that area of Asia Minor. However, a centralized Christian religion would not exist for a couple hundred more years. The followers of Jesus became the Christian Church when Constantine died in 337 C.E. The church remained strongly anti-sensual and opposed to these kinds of fertility cults since they glorified the current world rather than the next world. Early Christians were certain that the end-of-times was at hand, and they had been severely persecuted by these older religious groups, so they were focused on making the world ready for Jesus's soon-to-come triumphant return.

Earlier human societies were very interested in fertility and created entire religions, deities, and rituals surrounding it. During early human history, their lives as hunter/gathers and pastoralists often depended on the bounty and fe-

Figure 14 - Statue of Artemis of Ephesus
Statue with Annona fruit above the bull testicles. This statue is in the Archaeological Museum in Seljuk, Turkey. Photo taken by Jerrid Wolflick, used with permission.

cundity of the land. Later, after humans began truly settling down and becoming farmers, the harvests were very important to the entire community and region. This was a time without modern medicines, with its immense lifesaving ability, so the rate of infant mortality and death from relatively minor injuries was quite high. The priesthood was therefore interested in the many-seeded fruits as religious levers for maintaining abundant num-

bers and fe-
cundity of
livestock and
the produc-
tion of chil-
dren.

One ar-
chaeologist in
Ankara, Nil-
gun Sinan,
told me that
the Roman
Empire had a
goddess of
Fertility
known as
Annona. She
was a part of

Figure 16 - Annona Fruit
Hoysala Dynasty Statue dated to the 11th Century C.E.
Picture by Carl L. Johannessen.

the imperial cult rather than a goddess from older times and she guarded
the grains and granaries of the Empire. She was often depicted in a manner
similar to the Tyche of Turkey, with a cornucopia overflowing. Indeed, the
fruit for which this Goddess was named has the required multi-seeded
characteristic. The word annona in Latin means a year's supply of corn,
grain, or provisions. It is a first-declension noun that finds its roots in the
Latin word anuus or year. The original native Mexican name for it was *ati*.

Figure 15 - Close up of Artemis
This close-up shows the row of Annona fruits
in the row above the rows of Bull Testicles.
Photo taken by Jerrid Wolflick, Used with
permission.

So when was the
name, annona, given
to the American fruit?
We do not have
enough time-depth on
the name to answer
the question but it
gives us reason to
wonder just how far
back this Goddess,
Annona was wor-
shipped.

The sarcophagi
both in the museum
collection at Selcuk
and at the numerous
surrounding ruins,
currently set-aside as

study sites and tourist attractions, almost all show annona in the carvings. The annona are roughly to scale with the other fruits carved on the sarcophagi and they conform to the shape with its multiple lumps on the skin of the fruits. These lumpy fruits are essentially the same shapes as some of the sculptured fruits found in southern India among the Hoysala Dynasty temple sculptures and in the Hindu religion's murals. In the next chapter, we will look at the evidence for the sunflower and maize being present in India, carved on the same temples where the annona is found. With all three present in India, and Turkey, as well as Annona, peanuts, and maize in N.E. Timor millennia ago, the case for early contact between civilizations across the tropical oceans becomes far stronger.

MAIZE

I have been studying the presence of Maize in the Old World, especially in India for decades. In Hoysala Dynasty Hindu temples, located in Karnataka Pradesh, India, dating from between the 10th and 13th centuries C.E. there are hundreds of carvings of female figures holding a plant that has been repeatedly identified by renowned corn experts as corn. In Jain and Buddhist temples in India, dating from the same time and even further back to the 5th to 8th Centuries, male figures hold most of the large maize ears carved on the temples. The carving of the Hindu God Vishnu from the Cave Temple III at Badami, a town in the northern area of the Karnataka Pradesh, holds a maize ear horizontally. This temple dates back to the 5th Century C.E. and is one of the oldest examples of maize sculpture in India. It may date to the Chalukya Dynasty, which ruled the area between the 6th and 12th centuries C.E. A statue of another male Hindu God, Kubera the Lord of Wealth, holds a maize ear in his hand vertically. This statue may date from between the 5th and 8th Centuries C.E. Sculptors, who created the images of the gods, later followed this orientation when they carved the female maize holders in the Hindu temples of the Hoysala Dynasty with vertical ears of maize in their sculptures.

M.D.W. Jeffreys was a major researcher on the origin and diffusion of corn around the world and wrote many scholarly articles showing that corn appeared in Africa, Anatolia, the Middle East, India, and China long before the Europeans explored these areas. During my own travels in India and other Old World locations, I also had the opportunity to find corn types first identified by Jeffreys and reviewed the previous evidence in his writings. "Waxy" or sticky starch maize is found throughout the Corn Belt of China from Assam, India to South Korea. It is found between $5°$ and $45°$ north latitude. The Russians, when they studied Asia, found waxy, and dwarf maize all the way across Central Asia to Persia and into the Trans Caucasus region. Another curious growth habit of some of the Himalayan maize is that the ears and the tassels are wrapped in leaves at the top of the stem. As I traveled throughout the region, I rediscovered the many unusual characteristics of maize discovered by both Kuleshov and by Vavilov's teams. The sticky starch features are significantly different from American maize. Jeffreys documented the early presence of these distinctive forms in maize. Since these varieties are so widespread in Asia and are essentially absent in America, maize must have been in Asia for a very long time to evolve these distinctive forms and characteristics, such as sticky starch, and for them to spread across the continent without modern genetic help.

Jeffreys' also demonstrates that maize has a set of names in India, Arabia, and Persia that seem to be cognates of the same root word *makka*. My further research indicates that this root word *makka* actually derives from the Arawak language in the Amazon Basin of South America. I am not convinced that it is a misspelling for Mecca as Jeffries concluded. Jeffreys' research shows that maize came into Southern Europe from the Anatolian Peninsula according to the early 16th century C.E. herbalists in Europe who showed similar names for corn as well. According to Sauer's research, however, corn was being grown and used in Southern Europe long before Columbus' time. According to Carl Sauer's son, Jonathan Sauer, corn was introduced to the Po Valley of Italy through Venetian trade with Turkey around the 5th Century C.E. He noted that the southern German herbalists were highly competent

Figure 17 - Corn Ear Sculpture in India
This detail of a sculpture shows the typical alternating row pattern of corn kernels on an ear. It is found on a Hoysala Dynastey Temple. Karnataka, India. Picture by Carl L. Johannessen.

and had very good access to Venetian trade goods so their very accurate description of maize should be accepted as valid.

When depicting an ear of corn within the husk, without any kernels showing, the Hindu and Jain sculptors would carve a small J-like curve down from the top of the husk to represent the silk (stigma and style) that distinguishes maize. This symbolic representation has also been used to distinguish maize in the codices of Mexico and Guatemala whenever maize was portrayed in the husk in a diagram or sculpture. This identical symbolic representation is not a convention that artists on both sides of the Pacific Ocean would have generated independently of maize ears in the husk! Academics who adhere to the parallel invention belief system can no longer afford to ignore the evidence that maize has been a significant part of Indian culture for the last two millennia (9,800 years according to my research.) where the representations are extremely accurate. When maize ears were sculpted in stone a couple thousand years ago in Mexico, however, they appeared as rather rapid and simplistic sketches of how the ear looked. Perhaps, since maize was so common that everyone in the Americas knew what it looked like, it was not thought to be important to portray it in fine photographic detail as it was in India. In the Indian temples of Karnataka, for example, the execution of detail was often so much better that the sculptors frequently achieved images nearly photographic in their detail. All of these were completed long ago, before the last Hoysala Dynasty temple was finished in 1268 C.E. at Somnathpur. However, between 500C.E. and 1268 C.E., renderings of maize in the Americas, especially in Mexico and Peru, became more detailed and by circa 1268 C.E. were comparable to those found in Asia.

In Timor, Indonesia, an archaeological cave site record shows the presence of maize at 1000 C.E. China, too, has had maize for at least the last 2,000 years. Academia has ignored the work of their own botanists who wrote about these maize impressions. Unfortunately, the baked clay of the bird image with the maize impression has not been dated with thermoluminescence technology such as is available in the Shanghai Museum of archaeology. I am hoping that someday the archaeological artifacts of maize, peanut, squash, etc. in China will be dated with these new methods (39Argon/40Argon, for example). Science also needs to date the discoveries in regions in which the polymorphism in religious buildings are present and measured.

Assyrian Palace bas-reliefs, carved at the latest by 605 B.C.E. when the Assyrian Empire fell, were installed in large slabs of marble. These reliefs show that the artists and priests of the time knew maize, and that it was likely used in religious pollination rituals for the "Tree of Life". In Assyria 2,000 or 3,000 years ago, however, date palm may have been the "Tree of Life". The Eagle- headed deities are magically anointing the "Tree of Life" with something, but what the tool might be in these carvings is not clear. However, H.W.F. Saggs, a noted Assyrian scholar, interpreted the object as a cone (presumably a pinecone) which was used ". . . to asperge the king" with another symbol of fertility. The other authors and Assyrian scholars, however, did not describe what they thought the winged "Goddesses" held in their hands, but they certainly seemed to resemble maize ears. When I was in India, I checked with eleven different scholarly authors and this same lack of detail held true for all of them regarding references to the obvious maize ears held by the Goddesses, or Maize Maidens, and Gods in the Hoysala Dynasty temples in India, even though the written references in the books included illustrations of maize ears in their pictures of temple walls. The authors made no reference to corn though every other article on the sculptures was described in detail. As referred to earlier, Dr. Shakti Gupta (1996) has broken the Indian code of silence on the issue of American plants in early India.

The Assyrian Priests, in headgear impersonating the raptors of the area, are shown pollinating the sacred "Tree of Life", but the artistic license showing the design of a date palm tree almost stretched too far. On a cylinder seal used during the Assyrian Era, the artist and sculptor shows a series of fruits on that "Tree" and that a particular one seems to be a pomegranate tree. In the sculptures illustrated in several previous works the tool that the priests held in their hand to pollinate this sacred "Tree of Life" has the overall size, form, pattern, and shape of an ear of maize, American corn. The kernels of an actual ear of maize, as described before, are sometimes arranged in ranks (of two rows) that are paired side by side. The next two rows of two kernels are displaced by half a kernel thickness up or down the ear. The bas-reliefs in India have many of the sculpted ears of corn arranged in straight lines, the above-described alternating pattern known in botany as tessellate, or in a jumbled distribution of kernels. All of these versions of kernel distribution on the ears of corn are seen in the statuary in the Hoysala Dynasty India temples.

Paul Mangelsdorf, a world-renowned specialist on corn genetics and their mutations from Harvard, who died in 1989, knew that the displacement by half kernel thickness between ranks definitively identified corn. He made this feature a cornerstone for his identification of maize impressions in pottery and in art objects in the Americas. The fact that the arrangement of kernels sculptured in Assyrian sculptures is occasionally shown in a tessellate pattern has limited the recognition of maize as the object in the priests' hand, but it does not invalidate the identification as maize. They are carved approximately in the manner and design of the Aztec and Toltec sculptors in Mexico. The bracts (scales or seed pods) of pinecones, for example, and the scales (seed pods) of pineapples are never arranged in straight rows; they only appear as spirals around the central shaft!

Other archaeo-ethnobotanists have denied the validity of the Assyrian sculptural record to be valid, because they have not found caches of maize ears in the archaeology of the region. Although there is no definitive answer for why evidence of actual maize in the Chinese or Indian regions has not been discovered, we can posit one fairly simple explanation. Virtually all of the plant material thrown away around camps, villages, towns, cities, or temples, are thrown into the middens or rubbish heap. This is a perfect place for this material to rot and return to the earth as nutrients and fertilizer, as everything in the pile is rotting. Very few plant remains are discovered in archaeological digs for this reason. Moreover, only a very tiny amount of the Earth's surface has actually been explored and scavenged by modern archaeologists so to infer that a plant was not in a place because an actual specimen has not been found, is less than conclusive reasoning against the plant having been in the region, especially if there is other evidence to support maize being there. Most of the recovered plant remains in archaeological digs consist of seeds or burned remains. The burning actually preserves the plant better. If, in Assyria and other Middle Eastern countries maize was used in priestly fashion and illustrated in the temples, perhaps it was highly regulated and controlled by the religious brotherhoods and therefore not as likely to be found in general scrap piles. However, we have found copious amounts of other evidence for the presence of maize in other regions of South Asia and China, enough to allow a strong likelihood of widespread distribution in the Old World. It is, however, only rarely that archaeologists and other researchers find actual plant archaeological artifacts in Asia. I am certain that one day in the future researchers will find the physical remains of corn and other plants of American origin in ancient dig sites in Europe and Asia. It might be advantageous to the researchers to probe more carefully the locations of the sculptor's workshops who were commissioned to sculpt these deities. They may well have used ears of corn in many ceramic models for sculpture. A maize ear was used as the armature for sacrificial food, such as a ceramic bird as funerary offerings in China. It is found in the classical medical literature of China. All of this allows me to confidently challenge the conventional wisdom of older paradigm scholars as to the absence of maize before the European expansion in the Old World.

My mentor, C.O. Sauer, also challenged the conventional belief on maize with evidence from literature that maize was in Mediterranean Europe in pre-Columbian times. "Scholars" apparently did not take him seriously. However, Sauer did not find the report by Acosta on a comment by Pliny that maize was in the Roman region at the time of Pliny's writing. Pliny said that "maize" had come to the Roman Peninsula from the Middle East through Turkey. The ears of corn on the sarcophagi in Turkey are separate ears 'woven' into garlands on the upper side of the sarcophagi. After studying these giant sarcophagi with all the hundreds of "fruits and pinecones" many appear as annona and maize and a few, as mentioned, look like pineapple fruits (American plants). The menu of American crop plants in the Old World is growing and includes pineapple, annona and maize as new evidence for Turkey and the Tigris River Valley. We add to that list, my data on the sunflower (Johannessen, 1998). In addition, Gupta

Figure 18 - Carl O. Sauer.
Carl Sauer is often referred to as the founder of the modern study of Cultural Geography. Press picture.

(1996) had added cashew, chili, monstera, kapok, sunflower, magnolia, and more to this list.

If you do not realize it at this instant, you are perhaps caught in a corn-cob-web of evidence, as I have been. Did you ever think of getting caught in this cobweb of evidence, the way you have just been snared? We now need to start thinking about how we teach the younger generation about the prowess of the tanned skinned peoples of the tropical world prior to Columbus and the expansion of political control by the Northwest Europeans. We colorless folk were really late arrivals on the oceans, except for some of the Basques, Celts and Norsemen who came much earlier than the Norse have normally been given credit for. Our children will likely treat other cultures with more respect when the children gain the recognition of these kinds of facts and accept the tremendous number of discoveries and innovations that others cultures made before us.

CHAPTER 6: SEVERAL OTHER FOOD CROPS DIFFUSED ACROSS THE OCEANS

Although books could be written about the history of each of these plants, I am going to provide a quick overview of the available evidence for these featured plants. readers who are interested in a more detailed analysis of the evidence for all the plants we have thus far discovered are encouraged to read <u>World Trade and Biological Exchanges Before 1492C.E., Revised and Expanded Edition</u> (2013).

VARIETIES OF BEANS

In Gujarat and other northern India locations three kinds of beans, known to have originated in the Americas have been found in a number of archaeological digs that have been dated from between 1800 B.C.E. to 600 C.E. In 1996 archaeo-botanist, Anil Kumar Pokharia and paleo-botanist K.S. Saraswat discovered the common kidney bean, the lima bean and the phasey bean in Neolithic sites in Maharashtra, India. This site was dated to the 2nd millennium B.C.E. so it is over 3,000 years old. The seeds from the Custard Apple or *A. squamosa*, were also found at the site. The Custard Apple is also accepted to have its origin in the Americas. Since the annona was likely domesticated prior to originally crossing the oceans, these findings help document that annona returned to the feral form in China and India from domesticated shapes across much of India for millennia, therefore it was and is feral. In Sanghol, Punjab, India, these same researchers found seed remains of the Mexican prickle poppy, *Argemone mexicana*, which is another psychedelic plant with its origin in the Americas. This find dates to between 1100 and 1060 B.C.E. With these discoveries, we can infer that there was definitely contact between India and the Americas over 3,000 years ago.

SWEET POTATO

The amount and variety of research done on the sweet potato is amazing. Based on linguistic evidence there has been a long claim that it arrived very early in India. The common name for the plant was essentially the same in Columbia, the Philippines, and India. Researchers were aware of these names before the discovery of the charred remains of baked sweet potato in the Marianas, Philippines and New Zealand Island hearth sites. Since the Sweet Potato is commonly agreed to be a plant that originated and was first domesticated in the Americas, regular and sustained contact across the Pacific was essential for it to have been transferred across the island chains.

The sweet potato got a lot of recent attention in the academic community when a research team ran complex DNA analyses of sweet potatoes from around the Pacific Islands, South America, and China. This study found that it is very, very difficult to determine the direction and spread of the sweet potato across the Pacific because it has been bred back into itself so many times. However, it is a point of agreement throughout the scientific community that the sweet potato was definitely diffused among the Pacific Islands long before any Europeans got to the Pacific Ocean. To make matters even more confusing, the Portuguese picked up the sweet potato in South America before sailing across the Pacific, not knowing that it had already been spread across the Pacific and onto the Asian mainland and the Indian subcontinent, and so they, too, planted the sweet potato with its own DNA on islands as they crossed. This new introduction was bred into the existing stock, which already had a complicated DNA history, complicating the DNA chains even more. However, after a great deal of analysis and study, the team determined that the sweet potato was definitely diffused across the Pacific Ocean by ocean-faring folk, likely the Polynesians, who picked it up in South America and brought it with them on their return voyages across the ocean. It was a staple to the sailors of the Pacific so was repeatedly introduced and bred into local sweet potato stock through the millennia of sailing done before 1492 C.E.

THE COCONUT

Of course when sailors were moving on the ocean sometimes they took something from the other side of the ocean and sometimes from home, put it in the boat and sailed off. In the case of coconuts, it can easily be imagined that they took a whole bunch of them along so they could have something to drink when they were out of water and it had not rained for a while. Coconuts serve this purpose well, as anyone who has spent time in the tropics well knows. Coconuts tend to fall to the ground, and if you happen to have a machete handy, and are lucky enough not to be hit on the head by the falling fruit, you could accord yourself a tasty bit of refreshment. Of course a falling coconut is ripe and can be taken advantage of, however, if you were taking them along on a long journey you would have to include some green coconuts as well to be used as they ripened. However, you would have to be careful to be sure you were only drinking from the ripe ones, because if you happened to grab a green one by mistake you would end up paying a price for your mistake, namely, a bad case of diarrhea.

Coconuts arrived in the Americas long before 1492 and are widely distributed along the Pacific slopes from Ecuador to Mexico. Thus many early botany researchers, after much study and debate, had concluded that the coconut, *Cocos nucifera*, originated in the Americas. They concluded this because the coconut is so widespread and ubiquitous across the tropical and subtropical areas of the Americas. Apparently, this conclusion was not correct. After further research and many debates, most botanists have come to agree that the coconut actually originated in Asia or in the Eastern Pacific or Indian Ocean. These researchers became so certain of this that they further declared that the coconut was not even in the Americas until after the conquistadors. This declaration ignores the eyewitness evidence in the form of journals, diary entries, ledger entries, and the like from these very same Spanish adventurers.

According to the reports and journals of Vasco Núñez de Balboa, the famed conquistador, he encountered coconuts in 1513 while he was on the very first crossing of the Panamanian Isthmus by Europeans. These journal entries are from just before he was murdered by his father-in-law, the regional Governor. Balboa was becoming too powerful and popular for his father-in-law's comfort. More recently, coconut husk fibers have been found in ancient tombs at Ancon, Peru. This find dates back to 922 C.E. Coconut fibers and husks were also found in an archaeological site in Guatemala dated to 700 C.E. This dating indicates that the earlier discovery of coconut remains in Copan, Honduras was also likely valid.

Traditional archaeologists and biologists, even those who accept that the coconut was in the Americas earlier than the European conquest, have put forth the claim that the coconut seeds simply floated across the Pacific or Indian Ocean on their own and landed in fertile locations in the Americas where it could germinate. However, in an attempt to test these theories, Thor Heyerdahl, the famous researcher and adventurer, sailed across the ocean from Peru to Raroia in the Tuamotu Islands. He did this on a raft, the Kon-Tiki, which was designed in accordance with the drawings of Peruvian rafts that existed when the first Spaniards got to the region. Heyerdahl, along with a small group of Peruvian ship builders constructed the raft out of materials that would have been available to raft builders of that earlier time such as balsa logs, vine wraps, and the like. He carried a large number of coconuts on the raft, some on the top of the raft and some floating underneath the raft in the water. After 101 days on the ocean, the Kon-Tiki arrived at Raroia Island. Not one of the coconuts that were soaked in the saltwater germinated when planted on the Island. However, the ones that were carried on top and not exposed to salt water all germinated and grew just fine into tall coconut palms. This indicates that the idea of the coconut having arrived in the Americas via flotation from the Indian Ocean is false if not ludicrous; and, if it originated on some island or coral reef in the Pacific as seems to be the accepted theory, then it would have to have been brought to the Americas aboard a sailing craft.

THE BOTTLE GOURD

The large bottle gourd, *Lagenaria siceraria*, is a very useful item for water-faring people, whether at sea, or on rivers, or lakes. It is likely that every early fisherman in regions where this gourd grew would want them to use for fishing floats and water bottles while they were on the water. Given the utility and practicality of this plant, the sailors likely transported them around the world in their boats. Wild precursor plants to the modern domestic bottle gourd have been found in Zimbabwe, a landlocked country North of South Africa, indicating this plant likely evolved in this region. This plant moved out of Africa and into Asia where we find the earliest evidence of domestication. Some researchers believe that the bottle gourd may actually be the oldest domesticated plant in human use. For whatever reason, the gourd was not domesticated first in Africa, but rather in Asia some 10,000 years ago. In Africa, there is no evidence of domestication until 4,000 years ago. In 2005, researcher David Erickson and his team from the National Museum of Natural History in Washington, D.C. found that the remains of domesticated bottle gourds in Mexico dated from 10,000 years ago and that these gourds have DNA matches to gourds from Asia, where the plant originated. Radio carbon dating shows that the domesticated plant was in the Americas long, long before the European expansion.

Until recently, it was accepted by most botanists, anthropologists, and archaeologists that the bottle gourd floated across the Atlantic Ocean from Africa to the Americas and since it was domesticated very early in Africa, then the domesticated plant would have been the one to have arrived in the Americas. There was a very serious problem with this theory, no bottle gourds were found on the eastern coasts of South or Central America. In fact, there is only one East Coast location for the bottle Gourd and it is in Florida. Upon doing definitive DNA tests on ancient samples, researchers discovered that the bottle gourd artifacts from every location in the Americas that were dated to before the European expansion were a type of the Asian domesticated bottle gourds, not the African one. The only African-based bottle gourds found in the Americas was from gourds brought over by the Europeans. In other words, bottle gourds were domesticated in Asia and then transported to the Americas aboard a raft or ship in some manner. What that manner was has been open to debate. Some early researchers continued to propose that they floated across, although this was not taken very seriously. In 2005, a team of researchers proposed that the gourd was likely brought to the Americas with the early Asian migrants along with the dog. However, they cannot explain why the oldest domesticated gourds found in East Asia and Japan are only 9,000 years old. It could have been that the gourd was not transferred during the first sailing voyages. Another possibility arises with the discovery of domesticated gourds across the Polynesian and Pacific Islands from New Zealand to Easter Island, all prior to European expansion.

Domesticated bottle gourds are found in several locations on the West Coast of South America and in ancient sites in Mexico, including the Cuscatlán Caves in Tehuacán Valley dating at 10,000 years ago. After it was initially introduced into the Western side of the Americas, it is likely that it was picked up by sailors from Polynesia and distributed across Eastern Polynesia along with the sweet potato. However, there is no evidence of the bottle gourd being used on the Western Polynesian Islands (those closest to Asia) so it is hard to conceive of how they got to the Eastern Islands without touching the Western Islands of the Pacific Ocean. It is more likely that they were transported around the Eastern Pacific by groups of sailors, Polynesian or native South Americans. Whatever the specific case, it is generally understood and accepted that the bottle gourd, like the sweet potato, was regularly transported across the tropical oceans by sailors long before Columbus and the European expansion.

PEANUTS

Today we are aware of the importance of nuts, especially peanuts as supplements to our daily diet. During WWII, the U.S. army created peanut butter in order to increase the soldier's intake of protein and necessary plant oils in their diet without having to ship cattle or butchered beef across the ocean. Peanuts were much easier to transport and could be stored longer without spoilage.

According to the U.S. National Peanut Board, "The peanut plant probably originated in Peru or Brazil in South America. No fossil records prove this, but people in South America made pottery in the shape of peanuts or decorated jars with peanuts as far back as 3,500 years ago. European explorers first discovered peanuts in Brazil."

Other entities have claimed that the peanut originated in Africa and was brought to the Americas via the slave trade, and the peanut was, in fact, in parts of Africa prior to Columbus' voyage in 1492. However, the dates for the existence of the peanut in South America predates that of any African find.

It has also been claimed that it came from China, but again the evidence for that has been rejected making it clear that the original cultivation of peanuts took place in the Americas. However, the fact that it is also found in China and Africa with dates indicating its presence prior to 1492 C.E. is a further indication of transoceanic transfer.

CONCLUSION

In this chapter we have explored the evidence for several different plants, all of which show definitive transportation across the tropical oceans long before Columbus and the European expansion. They include maize, peanuts, annona, three varieties of beans, the coconut, and the bottle gourd. We also looked at the evidence for a couple of parasites. It would seem that rather than continuing to insist that the cultures and civilizations of the tropics were created in isolation, we should start recognizing the vast interaction between the early tropical civilizations and how much and what they shared with one another.

Let us then postulate how early mariners might have functioned. The ship captains surely needed cargo that was compact, light in weight in relation to value and resistant to spoilage or deterioration during transit. Metals, jewelry, tools, drugs, medicinals, spices, herbs, certain fibers, spices, perfumes, and certain objects of religious value would fit these criteria. Salt, sugar, alcoholic beverages, and slaves require special conditions for transport that would not have made them good candidates for earliest trade by sea. In addition, to successfully complete long voyages, mariners would have required plants rich in vitamin C, as mentioned above. The fruits of the annona, cashew (especially the aril), the leaves from the baobab tree, and perhaps the pineapple, that could be grown on board ship, would have been excellent choices, because of their nutritional action in preventing scurvy. The following chapter presents further evidence that such transfers did, in all likeliness, happen.

CHAPTER 7: SUNFLOWERS TAKEN TO ANCIENT ASIA

Every spring and summer across the world, we are greeted by the ubiquitous and lovely sunflower. In the modern world, when we talk about the sunflower, we tend to picture the large-headed, tall flower, which birds and small rodents use to eat their fill and spill some of the seeds for winter pantries. The sunflower is planted in gardens across the world. It is funny to think that this beloved and innocuous plant is one of the plants swirling at the center of this debate on early plant and animal transfers across the tropical oceans.

Although wild sunflowers covered much of temperate and subtropical North America for at least the last 500,000 years, the archaeological record of the plant shows that the domesticated sunflower seeds were unlikely to have been carbonized – the burning or scorching of organic materials, particularly plant remains such as seeds or grains, resulting in conditions of insufficient oxygen while burning for full combustion. This results in their long- term preservation in a fairly stable state and thus they are discoverable by archaeologists in the dig sites. The neo-tropical climate of Central and South America are not favorable for preserving the un-carbonized seeds. Many plants that were preserved through carbonization were those that were used as fuels, those that were roasted, or those that required fire or heat to be useful. The sunflower does not fit into any of these categories, and the seed shell is not likely to be used as a fire starter, both due to its small size and the fact that it is not very flammable. It is also possible that we have lost some archaeological evidence over the years since many archaeological research strategies in the past simply did not concentrate on or really look for plant remains. Wild sunflower seeds were apparently used by ancient people in Mexico, in the Vera Cruz area.

Early domesticated sunflower remains in Mexico were only recently discovered and were excavated by Mary DeLand Pohl and Kevin O. Pope at the San Andrés site in Tabasco, Mexico. The earliest discoveries of sunflowers were dated to 3575 - 2875 B.C.E. and also to 2867- 2482 B.C.E.

Figure 19 - Field of Sunflowers
This field is located in Southern India. Photo taken by Carl L. Johannessen.

in Mexico, not in the United States. They found another domesticated sunflower from Cueva del Gallo, Morelos, Mexico that may have been involved in a ritual activity such as a burial. One of the achenes (seed) in Cueva del Gallo was dated at only 290 ± 40 B.C.E. With these discoveries in Mexico, the sunflower could not have been limited to growing in the Southern and Southeastern United States as some researchers formerly believed. Some scientists thought that the Southern and Southeastern United States was the edge of its range. Given that domesticated varieties of the plant have been found far to the South of this location, it follows that the sunflower actually had a much larger range as a domesticated plant. Given that it is a very useful plant to both airborne and ground animals, it makes sense that it would have been spread far and wide by these creatures. Once people began to plant the sunflowers and carefully select the seed for the best crops in the next year, its range greatly expanded again. We can be pretty sure that the idea of planting sunflower seeds and storing the largest and meatiest ones to plant the next year spread from the areas of Mexico where it had been domesticated by the people living in the Mississippi Valley either by seafaring people trading up the Caribbean coast or by overland traders as they wended their way across the arid lands of Northern Mexico into the fertile plains and valleys of the Mississippi River flood plain.

Along with the sunflower (*Helianthus annuus*) researchers have found maize (*Zea mays*), common beans (*Phaseolus vulgaris*), two species of squash (*Curucbita argyrosperma* and *C. moschata*), chili peppers (*Capsicum annuum*), avocado (*Persea americana*), chayote or vegetable pear (*Sechium edule*), and hogplum (*Spondias purpurea*) in the same archaeological sites in Mexico. These plants were all found in the same strata or age area as the sunflower. This shows that the people of this region, Cueva del Gallo, Mexico, were serious farmers and had a robust and complex farming life. Five of these same domesticated plants were discovered in archaeological excavations and among other research data sources such as artwork and literature in India. All of the discoveries in India date to times long before 1492 C.E., indicating that there was extensive sailing contact between the Americas and the Old World before European Conquest began and that 50 plants were

Figure 20 - Sculpture of Parrot on Sunflower

This is a sculpture of a parrot sitting on a Sunflower bloom. The sculpture is carved on the wall of a Hoysala Dynasty Temple. Karnataka. India. Photo by Carl L. Iohannessen.

moved to India earlier than 1492 C.E. Across India, but especially in Karnataka Pradesh (Karnataka State) I have discovered images of sunflower blossoms in the sacred sculptural art as well as carved as bas-reliefs in temples of the powerful Hoysala Dynasty. This dynasty ruled most of Karnataka Pradesh and areas both South and West of India from about 950 C.E. until Veera Ballala III was killed at the battle of Madurai in 1343 C.E. The area was then turned over to other kingdoms and rulers.

Between these literary and artistic sources, we know that the plant and the flower were both closely associated with the Hindu Sun God, Suria. In fact, one of the sacred Sanskrit names for the sunflower was *suria-mukhi*. Whenever we find sculptures of the sunflower in ancient Hindu Temples, especially those from the Hoysala Dynasty, we find it relating to important annual solar events, such as Solstices or Equinoxes. The hundred temples located around Karnataka Pradesh are oriented to specific sunrise or sunset points on the horizon or associated with key calendar events. The flowers were also engraved on temple doorways, in the floors, and on images of Nandi, the bull, which served as Shiva's 'transport'. Thor Heyerdahl also found carved sunflower designs on giant stones on the Maldives Islands south of India. These islands and the stones on them are located precisely at the equator which could make them part of this South Asian complex of ideas relating to the sunflower representing solar conditions, solar events, and annual solar cycles. It is obvious from several carvings that Indian artists had access to living sunflowers as models for their bas-reliefs and other carvings. This is very easily seen in an unmistakable sunflower carving on an ancient temple pillar inside the Virupaksha Temple at Pattadakal, in Karnataka Pradesh. We can see that a long-tailed Indian parrot is carved sitting atop the seed head, eating the seeds of a very large sunflower. There is no other flower in the world that has a flower that could support the weight of the parrot, as shown in this carving, to create such a unique seed head formation except the sunflower. We can, therefore see and accept that the person who carved this in the 8th Century C.E., had to have observed a scene similar to this perhaps in the wilder areas surrounding the temple.

Tewari, an epigrapher in the epigrapher's office in Mysore, India found a number of references to the sunflower in literature from ancient epigraphic writings in India. He had actually discovered the sunflower references and interpretation in early epigraphic transcriptions before I had made my discovery of sculptural sunflowers in the temples of India. The other officials of the Office of the Epigrapher in Mysore, India concurred with both Tewari's and my interpretation of the epigraphic and sculptural evidence. The Director of that Epigraphic Office for the Government of India, Dr. Katti, asked me to go with him to Somnathpur Temple (40 km to the east of Mysore) and showed me the sculptural evidence of sunflowers in this temple. There are definite sculptures of sunflowers at the horizon level at the feet of many of the sculptures of gods and goddesses. (Horizon level refers to the level of the ground when the sun is on the horizon.) Many of these figures are also holding ears of corn (Zea mays), a second crop that originated in the Americas. I observed maize images in temple statuary along with those of sunflowers in Hoysala Dynasty temples of 11th to 13th Century C.E. This widespread use of two American species together in a single ritual context is extremely strong evidence for regular and continuous interaction between the tropical cultures of India and the Americas. In Karnataka, sculptured female figures on temples are depicted holding ears of maize. They also have sunflower

Figure 21 - Sunflower Carvings at Goddesses Feet
These sunflowers are carved at the feet of bas relief maiden statuary in Hoysala Dynasty Temples. Karnataka, India. Photo by Carl L. Johannessen.

blooms sculpted below the bottoms of their skirts (Fig. 22). These were meant to symbolize the sun on the horizon. Different figures show whole, half, or quarter images of the sunflowers (the sun) below the goddesses' skirts. I suggest that these images communicated information about the ritual calendar and daily life of giving offerings.

At the Hoysaleswara Temple in Halebidu, Karnataka Pradesh, India, there is a massive Nandi the Bull figure lying under a canopy. Nandi is the 'mount' of the god Shiva and the gatekeeper of Shiva and Parvati. Nandi is also the chief guru of the eighteen masters, including Patanjali who is said to have authored the Yoga Sutras around the 2nd Century B.C.E. If one looks closely at the tail of this particular statue of Nandi, there is a set of six sunflowers carved on the material matrix between the tail and the flank of the statue. The sunflowers are carved on both sides of this matrix beneath the tail. These sunflowers, six on each side of the tail, are fully illuminated when the sun rises on each solstice, summer and winter. The left group of sunflower carvings under the tail is illuminated during one solstice and the opposite side during the other. The sunflowers on the tail, during the sunrise of the equinoxes, are clothed in total shadow from the tail itself. This same statue has another sunflower carved on it. The dawn light at the equinoxes passes over a large sunflower that is 16 ½ cm in diameter sculpted below its left horn and above its left ear. The shaft of light passes over the

Figure 22 - Sunflower Blooms
This photo compared the sunflower bloom to a Sunflower carving just below the ear of a Nandi statue. Karnataka, India. Photo Taken by Carl L. Johannessen.

sunflower above the ear and below the horn and down a long narrow hallway in the temple to illuminate the large Shiva lingam located deep in the recesses of the inner sanctum of the temple for just a few minutes. The positioning of the various sunflowers on the Nandi serve as a calendar based on light and shadow so the knowledgeable priests at the site can effectively and accurately perform the correct rituals at the proper times. The priests never spoke of the relationship to me, but we ascertained this during our long and careful observation.

Other Shiva temples in Karnataka Pradesh are oriented in differing solar directions using the rows of columns supporting the stone roof running down the middle of the temple. At one temple on the appropriate date, the First Quarter Day, which is the day half way between the winter solstice and the spring equinox, the dawn sun shines down the hallway for about five minutes over a small Nandi and onto the Shiva Lingam of that temple. This Nandi has a sunflower carved on each side of its head and the sun shines directly between them to reach the Shiva Lingam. Other temples are oriented to yet different days or to the sunset instead of the sunrise. They typically share the feature of having the sunflowers carved on the head of Nandi, if the Nandi statue is still intact and is in existence at the temple.

During my travels in India, I had several assistants and associates that helped me discover some of these temples. A most promising young man, who was a vocal proponent of my ideas while I was researching in Halebidu, invited me and my research associate to visit him in Bangalore, capitol city of Karnataka Pradesh and a city filled with ancient temples. In Bangalore there is a more complicated temple that is oriented so that sunset light at the equinox shines through a solar arch, parallel to the west side of the temple in the front of the temple, and the sun shines past the temple directly on a sunflower etched and painted on the back concrete garden wall. Also, on the solstice the sun shines through the same solar arch, through a window to the outside on the west temple wall, then through another window in the first room to the inside of the temple, across an underground room, then over a Nandi's horn and over a sunflower carved in the floor in front of the holy sanctum and on to a small Shiva lingam inside the sanctum for about five minutes at sunset on the Winter Solstice. Unfortunately, the audience of Indians waiting to see this solar passing stood up and blocked the sunlight and destroyed the scene while we were attempting to make a video of the view.

In the Mexican Otomi, Nahua, and Popoluca cultures, the sunflowers were also used in religious ceremonies and as religious adornments on altars, shrines, and in cemeteries. The Spanish terminated sunflower use under threat of punishment under the Spanish rules because of the use of the sunflower in Mesoamerican art, its religious use, and its supposed aphrodisiac powers. These acts and ceremonies, which conflicted with the Catholic's power of religion and their need to destroy the traditional Indian religious customs, likely continued underground without the Spanish being aware of it.

We have found archaeological evidence of sunflowers in India, Turkey, and Mesopotamia, and discovered specific shapes of sculptural evidence of sunflower in their solar-oriented temples. These discoveries can only be reasonably interpreted as the presence of the sun-following sunflower as indicating the certainty of our interpretation. The uses of the sunflower in both ancient Mexico and 11th to 13th Century C.E. India were similarly oriented for religious uses. In both regions, they were used as adornment in religious ceremonies as well as their use as food and medicinally for several illnesses.

Some researchers have proposed that the sunflower sculptures in India, Turkey, and Mesopotamia are actually carvings of the local Lotus flower, which is used, in a fashion similar to that of the sunflower. However, the many other sculptures of the Lotus flower carved in all three regions showed flowers with a clear set of circular markings in the center of lily fruit, including carved seed marked as circles and showing under the circles on their tops. This shows the way that the center of the Lotus flower looks. The sunflower does not show these distinct circular holes in the fruit head as the Lotus flower does. Instead, it has a complex spiraled seed pattern. It is the spiral pattern that is seen in many of the sunflower carvings in these same regions. Since both the sunflower and the Lotus are used in similar fashions in these cultures, it would make sense to compare the sculptures in the temples to see the distinct differences. When we do this, we find flower sculptures with the distinct round circles carved in the center of the Lotus fruit, the Lotus characteristic, and flowers with a complex spiral pattern or a flat, smooth

Figure 23 - Lotus Flower Sculpture.
Hoysala Dynasty Temple. Karnataka, India. Photo by Carl L. Johannessen.

center, character-istic of the sun-flower. If only one of the flowers existed in the re-gion, then why are the sculptures different enough to be identifiable as different flow-ers? The most likely explanation, especially given the evidence that we have already discussed, is that both flowers were present and used in the region.

The term achene is a tech-nical term for the fruit we see when we look at sun-flower seeds. The actual seed of the sunflower is the soft interior mass inside the hard outer shell. The

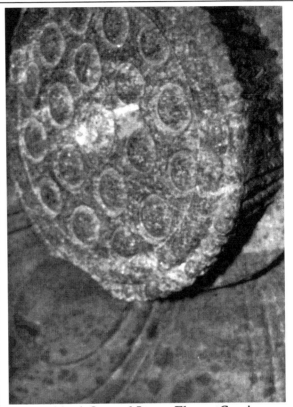

Figure 24 - A Second Lotus Flower Carving.
The Fruit with Seeds of the Lotus is shown. Hoysala Dynasty Temple. Karnataka, India. Photo by Carl L. Johannessen.

achene is the entire hard shell. There are other flowers that produce achenes, but the sunflower is by far the most famous along with the helicopter seeds of the maple tree. As we domesticated the sunflower, we would have selected the achenes from plants that produced larger seeds. Since the seed is trapped inside the achene, it would make sense that we would tend to select for larger achenes. In both the Old World sunflower specimens and the Mexican specimens, we found considerable variations in the length of the achenes, up to about 20% of its length (6.3 mm – 8.8mm). These variations may give us a clue as to potential differences in the lengths of the sunflower achenes in China, India, and Iraq. When I was in Xian, China, I collected and measured 55 achenes. They averaged 22 mm long (with a range from 16 mm to 25 mm) and 7 mm wide (range from 5mm to 9 mm) at the widest portion of the achene, significantly larger than the

Mexican plants. It is possible that the early Chinese sailors selected seeds that were particularly long when they initially transported them to China from the Americas. We may be able to ascertain where the original sunflowers came from in North America or from Mexico from this information. However, sunflower seeds may have been transferred from the Americas to the Old World so long ago that the Old World achene sizes have all been altered significantly from the original introductions due to farmer selection of long seeds. All of the Old World seed is significantly longer now than its American contemporaries.

A DNA analysis of the Asian sunflowers shows that the sunflowers in Asia have to have been there for a very long time. We know this because changes, or mutations, in DNA are seen and can be mapped backwards in a known timeframe. As a result of the multiplicity of the types of sunflower's DNA, which are evident in the west Asian characteristics, great age is further demonstrated because they were so much longer in the Old World. The distinct types of DNA that exist in these countries in comparison to the DNA of the sunflowers in the United States, both wild and domesticated, demonstrate that sunflowers on the other side of the ocean were subject to a very different selection process than those in the United States and Mexico. These differences in the DNA are shown by D.M. Arias – a researcher at *Centro de Investigación en Biotecnología, Universidad Autónoma del Estado de Morelos* – and Loren Rieseberg – Professor of Botany at the University of British Columbia, Distinguished Professor of Biology at Indiana University, and head of the Rieseberg Lab at UBC – in their 1995 graphs of three segments of DNA. The differences in these segments are so great in Russia, Turkey and France especially, that they are unlikely to have had time to evolve the level of DNA differentiation entirely after the Spanish conquest of Mexico. Arias and Rieseberg apparently never considered a pre-Columbian introduction of the sunflower into Asia as a possibility for the explanation of the extreme differences in the DNA, though they do recognize that the distributions were very different from the wild and domesticated sunflowers in the United States and Mexico.

Throughout both India and Mexico, many of the names under which the sunflower is categorized refer to the sun. There is some evidence that at least some of the Indian names were borrowed from ancient Mesoamerican languages. Sanskrit is the sacred language of Hinduism, the language in which all ancient Indian scripture was written. Moreover, although Sanskrit is technically one of the official languages of India, even today, it is rarely spoken and when it is it is for religious festivals. We know that words added to Sanskrit after the 11th or 12th Centuries C.E. are nearly all loan words, and not original Sanskrit. That there are many names for the sunflower used in sacred Sanskrit texts, as well as other Sanskrit literature, indicates that the word entered into the religious lexicon prior to this time, as several of the words seem to be sourced from Sanskrit rather than as loan words, words borrowed from other languages. It is also important to note that Hinduism, like other major religious institutions around the world, is conservative in adding new elements to the religious iconography. Given this, that we find carvings of sunflowers at the feet of bas- relief statues on Hoysala Dynasty Temples and the clearly thought out carvings on the tail and behind the ear of several statues of Nandi (thought out because they mark specific solar events through the year), it is clear that the sunflower had to have been introduced to the Indian subcontinent long before these religiously significant carvings were formed, which was before the time that Sanskrit quit adding unique nouns to its vocabulary.

The names for sunflowers in India include *suria mukhi, suryamukhi*, meaning literally "sun-flower" and *adityabhakta*. In Mesoamerica the names include Otomi's *dä nukhä* ("big flower that looks at the sun god"); Uto-Aztecan's *chimalacatl* ("shield flower"), *chimalxochitl* ("shield reed"), and Uto-Aztecan *tásai* ("sun"); Mayan *met' al a k'i:icha*: ("looker at the sun"); Mixe-Zoquean's name is *ama gahama* ("look at the sun"). Note that the Sanskrit *suriya mukhi* and the Otomi language group *dä nukhä* have homologous last words, both likely meaning flower coupled with a first noun/adjective that relates to the sun or a sun god. Linguistics is a strange and complex science, one that often seems to be comparing words that do not structurally sound the same but that have roots that are the same. This occurs because there is a known way in which sounds change over time in a language or in a word that has been adopted by one language from a different language. Given these known changes, a linguist can look at a group of words across several languages, usually words that mean the same thing, and they can see patterns and similarities that allow them to see that the languages are related. They can often even create language families based on these similarities.

Sunflowers in India are shown to have been used regularly by, at the latest, the 11th to 13th Centuries C.E. in Hindu temples. It is also worth noting that the sizes of the sunflower seeds currently found in Asia are frequently longer than their counterparts, both wild and domesticated, in the United States and Mexico. It is good to note that North America is accepted as the source of the sunflower. The DNA components of sunflowers in Russia, France, and Turkey are dramatically separated from the sunflower's DNA in the United States in Arias and Rieseberg's DNA graphing. We have names for the sunflower in the Sanskrit and Otomi language families that are close enough to be derivatives at the time of the early contact. It is very easy to conclude that there were significant pre- Columbian exchanges of plants between the Americas and the Old World. Further, before a plant is incorporated into the religious structure of a culture, a significant history of recognition and use has to have taken place, as it did in Asia and Mexico, in order for it to exist. Again, we have to accept the fact that tropical mariners were traveling to American shores and sailors departed with sunflower seeds in addition to the other 84 tropical plants that were transported to the Old World. This greatly expanded the distributional range of sunflowers, and the existence the other 83 American plants in the Old World before 1492.

CHAPTER 8: TOBACCO, COCA, AND CANNIBIS

In 1992, one of the most contentious and divisive chapters in the search for answers to the question of early tropical human interaction across the oceans began. It is contentious and divisive because it draws a highly respected and world-renowned scientist into a debate in which she was not even involved, or in fact interested. It shows the lengths to which some people, even professional scientists, will go to maintain the status quo rather than follow good scientific procedure by altering an old hypothesis to fit the new facts, or to discard it altogether. As we have stated repeatedly throughout this book and in other writings, we did not set out to change the way in which we, as modern people, view the rise of civilization. Scientists do not get up each morning determined to change the world, or to topple long-held beliefs, or even to cause intellectual revolutions.

Figure 25 - *Cannabis sattiva* or Marijuana.
Wild example in Asia. Photo by Carl L. Johannessen.

Figure 26 - *Erythroxylum novogranatense* or Coca bush.
Wild example. in Columbia. Photo by Drug Enforcement Officers. Public Domain.

The truth is that scientists are generally quite conservative in their views. They look at facts, and assume that if something does not fit into a well-established hypothesis, that the new research, new data, and new findings are likely to be incorrect. Scientists assume this and they will do everything in their power to correct any mistake that they or other researchers are thought to have made. Only after the researchers prove to themselves that the new data is valid and has been interpreted correctly, often through talking with other researchers or letting other researchers look at the data independently, do they look up and realize the importance of their research or discovery; and then, and only then do they publish and push the new idea.

This is what should have happened in 1992 with Dr. Balabanova's ground breaking discovery. However, it did not. Instead of accepting her work as valid research, and her results as a possibly paradigm changing reality to be checked and re- checked and then validated or discarded, her data and conclusions were rejected out of hand. But I'm getting ahead of myself, so let's revisit what actually happened in Ulm in 1992, and put a face on both the professor and her findings that ended up being so controversial.

The University of Ulm was founded in 1959 in the southern German city of Ulm. Ulm is on the Danube River at the point of confluence with the Blau River. It is an ancient city, with early ruins dating back as far as 5,000 B.C.E.

Figure 27 - *Nicotiana tabacum* or Tobacco Plant.
Domesticated example. Photo by Jerrid M Wolflick. Used with permission.

and the city itself being mentioned in records dating back to 854 C.E. Ulm has long been known as a manufacturing city and a city of classical industry. With the establishment of the University, which focuses on biomedicine, the sciences, and engineering, Ulm became an important research center in the high tech industrial world. Intel, Nokia, and Siemens all have major facilities in and around this ecologically friendly and industrial powerhouse. Ulm is considered by many people in academics and research to be one of the most respected research universities in Germany and in the world. Dr. Svetlana Balabanova is a world-renowned and highly respected pathologist and forensic anthropologist who was working at the University of Ulm in 1992. She specialized in discovering how people died, especially relating to toxic substances (poisons), and some of her pioneering toxicology tests are still used to this day in criminal investigations and crime lab research around the world. Dr. Balabanova did a lot of criminal investigation work relating to testing bodies for lethal substances, including drugs and poisons, to discover how they died. She was a regular and highly regarded witness in the German courts as well as other criminal courts around the world.

Just a few hours away, at the Munich Museum, the museum's Egyptologists had begun to suspect that the Egyptian pharaohs and upper class had imbibed opium and other mind-altering substances (including the lotus flower), for recreation and/or religious purposes. It had long been recognized that the recurring use of the lotus flower in Egyptian art was religious and symbolic, but a group of researchers suspected that it might also indicate that the intoxicating properties of the plant were well known to the ancient Egyptians. It made sense for these researchers to bring in a highly regarded forensic researcher to do any toxicology tests on the mummy remains that were in the possession of this Museum. It was logical for them to bring in Dr. Balabanova whose accuracy, care, and attention to detail was so well-known that her testimony was asked for and respected in criminal courts around the world.

Dr. Balabanova gladly took on the challenge and went to Munich to take samples of the nine mummies in

Figure 28 - Egyptian Mummy
This Egyptian mummy is dated to the New Kingdom. Photo by Jerrid M. Wolflick. Used with permission.

their collection. She returned the samples to her lab and, using the well-established and accepted techniques she had pioneered in forensic pathology, tested the samples using across the board tests. She did this to insure that they didn't miss any substance that they might not have considered as possible. In a word, she was being thorough. She did not expect to find anything outside of some possible opium and lotus flower traces. She also thought that she might be able to further understand some possible causes of death in this ancient country. The technology of modern forensic analysis had not yet been brought to bear on these ancient remains. Imagine her surprise when she got the test results back and the mummies showed definite use of Coca and Tobacco in addition to the expected chemicals. To a lay person it may not seem like a big deal that she found traces of powerful drugs in these mummies; after all, is that not something we expect from the rich and powerful from every era? And it would be true, except that neither of these plants could have been 'available' to the Egyptians, according to traditional scholarship. Both of these plants are known to have originated in the Americas (the only place where Coca is still grown to this day) and not introduced to the old world until after the beginning of the Sixteenth Century by European explorers. Since the mummies dated to between 1000 B.C.E. and 400 C.E. it was not possible for the metabolites of either Cocaine or Nicotine to be in these mummies; and yet, the tests showed that they were both present.

Dr. Balabanova, being a conscientious and careful scientist, looked at the results and knew that her lab must have somehow been contaminated. If her lab was not contaminated, then the samples had to have been contaminated. After all, everyone knew that there had been no contact between the Americas and the Old World, except possibly between a few Vikings and Canadian tribes, until the European Age of Discovery sent Christopher Columbus across the uncharted oceans in search of a quicker way to the Spice Islands. There was no evidence to the contrary, according to most accepted scientific venues. Dr. Balabanova went through her entire lab with her team, recleaning every surface, every container, every machine so that when she reran the test, she could be certain that there was no contamination from the lab equipment. When the tests were rerun, the same results occurred showing the same levels. Dr. Balabanova was forced to conclude that the contaminant was not from her lab. That there was a contaminant, she was certain, but that contaminant did not come from her lab. She reran the tests again, after doing some more research and the results came back the same. She went to the Museum curators and, after a lot of discussion, was convinced that the provenance of the mummies was valid; that they were in fact Egyptian mummies from long ago.

After all the care and attention to detail she followed, Dr. Balabanova concluded that somehow the ancient Egyptians had access to New World Coca leaves and tobacco long before it was previously thought that these were introduced to the Old World. She and her team published their findings in *Naturwissenschaften*, a peer-reviewed journal from Germany. One would think that the findings would cause an international stir in the academic community. Dr. Balabanova, already highly respected and trusted, had taken so much care to insure the accuracy of her findings. She had started as a skeptic of her own findings, putting them through exceptionally harsh regimens to make sure that no errors had occurred on the part of either her or her team. When all was said and done, she had taken the advice of Sherlock Holmes and recognized that when all other possibilities had been exhausted, the only explanation left had to be the accurate one, no matter how insane or unlikely. In the short article to the journal, Balabanova impartially presented her findings and conclusions.

Did it cause a stir in the international scientific community? Oh yes it did, although not one that Dr. Balabanova or the Munich Museum expected. They were attacked from every side. Dr. Balabanova, the same scientist whose testimony and evidence was regularly accepted into the records of criminal courts, was called a fake and a fraud. Scientist scoffed at the research, impugned her credibility, and even attacked the provenance of the mummies from the museum. The attack was so severe that the Museum began refusing everyone access to the mummies.

In the meantime, Dr. Balabanova had become deeply interested in finding out whether or not her discovery really was accurate; that underlying conservative side of scientific research rearing its head. She requested, and received, samples from mummies in museums and private collections from across Europe. She also asked for access to collecting her own samples from other mummies, including many naturally created mummies from the deserts of the Sudan. She also later tested Peruvian mummies of the same age so she could get an accurate baseline for the chemicals in mummies that researchers had strong reason to believe had used Coca in life. After testing thousands of mummies, some created through the Egyptian processes and others from naturally occurring mummification in extremely harsh conditions, she came to a shocking conclusion. The evidence was overwhelming that the Coca plant and Tobacco had both been present across the Old World long before Columbus. Moreover, the mummies in Peru also tested positive for the metabolites of THC, the mind-altering substance found in Marijuana (a plant originating in the Old World). These Peruvian Mummies dated to between 5 B.C.E and 1400 C.E. therefore crossing over the timeline of the Egyptian mummies by 400 years. Mummies from Jordan, Asia, Egypt, and the Sudan all tested positive for the metabolites for marijuana, cocaine, or both drugs and tobacco. There could be no doubt about the existence of these plants in

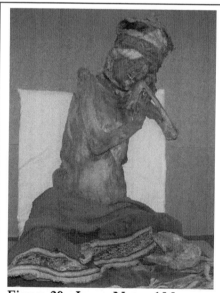

Figure 29 - Incan Natural Mummy. This example of an Incan mummy is dated to the early 8th Century C.E. Photo by Jerrid M. Wolflick. Used with Permission.

both hemispheres prior to when it was accepted that they were introduced. However, the heckling and disbelief didn't stop. It got so serious, in fact, that Dr. Balabanova was told not to discuss the findings with anyone. The credibility of the Ulm laboratories was at stake.

During the early days of the Egyptology craze in Europe, many mummies were bought, looted, or 'borrowed' and brought back to the many museums and collections in Europe. So many, in fact, that it was obvious that many of the alleged ancient mummies were modern forgeries. Although Balabanova accepted the authenticity of the mummies based on the statements of the curators, not all researchers were so kind. One such curator was Rosalie David, Keeper of Egyptology at the Manchester Museum in England. She was certain that the mummies had to be Victorian fakes, especially after Dr. Balabanova had rerun her tests using a very, very accurate and accepted process known as the hair shaft test. This test is still used by police departments worldwide to absolutely confirm drug use. David went to Germany to confirm the provenance of the mummies in the Munich Museum. Even with her exemplary credentials, Dr. David was not able to see the actual mummies that were tested. However, after a long discussion and assurances, she was given access to all of the records related to the mummies. These included purchase receipts, archaeology notes, research notes, preservation records, and anything else that the museum had regarding the mummies. It seems that the old stereotype of German order and organization proved true in this case. After studying the immense pile of available records for the Munich mummies, Dr. David concluded that there was no doubt in her mind that the mummies were of ancient origin and that their provenance was authentically ancient Egyptian.

Dr. Balabanova had continued to test samples of mummy hair and tissue from museums and collections across Europe, Africa, and the Middle East (a total of over 3,400 samples in the end). Although the fewer and fewer of mummies testing positive for the coca metabolites, nearly every mummy tested positive for the nicotine metabolites at a level impossible to explain using the plants of the Old World that also contained miniscule amounts of nicotine. There were some researchers that refused to accept the Coca findings at all but were postulating that the plant from the Old World that did contain small amounts of nicotine could explain this discovery. Dr. Balabanova's extensive and detailed tests revealed that this was simply not possible as the concentrations of nicotine in the mummies were too great for these other plants to have been the contributors to these chemicals. That few mummies tested positive for the metabolites of Coca makes a lot of sense if we think about it for a minute. Coca would have been far less available to the traders who traveled across the oceans to procure these products for the Old World markets than Tobacco. Tobacco grows on the eastern and western coasts of the New World and has a very large growing region. Contrasting this is the very small and difficult growing region of the Coca plant. This plant grows almost exclusively in the northern and western areas of South America (primarily Columbia, Peru, and Bolivia) and is concentrated in the Andes mountains and jungles of these regions. The leaves have been picked and chewed by local tribes for many millennia, likely soon after the first person tried it and discovered that it gave them energy, decreased pain, and induced mild euphoric states. Since this plant is not really present in any frequency on the Eastern side of South America (places where the Atlantic Ocean touch the shore) it would have to have been traded across various tribal lands and communities to get it to the places where Egyptian traders would have had access to both sampling the product, buying it, and then selling it in the Mediterranean Basin. Given that Egyptian nobles and royals already used poppy and lotus residues to achieve either euphoric or religious states, Coca would have seemed a perfect product to add to the potential trade inventory of a smaller ship. Given that it was found in mummies covering a 1400-year timespan, and that there is no evidence of planting it in the Old World, we have to conclude that this powerful mind-altering substance was traded across the Atlantic Ocean between the Americas and the traders in the Mediterranean along with tobacco and marijuana.

In the case of Dr. Balabanova, the male-dominated research world simply ignored the very overwhelming evidence from their female counterpart. Dr. Balabanova, more than many researchers, took every precaution to guarantee that the information was as accurate as was humanly possible to obtain. But rather than all of this creating an entirely new way of understanding human history and cultural interaction, she and her highly qualified team were ignored and vilified by the establishment scientists who were perhaps bent on maintaining the status quo, and maybe even a little afraid of giving this kind of power to female researchers. The director at the laboratory where Dr. Balabanova was a head researcher went so far as to order her not to travel overseas to give lectures and presentations on her findings. He was afraid that the reputation of the laboratory, at the time one of the most respected labs in the world, would suffer from a concerted attack by those who refused to accept Dr. Balabanova's findings.

When I had related this story to one person, a Brit, he quipped, "If cocaine and tobacco were both found in the Egyptian mummies, what about the Egyptian daddies?" I guess some folks can find humor in every situation. At least he got a laugh out of me.

The most secretive of the traded products were surely the drugs and mind-altering chemicals. Tobacco (*Nicotiana tobaccum* and *N. rustica*), cocaine, and marijuana products are among the earliest substances for which we have a positive identification in Egypt. Datura, Mexican prickle poppy, and Convolvulus seed (possibly sweet potato seeds) were also traded. All except marijuana are from the Americas. We are still researching the extent of the use of opium poppy, and mushrooms, San Pedro cactus, and other drug-related plants on both sides of the ocean need more DNA attention for more accurate identification.

Tobacco leaf and powder and tobacco-leaf insects were found in the wrapping of the mummy of Ramses II. The tobacco was not dated because the archaeologists who found it knew it originated in the Americas and therefore assumed it had to have been introduced subsequent to unpacking the mummy. It is true that the tobacco insect parasite is now distributed worldwide, but the question is, was it dead inside the original mummy wrapper? The tobacco material dating should be dated again, but so far, the Egyptians have seemed reluctant to cooperate. It is time for a change in attitudes for the honest good of science.

The plant substances that produced the chemicals found in these mummies can only have been obtained in two ways. Either they were the result of direct contact by mariners with people at the sources of such substances; or mariners were in contact with the source or through intermediaries at weigh stations, such as the Azores, Canary Islands, or the Polynesian Islands or India, that were used in the dispersal process. It is too soon in the development of this new evidence to know for certain how the oceanic transfers occurred. It seems likely, however, that drug runners were widespread in earlier millennia and that they were as secretive then as they are now. They apparently did not leave their ship's logs open for all to see.

Other drug-containing medicinals and hallucinogens, such as Datura and the Mexican prickle poppy were transported to the Old World from the Americas. They are recorded in carbon-14 dated archaeological strata in India and South America. Once on land, traders surely carried them between temperate and tropical zones, north and south. Since these cultivated plants are the 'footprints' of the passage of humans, it should be possible to gain further insights about trading patterns in the future as we learn more about the successive occupants of ports and interior trading stations worldwide. For instance, the Neolithic culture unearthed in Xian, China from 6,000 years ago had amphorae and three legged pots that are similar to Eastern Mediterranean amphora and pots. These are highly individualistic and demonstrate trade between the regions. We remain searching for the original source regions of the two drug items.

CHAPTER 9: PRE-1492 DIFFUSION OF WEEDS ACROSS THE TROPICAL OCEANS

According to the Columbia Encyclopedia, a weed is, "the common term for any plant, particularly an undesired plant, growing in controlled or cultivated ground, where it competes with crop plants for space, soil nutrients, other energy, water or sunlight." According to Biology Online, a life science dictionary, a weed is: ."any plant that is growing in a place where a human wants a different kind of plant or no plants at all. Any plant that crowds out cultivated plants. Plants that are considered a nuisance to man because they compete for resources in the same local environment as the crops we intend to grow for our own species." Unlike the many valuable crop plants and trees that we know were transferred across the oceans, and of which we have ample and abundant evidence, we only have evidence for a few weeds that were also carried by early mariners across the oceans. Of course, this is because of the nature of weeds. Early explorers would have likely shown no more interest in them than the native population with which they were trading. Moreover, the native population would likely not have really said anything about them except in the context of pesky new plants growing in the way of their crops. The domesticates (purposefully traded and cultivated plants) were improved and their usefulness increased through millennia of selection and maintenance of the selected genetic lines. These plants had useful characteristics that were recognizable. Of course, we assume that the farmer attempted to maintain and save the seeds of the plants he or she selected during his or her lifetime, especially those plants that improved over that time. When I lived with farmers and other peasant populations while I was in the field studying, I discovered that the giving of seeds to a new person (the trader in this instance) was essential. It was something not only deemed appropriate, but also very important, a duty almost. Therefore, it is likely that the local farmers would have given seed samples to the foreign traders who took them back to their homelands and planted them in the appropriate zones. The seeds of their weeds likely traveled as unknown hitchhikers on these journeys as well.

When seeds were traded, transported, or stored, it is likely that early farmers, in a manner similar to that of their counterparts around the world during a later era, gathered and packaged their "seeds" in cloth or woody containers and packages. Unlike the modern world where we have machines and computers to help ensure accuracy, seeds were sorted, stored, and maintained by hand by the farmers and their families. These bundles of seeds would often contain unwanted smaller seeds of other plants that grew either in or near the fields where the crop plants were harvested. Even today when we buy seed packets for flowers we still occasionally get odd seeds in the seed packet along with the intended flower seeds. Even if on the rare occurrence that the seeds were sorted perfectly, as could be the case with a simple large seed like maize, the barbed seeds of weeds could stick to the surface of the storage containers whenever they were placed on the ground, either in the fields or during sorting and final storage. The seeds of certain plants are heavily barbed specifically for the purpose of clinging to a passerby and being transported somewhere else. This is evident to anyone who was ever owned a dog or walked through the tall grass during certain times of the year. Getting rid of the tenacious burrs and spears is nearly impossible and you never get rid of every one of the pesky things. These unintended seed tagalongs would have attached to trade goods and to the clothes of the traders and would then be carried along across the many land and sea trade routes around the world, landing in fertile ground in the fields of many farming civilizations. They would arrive unrecognized alongside the intended trade goods for the city, town, village, or farm. The burred and hooked seeds of weedy plants would also attach themselves to the hair, clothing, and bedding of the transoceanic mariners, traders, passengers, and their animals; they also were transferred throughout the oceanic trading routes of the traders from original civilization. This includes being transported across the oceans to the other hemisphere.

Weeds tend to be quite hearty and robust plants, often far more so than the cultivated plants being traded. When the seeds were deposited unwittingly on the soil in a new location they often prospered without further support, tending, or protection. The next year the weed would return quite easily to that same site in spite of every effort made by the farmers to kill it. Anyone who has ever dealt with dandelions in their lawn can attest to the difficulty of actually getting rid of them over the years. Even if you get rid of every dandelion in the yard, you will still see new dandelions, which were blown in from a neighbor's yard, shoot up the next year.

Another source of these seeds could have been the packages of fruits and vegetables, which were brought on board for the sailors, traders, and passengers to eat during the voyage. The unwanted seeds may have attached themselves to the storage packages or the consumable produce itself and could very easily have gotten rubbed off or dropped and stuck in the crevices between the ship's deck boards. These stray seeds would have been later washed off when the ship returned to home port, or when it was put into dry dock, or even when a smaller craft was pulled up onto the beach to be cleaned, parked or repaired.

The underlying problem with documenting the weedy plants we are looking at as well as the animal pests we will discuss in a later chapter is that we have had five hundred years of Post-Colonial history and significant ocean travel that could have, and likely did contaminate every square inch of the inhabitable planet with these very same pests. However, we have a science that helps us sort the post-1492 contamination of the Earth from the pre-1492 contamination. It is Paleontology and the subspecialties of this branch of science: paleo-botany, paleoecology, and paleozoology. Paleontology is the scientific study of prehistoric life, generally excluding human history. Paleo-botany is the branch dealing with the recovery and identification of plant remains from geological contexts, and their use for the biological reconstruction of past environments (paleogeography), and both the evolutionary history of plants, with a bearing upon the evolution of life in general. Paleozoology is the branch dealing with the recovery and identification of multicellular animal remains from geological (or even archeological) contexts, and the use of these fossils in the reconstruction of prehistoric environments and ancient ecosystems. Paleoecology uses data from fossils and subfossils to reconstruct the ecosystems of the past. It involves the study of fossil organisms and their associated remains, including their life cycle, living interactions, natural environment, and manner of death and burial to reconstruct the paleo-environment. These three scientific pursuits are perfect for the search for, and identification of weeds that were transferred before 1492.

Up until recently, archaeological sites did not regularly collect, label and sample soil remains from the various strata of their dig sites. In order to truly begin extensive research on accidental transferals, this soil collection would be a necessary addition to the archaeological routine. This addition would mean that we are planning for the potential discovery of unknown weeds of all kinds, as well as other domesticated plants, at each archaeological site being excavated everywhere in the tropical and subtropical regions of the world. It is, admittedly, a long and tedious process, but the effort should pay off admirably in the long run. I suggest that this process should be as follows: Archaeologists at each site collect and save a few cubic centimeters of soil from each accurately dated layer of the excavation. There are several accepted dating methods used by researchers. These sealed and verified samples would then be sent to a paleontologist or paleo-botanist along with the comprehensive list of the plants found growing on and around the site, needed on any reputable excavation. This botanical inventory of current plants will greatly accelerate the researchers' ability to identify the species in the soil samples by their seeds and leafy parts only. The researcher uses the list to find these plant remains, as fossils, in the soil samples from the several layers of the site. Using floatation or another method of separating the actual mineral dirt from the organic detritus in the soil layers, researchers will have access to potentially identifiable the organic materials specifically. The person in charge of each site and its examination should put into their financial applications (grants, fellowships, etc.) sufficient funds to pay for the analyses by the paleontologist for every depth level of their excavation. With this system in place, the paleontologists now need to develop a working relationship across all archaeological branches of the field and cooperate with them to accurately identify all organisms at each dated level.

Professor John Sorenson and I have already identified 100 plants moved across the oceans in our book: World Trade and Biological Exchanges Before 1492 C.E. Revised and Expanded Edition, published in 2013 for the academic audiences. Our research has confirmed that at least nine weedy plants were diffused across the tropical oceans before the 15th Century C.E. There may well be more but we found definitive evidence for these nine weeds. These include alligator weed (*Alternanthera philoxeroides*), bulrush or totora reed (*Schoenoplectus californicus*), carpetweed (*Mollugo verticillata*), fleabane (*Erigeron canadensis*), goatweed (*Ageratum conyzoides*), milkweed (*Asclepias curassavica*), spiny amaranth (*Amaranthus spinosus*), phasey bean (*Macroptilium lathyroides*), and purslane (*Portulaca oleracea*). Some of these plants have been found in the carefully dated archaeological digs in both hemispheres. Others are mentioned in ancient writings from the hemisphere to which they were transported. Still others have been found on formerly uninhabited islands in the Pacific Ocean that were likely used by early tropical mariners as stopping points for water, rest, repairs, or other reasons during their travels.

Phasey Bean, Purslane, Totora reed, and Carpetweed are all wild plants that have been found in archaeological digs dating to before the 15th Century C.E. In 1974, Jefferson Chapman, Robert Stewart, and Richard Yarnell studied Purslane and carpetweed in the archaeological digs of the temperate Eastern North America, specifically at the Salt Cave site in Kentucky and the Icehouse Bottom Cave site in Tennessee. They discovered the carbonized remains of Purslane seeds dating back to the 1st Millennium B.C.E. in the Salt Caves and carbonized remains of the carpetweed seeds dating to 1170 ± 140 B.C.E. in the Icehouse Bottom Caves and the 1st Millennium B.C.E. in the Salt Caves. Both were recovered using water flotation, using gently bubbling water to process soil to recover tiny floating artifacts like seeds and woody remains out of pulverized material from the site. Moreover, both plants were reported to have been discovered in the fire level at the bottom of the Great Mound at the Troyville site in Catahoula Parish, Louisiana, dating to 500 C.E. Most scientists agree that Purslane likely originated in Southeast Asia and was transferred across the Old World to Europe long before the present time. History records the uses of Purslane as a food product and medicinal herb in both Roman and Greek writings. In fact, when very early French settlers noted that Purslane was growing among Native American maize crops, they were puzzled by why the Native Americans did not think to eat it as it was a sought-after delicacy in France. This indicates that the plant was not introduced purposefully to the Americas by any European group as all of the European groups used it as a source of leafy greens, both cooked and raw. It is likely that Purslane was accidentally introduced to the Americas by early travelers and traders.

Figure 30 – Blooming Purslane
Photo by Jerrid M. Wolflick. Used with permission.

Figure 31 – Blooming Carpetweed
Photo taken by Jerrid Wolflick. Used with permission.

Weeds such as Purslane and Carpetweed emphasize the potential of and the need for cooperation between scientists in various disciplines and fields. Paleo- botanists can contribute much to the understanding of plant histories and the plant's relationship to people. Often, as we have shown in our cross-discipline and cross-science research, each field of study has some information about a subject that is often unknown or missed by others in different fields. Scientists in different specialties, even those quite closely related, do not often compare research, and the researchers may not often read research outside of their field, as they are usually lucky to have time to read the current research in their own specialty. It is no wonder, then, that we often miss the larger picture of human interactions with nature and cultures across the oceans centuries and millennia ago.

Totora, a reed used in making woven baskets and bundled together to make reed rafts/boats in highland Peru, has a long and fruitful history across the Pacific Ocean. In 1770 the Spanish Gonzalez Expedition from Peru, definitively identified the Totora reeds in the crater lakes of Easter Island's volcanic caldera

Figure 32 - Totora Reeds
Photo taken by Carl L. Johannessen.

as the same species as those in Peru. According to the inhabitants of Easter Island, this reed, the Totora from Peru, was brought to Easter Island by early ancestors of the current inhabitants, not by European sailors. This places the species on Easter Island long before any European sailors visited. Further evidence of the Totora on Easter Island was found in the tomb beneath *Ahu Tepeu* (in a lava cave on the western side of Easter Island). At this time the discovery was declared a separate species, but Skottsberg eventually concluded that the remains were of the same species as those found in Peru. Later, in 1998, a team of researchers, exploring the impact of *moai* quarrying on the inhabitants of Easter Island ran several core samples and during the analysis found that the Totora reed was present in the strata dating to around the middle of the 4th Century C.E. Given that the Polynesians first arrived at Easter Island sometime during the 5th Century C.E., it seems that sailors from the western part of Peru arrived on the island first. As Peruvian sailors would have sailed the oceans in rafts made of the Totora reed and Balsa; it makes sense that they would have put seed of

some of this weedy reed in lakes and swamps at various remote locations along their sailing routes. This could have been used by later sailors as repair materials, since they seem eventually to have cut down all the woody trees used for building boats and rafts elsewhere on the islands.

The Phasey Bean, once considered a part of the *Phaseolus* genus but later reclassified under the *Macroptilium*

Figure 33- Phasey Bean Blossom.
Photo taken by Jerrid M. Wolflick. Used with permission.

genus, is a plant that has its origins in the Americas. Traces of this plant have been found in Peru and date to at near 3,000 B.C.E. Other organizations claim the plant may actually be native to and have originated in India. Given the age of the findings in Peru along with potential claims by some researchers that it originates in India, it is impossible to pretend that this plant wasn't present for millennia on both continents. It is considered a weed nearly everywhere that it grows but certain places in Australia actually use it for a food product. This weed has been found in numerous archaeological sites relating to the Malwe and Jorwe cultures of Diamabad, Ahmednagar District, Maharashtra Pradesh, India dating from 1600 - 1000 B.C.E. As this weed grows alongside other, cultivated beans in the Americas, it is logical to suppose that it was transferred by mistake along with the intentional trade and planting of the crop beans. The Phasey Bean is similar after all and is used as food during disasters like droughts, for instance.

These four weeds have been definitively identified in archaeological strata long pre-dating the arrival of the modern European explorers of the 15th Century C.E. and later. They were all positively identified by reputable researchers to have grown on the hemisphere not of their origin. Those that originated in the Americas were all found to have grown, and to still be growing, in the Old World and vice versa in the Americas. These discoveries require that researchers give a reasonable and consistent explanation for the appearance of these weeds on both sides of the oceans. There have been many attempts to explain these transfers including migratory birds, floating seeds, and the winds. None of these ideas has successfully explained the transfers after extensive experimentation has cast reasonable uncertainty on the efficacy of them as transfer possibilities. For example, the idea that birds in the tropical regions, from which all these plants originate, eat the seeds or get the burred seeds on their feathers and carry them across the oceans while migrating, is flawed. These birds simply do not migrate East-West across the oceans. Northern latitude birds that migrate to the tropical regions during the winter, migrate North-South, usually over land and therefore they would drop seeds in soils that could not sustain the weed since weather, temperature, and seasons are a factor in a plant successfully being transferred. In the case of seeds floating across the oceans on the currents, the seeds are soaked in the saltwater. Many researchers (including Charles Darwin) have floated seeds in briny water similar to ocean water, if not ocean water brought to the lab, to try and confirm the likelihood of transfer by flotation. Although many seeds will, even after sustained contact with the brine, germinate, every one of them rapidly sinks to the bottom of the container. This indicates that even if they did manage to survive the ocean's salty mix long enough to get to a new land mass, they would have sunk to the bottom of the sea long before they could have reached it!

Four of the other nine plants listed above, although they have not yet been found in archaeological remains, have definitive names and have been mentioned in the literature of the other hemisphere, in this case Classical Chinese or Ancient Sanskrit. (See chapter on Linguistic Evidence)

SECTION 3: FAUNAL EVIDENCE FOR TRANSOCEANIC DIFFUSION BEFORE 1492 C.E.

CHAPTER 10: INSECTS AND ANIMALS

Archaeological evidence for Pre-Columbian Transoceanic Diffusion of various animals and parasites is quite compelling. If a plant, parasite, or animal evolved in one hemisphere's environment and shows up in a similar environment across the vast stretches of oceans that separate the Old World and the Americas, we have to be able to rationally predict and explain their presence. Moreover, if there are reasonable cultural similarities like religious rituals, games, or architecture between the cultures that traded the plants or animals, then we can infer that these were likely transported at the same time. We no longer need to rely on the idea of independent invention to explain these many similarities in cultures. For the last several hundred years, much of the academic world has accepted the idea that the early European traders transported these various biotic species after Columbus "discovered" the Americas and that any similar traits were created independently by the separate cultures to fill a similar need. Given the amount of modern archaeological evidence that we now have showing species have been present, accessible, and regularly used by early tropical population far across the oceans from the site in which they originated and evolved, scientists have to revisit their original hypotheses of post-Columbian transfer and reorganize it to explain the anomalies.

In this chapter, we will look at the archaeological evidence for animals being transferred across the oceans from the Old World to the Americas as well as in the other direction, long before 1492 C.E. Of the many animal remains that have been discovered in archaeological digs dating to before 1492C.E. nine animals have been found that originated on continents, which are separated by the Atlantic or Pacific Ocean and were therefore transferred to the other hemisphere across one or both of the oceans. Five of these nine animals are pests that were likely in the crop seeds that were transferred either as trade goods or as shipboard food. These are the lesser mealworm (*Alphitobius diaperinus*), the live clam (*Mya arenaria*), the rat (*Rattus rattus*), the South American lesser grain borer (*Rhyzopertha dominica*), and the drugstore beetle (*Stegobium paniceum*). The four others are the domestic dog (*Canis familiaris*), the domestic cat (*Felis catus*), the domestic chicken (*Gallus gallus*), and the Turkey (*Meleagris gallopavo*). The rational explanation for these discoveries, knowing what we have learned about the transportation of plants, is that regular, repeated, and sustained interaction between sailors and people of the Old World and the Americas occurred prior to 1492. Of course there is always the possibility that the Extra Terrestrials in their unidentified flying vehicles carried the seeds and the animals, but this possibility may be close to hyperbole.

The Lesser Meal Worm, or *Alphitobius diaperinus*, is a native pest of the Old World where it was responsible for the destruction of flours, cracked grains, and other meal products. Although it was likely not a major economic issue in human populations for this reason, it is a major carrier of diseases and parasites that can decimate a chicken flock. Pests in general are not as likely to show up in widespread archaeological sites, rather in narrow

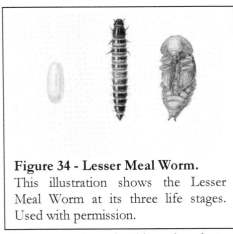

Figure 34 - Lesser Meal Worm.
This illustration shows the Lesser Meal Worm at its three life stages. Used with permission.

environments where the things they destroy were stored and buried, often mortuary sites like the pyramids of Egypt or the burial chambers of the Mayan or Incan leaders. This is because in older funeral rites, it was common to bury the dead who were wealthy or important enough with plenty of provisions for the journey through the afterlife or the land of the dead. These burials often included foods, drinks, statues, and household items. These pests will infest the foodstuffs of the burial chamber and they have been discovered in a similar mortuary context in the New World as well. Panagiotakopulu reports finding lesser meal worm in the British Isles in a second-century C.E. burial and in Egypt with a mummy dating to 1350 B.C.E. In Peru, the same worm has been found in a 1240 C.E. mummy bundle. One can hope for more discoveries once this possibility of its presence is recognized.

This association of pests with burial practices in both hemispheres appears less startling when we recall the mortuary context of the discovery of tobacco and coca chemicals in Egyptian mummies dating from the second millennium B.C.E to the fifth century C.E. In addition, the chemical residues of metabolized Cannabis sativa, an Old World plant, have been found in Peruvian corpses. It is not so surprising then, that a beetle and a worm from Eurasia should show up in graves in Peru. Humans traveling on boats provide the plausible means by which the two areas, halfway around the world from each other, could have been so linked both biologically, chemically and, apparently, culturally.

K. S. Petersen and his team report that shells of a live clam, *Mya arenaria*, have been discovered off the Danish coast that dated to before the sailing of Columbus. Researchers agree that the Vikings would likely have eaten the clams on their voyages, but have not agreed on why they would have brought live clams back to Denmark. Some researchers posit that the clams became attached to the boats and were transferred accidentally. Until now, the view had been that it was distributed only in the Americas. A radiocarbon date of the shell from the 13th century has been obtained for a specimen of shell that leaves only "very slight probability" of its having been brought to

Figure 35 - *Mya arenaria*. Clam.
Photo in the public domain.

Denmark after Columbus's voyages. Since the transfer had to have involved human voyaging (presumably involving the clam only inadvertently), it "could have been transferred from North America to Europe by the Norse" (Petersen et al., 1992). What makes this case so interesting is not really that the clam was transferred or whether or not it was transferred on purpose, but that most researchers accepted the evidence out of hand. This is important because the amount of actual evidence for this transfer was actually very scant. Of the shells that the team dated, only one shell dated to before Columbus. Unlike the negative reaction to the transfers that we have seen that had far more available evidence, the larger body of academics accepted this single shell as sufficient evidence of early travel across the oceans. It is interesting to note how easily the researchers accepted early European travel on scant evidence while they deny Southeast Asian, Middle Eastern, and Indian travel that has far better evidence.

Recent studies of the spread of rats in the Pacific basin have taken advantage of the obvious fact that the distribution of rats, or *Rattus-rattus*, must be explained because of human voyaging, since rats do not swim at sea. Thus when we find that rat bones were excavated over 30 years ago from an archaeological site at Tlatilco, a site west of the Mexico City that shows indications of Asian cultural influence, the explanation for their presence might come from a transpacific vessel on the Pacific coast of Mex-

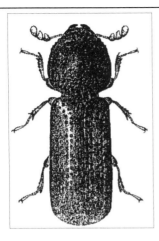

Figure 37 - South American Lesser Grain Borer Beetle.
This drawing was found in a classic text on wheat pests. Picture is in the public domain.

ico. The data is similar to that of the information on the cat and the chicken at Tlatilco. Polynesians allowed rats on their ocean-going crafts and may have used them to eat and spare themselves death from scurvy.

Some authors had apparently supposed the South American lesser grain borer, or *Rhyzopertha dominica*, to be from South America. Kislev and Panagiotakopulu have stated without any supporting information (so said also by Potter, see below) that it came from India. If it came from the Old World, then transoceanic transport in antiquity cannot be claimed, but if it came from South America, then an explanation for its presence in Eurasia is called for. An explanation for its presence in Old World archaeological sites would be necessary as well. It has indeed been found at the Minoan site of Akrotiri on the Island of Thera as well as in a Roman site located in Egypt. While commonly referred to as the 'South American lesser grain borer,' Panagiotakopulu lists the origin (in the table on page 9 of their book) as "India." It was also found in Kahun in Egypt (1900–1800 BCE), and in a vessel from Tutankhamen's tomb dated at 1345 BCE. It is a usual pest found in grain in warm countries, and it has been recorded to have been found in a wide variety of crops, such as wheat, barley, millet, rice, maize, and sorghum as well as other products. It was originally recorded in the literature as having been from South America, but now its origins seem to be becoming more cosmopolitan in nature. More accurate dating is

Figure 36 - Drawing of *Rattus rattus*
This drawing of the the House Rat or Black Rat was done by Carl Linneaus, 1758.

definitely needed.

The drugstore beetle, or *Stegobium paniceum*, is a pest usually found in dried, stored vegetable matter, is documented in both Egyptian and Peruvian ancient burials. Greater incidence and earlier recognition of the species in the Old World favors that hemisphere as the place of origin. In Peru, S. paniceum was found with mummies dated at least to the 13th century CE. Burials in

Figure 38 - *Stegobium paniceum* or Drugstore Beetle.
Also known as Biscuit Beetle or Bread Beetle. Used with permission.

Egypt as early as 3400 BCE have revealed this same 'drugstore' or 'biscuit' beetle. It was also present in both Roman and Bronze Age England.

Among the animals that have found their way across the oceans to or from the Americas, many are related to the shipping business. Cats were likely brought on board ships to help control the endemic rodent population resulting from grain and foodstuff being on ships. The insect pests were often in the food stores of the sailors or the foodstuffs being used for trade goods (beetles and insect larvae). It is unlikely that any of these animals would have gained a real foothold in the transplanted location without repeated and regular contact between the Old World and the Americas. Given the number of animals, plants, parasites, and diseases that now have been discovered by me and Professor Sorenson in Pre-Columbian archeological sites we can conclude that there was sustained and regular transoceanic trade between the continents long prior to 1492. These facts further emphasize that the same sailors brought the other components of civilization's development as they intermingled with

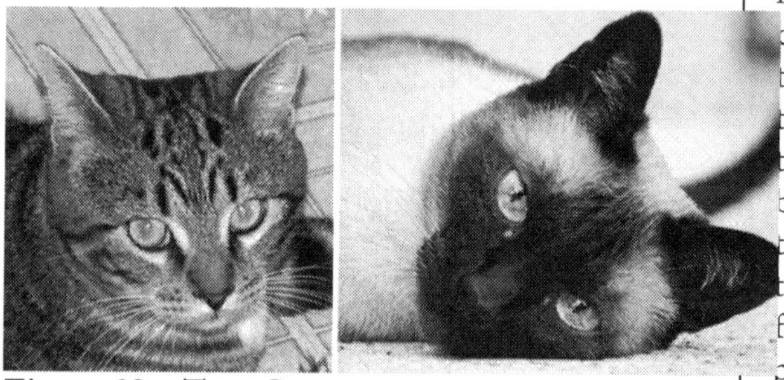

Figure 39 – Two Cats
American Short-hair with traditional tabby markings on left and Traditional Siamese with blue eyes on the right. Photos taken by Jerrid Wolflick. Used with permission.

local people on all sides of the oceans. This integrates all the tropical and subtropical peoples together as part of a similar contact. The data assembled by Sorenson and Raish (1996) is indicated as being highly relevant to the study of diffusion across the oceans over the last 8,000 years.

At the Middle Pre-classical archaeological site of Tlatilco, to the west of Mexico City, excavations conducted over 30 years ago revealed the bones of the domestic cat, or *Felis catus*. There is no actual evidence to suggest contamination of the archaeological remains by post-Castilian mixing of archaeological deposits for the faunal bones, although that was the claim of the archaeologist at the time of excavation. This Middle Pre-classical settlement and burial ground produced a single cat jawbone, [as far as is reported all archaeological material from Tlatilco hitherto has been dated between 800–400 B.C.E. The single jawbone came from level "F", the sixth deepest sub-stratum (of nine) within the stratum III or deepest master stratum of the archaeological site. Dr. Joaquin Arroyo-Cabrales of *Laboratorio de Arqueozoología, Instituto Nacional de Anthropología e Historia*, showed the jawbone to us although surface and intermediate strata, and a few deeper substrata, show the presence of horse, cattle, and goat bones so these bones need to be dated with C^{14}, but that has been difficult to carry out. Bones of the domestic cat have appeared in five archaeological sites in Mexico. In two of them, at Tlatilco and Cuanalán, they were found in bottle-shaped pits. Three other sites with cat bones were of Colonial Spanish age. Ticul Álvarez and Aurelio Ocaña suppose that the cat bones should be explained by either stating that the bottle-shaped pits were used after the Conquest when European cats had been introduced, or that digging/tunneling rodents introduced the bones in the deposit "by accident," or by the redepositing of post-Conquest remains due to churning of the deposit. Neither suggestion is entirely realistic in the case of deposits under several dwelling floors. We continue searching for functional permission to date the bones.

The dog, or *Canis familiaris*, is commonly assumed to have been brought to the New World by early hunter-gatherers via Beringia, but there is very slim evidence that this accounted for all of the dogs that arrived early in the Americas. Mair's round up of data from Asia suggests that

Figure 40 - Statue of Fattened Edible Dog

These dogs were likely for sacrifice and dated to Pre-Columbian Mexico. Photo by Carl L. Johannessen.

the reality of dogs living in the company of humans in the Old World is not particularly ancient. The earliest domestication (or taming) of the wolf to dog for which we have archaeological evidence occurred in the Near East during the Natufian era only around 12,000 years ago. However, recent DNA evidence suggests that the split between wolf and dog was at least 27,000 years ago and upwards of 40,000 years ago. Scientists took samples from a 37,000-year-old Siberian Wolf bone and sequenced the DNA. The results allowed researchers to recalibrate the DNA mutation frequency and rate for canines. This work showed that the dog genetically parted from the wolf between 27,000 and 40,000 years ago. Dogs in the European Mesolithic period date on the order of 7000–4000 B.C.E. The earliest dog remains in China are around 2,000 B.C.E. Moreover, the common hypothetical root words for dog in ancestral language groupings like Nostratic and Afro-Asiatic appear to date "closer to 6000 B.C.E than to 10,000 B.C.E". Turner says a dog skull dated to 12,000 B.C.E was found in a cave in the Altai Mountains, but it was not associated with evidence for human presence in the area. These data mean that it is a stretch to imagine domesticated dogs being available in northeastern Asia to accompany the presumed earliest walking immigrants to the New World via Bering Strait surface, even if it was taking place while or after the strait was landlocked. The people of the northern most areas of Siberia were obviously able to travel over snow and ice and the Arctic Ocean has regularly frozen in the wintertime throughout all of history. Snowshoes and skis as well as walking on the snow allowed people to travel on the marine edge of the glacial and land based ice where they could obtain fish, birds, and marine mammals as they needed them, for their culture's existence. More likely the people of the earliest influx entered the Americas in dugout canoes or boats paddled along the ice front on the Pacific or Atlantic Ocean to the north or south of the hemisphere in the full Pleistocene.

So where did American dogs come from? Although it is possible that the animals might have been independently domesticated in the Americas from wild canids, evidence, that even hints of domestication, are all but absent. Some dogs may have come from Japan where wool-bearing dogs existed and were kept. The natives of the islands of British Columbia also kept these wool- bearing dogs. Others, such as the edible-dog, may have come from China to the Mexico area. There is ample cultural evidence of the edible dogs in China and the edible dogs in the Americas were being raised for and used in temple sacrificial rituals as well as being eaten. Conventional wisdom among many zoologists holds that chickens, or Gallus-gallus, were absent in the New World until introduced by the Spaniards. If that had been the case, the chickens in the hands of Amerindians after the Conquest ought to have been strictly of the Mediterranean type, but they were not. Many of them looked like Chinese or Malay chickens, very different feather color, body shape, feather distribution, color of eggs, and behavior from the Mediterranean variety of chicken present in Europe. Evidence from physical characteristics of fowl, documentary history, ethnography, the uses to which the fowl were put, and the distribution of vernacular names combine to establish that the reputed introduction of all the types of chickens by the Spaniards is contrary to the facts. Instead, multiple introductions of fowl across the oceans, in addition to the later Spanish importation, are indicated.

In the early 1920s archaeologist Richard Latcham observed that in Chile, Bolivia, and Peru, at least three indigenous domesticated varieties or chickens were known. The people there had not adopted the Spanish terms for 'cock,' or 'chicken,' for those birds "because they have their own names."

Three kinds of chickens were definitely present before the Spanish Conquest and are still represented among the fowl kept by the Araucanian Indians of Chile. Some lay blue or olive-green eggs, are tailless, and have tufts of feathers in the form of a ball at the sides of their heads, as do fowl in China, which also laid blue eggs. Later I also examined chickens in Chile and found fowl similar to those just described. In 1929, archaeologist Carlos Aldolfo Finsterbusch agreed that these were pre-Columbian chickens. In 1921,

Figure 41 - Black-Boned Black-Meated Chicken
This example of the BBC was found in Guatemala. Photo taken by Carl L. Johannessen's assistant on the trip. Used with permission.

Professor Salvador Castello went so far as to identify four types (varieties) of Chilean chickens which differed from the common European fowl but showed Asiatic features, such as blue-egg laying and black meat. The chicken will be looked at in detail in Chapter 18

It is now clear that the quintessentially American fowl, the turkey or *Meleagris gallopavo*, was being kept in Europe in the late Medieval Period. In 1940, an observer claimed that an American turkey could be seen in a painted frieze at Schleswig Cathedral, which had been built about 1280 C.E. In 1940, Erwin Stresemann showed that the mural had been restored in the 1800s and 1900s rebutted that claim. Given the restoration, the rendering of the turkey as it existed in 1940, when he saw it, could have depended on knowledge acquired after Columbus. Nevertheless, findings since that time have restored the possibility of a pre-Columbian origin for the Schleswig representation. Hungarian archaeologists found bones of a turkey in the 14th-century royal castle at Buda. Turkey bones have also been excavated from a carefully dated 14th-century-site in Switzerland. Other Hungarian sites of the 10th to 13th centuries have yielded signet rings engraved with images of the turkey that show the fleshy pendant growth on the turkey's neck. Furthermore, a letter written in 1490 by Hungarian King Matthias, who died later that year, requested through an envoy that the Duke of Milan send him turkeys ("galine de Indie"). The king wanted to acclimatize the bird in Hungary. He also asked that a man who knew how to care for turkeys be sent with the birds. Obviously, the fowl was in Europe before Columbus' first voyage.

As an amusing anecdote, it seems that the early settlers to North America brought the turkey with them as a food crop. So, the turkey was originally domesticated in Mexico at some early date that has not yet been determined, transferred to Europe sometime before the 11the Century, and then transported by early European settlers back to North America as they were not aware that the Americas already had a population of both domestic and wild turkeys. Moreover, at some point in time after the initial domestication in Mexico, another group of aboriginal Americans in the US Southwest domesticated a different breed of turkey for use as food. This was discovered by Camille Speller and her team in 2010 when they were studying ancient turkey bones.

These larger animals, along with the other noted here in the Appendix in Table X, have been transferred across the oceans by sailors, traders, and adventurers since long ago. Cats and dogs were brought onto the boats as passengers that earned their keep by keeping the vermin population in check. Rats came on board ships surreptitiously because of the availability of food both from the sailor food stores and from the trade stores. In addition, the Polynesian sailors intentionally brought rats on board their boats for the purpose of adding a protein food source during the voyages. The insect pests came on

Figure 42 –*Meleagris gallopavo* or Wild Turkey
This species is originally from the Americas. Photo taken by Carl L. Johannessen.

board as part of the cargo or supplies. Sailors would have transferred all of these as they landed in new ports, traded with various civilizations and cultures, or simply landed to explore new lands. In conjunction with the many plants that we have already shown were transported across the oceans, these animals strengthen the case even further for regular and sustained transoceanic voyaging before Columbus.

.

CHAPTER 11: RAT AS TRANSPORT FOR GANESH

Government housing is available in India for scientists on low budgets. It is a wonderful assist when one is in India doing research in their temples without any grant money. I was at Halibidishfara Temple studying bas-relief carvings with the corn carvings in the stone panels on the outside temple walls and since Halebid had practically no recreation activities in the evenings to divert one from getting sleep, researchers, such as me, just crashed at night and woke up early in the morning. In fact, this was on December 20 one day before the winter solstice (the shortest day of the year). I awoke just before dawn and found I had a "visitor" in the dimly lit room. We were not expecting a rat to show its head at the edge of Ganesh's picture that was hanging on the wall. We were not expecting the little pointed nose and a beady little eye that was looking at me lying in bed.

Waking to see the nose of a rat behind a picture of Ganesh hanging on the wall of our room in government housing in India was enough to make me curious and a little distressed. In our existence in the US, we rarely appreciate the significance of a rat in our bedroom appearing behind the picture of Ganesh, but in India the rat is considered to be the transport of Ganesh -- the elephant- headed god, the remover of obstacles, the patron of arts and sciences, and the deva of intellect and wisdom. The fact that the rat was behind the picture of Ganesh, made the myth "come alive" for me, to an extent at least.

When I moved my hand, the little tiny nose sucked back behind the picture. I waited and was still and the rat poked his nose out from behind the picture again. One finger moving was enough to cause the rat to move behind the picture. When I was still, he would poke his nose back out again. What to do? I wiggle a finger and he goes back. Then I got up and was able to push a chair in beneath the picture of Ganesh. I started standing on the chair and then put one foot on the table and then the other foot to get a better pressure as I was going to push the picture, which would push against the rat. He began to wiggle when he felt the pressure, I pushed harder, and harder and finally, he quit wiggling and was quiet. I hoped that I was extinguishing the rat.

I did not want him in my sleeping room so I pressed some more in an effort to totally control him, perhaps kill the little beast. I got tired of the activity, so pressed a little harder just to make sure to control the pestiferous animal in "my" bedroom. I held it behind the picture for about four minutes. Yet, the only trouble was that the force from my feet worked the joints loose in the table and it collapsed under me with a terrible bang. That took the pressure off the rat before my murderous intent was fully successful and he fell to the floor from behind the picture into the debris from the broken table.

I was a bit distraught by having the table collapse under me and by the time I recovered, so did the rat, and it bounded onto the windowsill from the floor and out the window. The noise of the collapse awakened my companion with a start and she too was able to see the rat bounding away, but she was not about to arise so early, before actual dawn.

My partner went back to sleep and I got my notebook and camera, field gear and kit bag and quietly left the room to cross the street to the temple. Instead of going in the front of the temple where priests or guards may wake, distressed by my entry, I circled down the road and came in from an unofficial entry route by the back entry to the temple. As dawn broke and sunlight began to shine in the temple I moved from room to room to see if any of dawns light was shining into some corner that would indicate it had been specially built to notify the priests that the Winter Solstice sun was about to arrive at dawn the next day. I found a spot where a light was just three centimeters out of the corner of the room at the floor and I took it as a good sign that the marking angles of the light in the room were probably deliberate designs. The other rooms turned out to be of little interest. There were no guides and no priest to be distressed with my entry into the holiest location in the temple. I put my back up against the surrounding stone circle in which the *Shiva Lingam* stands erect in the middle in order to identify any light route that dawn sunlight might take to shine on Shiva, or on Shiva at some other time of the year as well.

We were not blessed with sunshine directly into the doorway to the inner sanctum at dawn on the solstice but I was able to make use of my Brunton compass and took a reading on the two and half meter tall, stone statue of Nandi, the bull, that was visible through a doorway under a separate roof to the east. I realized that on the equinox that arrangement would allow dawns light to shine from due east over the head of Nandi, the bull, which is the transport of Shiva in this Shiva temple. What I saw was that, towards the east I presumed the line of sight to the east would be roughly between Nandi's horns and on to Shiva's lingam inside the temple. With my Brunton compass the bearing of due east was not over the horns but just below the left horn and above the ear and from this point there was a view of a small nick point at that edge of the Bull's head. East was in that nick point, which meant that the sun, when dawn arrived on the equinox, light would have shined on Shiva's lingam over that nick point beside Nandi's head for just a couple minutes on the equinox.

I went out to see what was there because I had not been aware of anything on my first passage around Nandi the bull the day before. On arrival at Nandi in its own open-air room, however, I found that it was a sunflower that had been carved in stone just above eye level. It turned out no one had been looking and making the association of the sun rising over a sunflower. The sunflower was about 16 centimeters in diameter with about 16 petals and a smooth round gently curved head of potential flowers at its center with a smooth ring surrounding the circular head of the sunflower. Somewhat elated, I went back to the room and had breakfast with my partner at the housing restaurant. I wanted to show my traveling partner what I had discovered. After breakfast, cooked by people running the housing for scientists, we returned officially to enter the temple. While we were examining Nandi's head, my partner said, "But Carl, sunflowers do not have a ring on top of their seed heads." I said we should wait to find the actual sunflower before judging harshly.

I deeply appreciate the fact that my partner went to the other end of the bull and called to me to say 'come and look, there seems to be sunflowers under the tail'. There were 5 or 6 on each side on the vertical support for the tail and on the south side at mid-morning the sunflowers under the tail were totally illuminated as it curved around the rump – I reasoned that the priesthood could tell how close it was to the winter solstice. It seems that when one side of the tail had all the sunflowers totally illuminated at dawn then the official solstice was one day away. When the sunflowers on both sides of the tail were completely illuminated, then it was either the summer or winter solstice. This would occur in December and June. Contrariwise, on the equinox, the sunflowers on both sides of the tail would be completely shadowed. This would occur in March and September. By simply reading the light and shadow on Nandi's tail, the priests would know the proper time to begin planting, or harvesting the crops. This knowledge then helped them maintain their aura of omniscience among the uninitiated.

A little later in the morning before going to the next temple a group of pre-teens clustered around us. In the children's minds, they had an offer they could not resist when I told them they could each have a dollar if they could find a sunflower....and whoosh they left. It was about ten minutes later when they came back; three with sunflowers so we made use of those sunflowers, picked at random to show that they do, in fact, have little florets on the outside of the seed head as a ring next to the petals, early in their development. So at least, I was thoroughly convinced that the American sunflower, perhaps from Mexico or Veracruz area or southern US, had been present early enough so that the sculptors recognize that the sunflower could be used to follow the sun in its calendric path.

Upon returning to Mysore City, I went into the Epigraphic Office of the Indian Archeological Survey to tell them about my discovery since they had been very helpful. I had only just exclaimed about the sunflower when one of the epigraphers jumped up and ran back to his office to get his most recent reprint. He had recently published it with the statement that a particular Sanskrit name, *suryamukhi*, could have meant sunflowers even though the entire profession recognized that sunflowers were an American plant, yet that the temple had been dated to a couple hundred years before Columbus' trip to the Americas. His supposition was verified and I was pleased that we now had an actual set of carvings of a real setup of the orientation of the sunflower heads and series of sunflowers.

The next person I wanted to share this information with was the Head of the Geography Department at Mysore University, Professor P.D. Mahadev, a Brahmin who one does not physically touch. However, he came out of his house to meet me when I arrived at the gate to his yard and when I mentioned that I found a sunflower sculpted on the temple. He reached out and grabbed me by my shoulders and we went round and round in his driveway. He was ecstatic. The sunflower had to have come to India very early to be carved into the temple in the 12th to 13th century C.E. because Hinduism, like most established religions, is so conservative when it comes to introducing new plants to the religious symbolism of a deity.

The following day we went back to the epigraphic office located next to the University of Mysore and Dr. Kati, the Director of Epigraphy at the central office, met me with a proposal that we go together to visit the temple at Somnathpur, 40 kilometers to the east of Mysore down a paved curving road on the flat of the plateau. What do you suppose we found? We found that the corn maidens, 80 of them around the temple frequently were sculpted in the panels that made up the side of the Somnathpur Shiva temple. Many of these corn Maidens with corn ears in their hand had long flowing skirts or dresses with sunflowers carved at the ground level below the skirts. The carvings generally consisted of the entire blossom but sometimes only half of the blossom showed above the horizon or above ground level. Dr. Kati was very pleased that he was able to assist in the discovery process related to sunflowers in India prior to 1492, and I appreciated his interest and enthusiasm in showing me the sunflower in the last temple constructed by the Hoysala dynasty around 1268 C.E.

In late 1994, I was in Karnataka Pradesh, India near the Hoysala Dynasty (1006 C.E. – 1346 C.E.) Temples of Halebid, on my seventh research trip

121

studying the sculptures and statuary of the many ancient Hindu, Jain, and other temples that dominate the Indian subcontinent's landscape. My purpose was to find more evidence of artistic representations of plants that originated in the Americas among the numerous statues in the many temples surrounding the ancient Hoysala capital of Halebid. For years I had been travelling across this area of India photographing the many statues carved from welded schist, a stone that is relatively easy to carve when it has been freshly extracted from the earth but which becomes extremely hard upon exposure to the sun. In the hands of many of the male and female statues, I had discovered carvings that could be definitively identified as maize ears.

During my travels in India, I had discovered other plants that had originated in the Americas carved on temples of the same era. These temples were completed long before Columbus reached the Americas, or in fact,

Figure 43 - Hoysala Dynasty Temple Construction
These photos show the materials and technique used in Hoysala Dynasty temple construction. Note in the middle picture that the bas-relief panels made of schist rock are holding up the stone roof, and therefore cannot be easily replaced. Photos taken by Carl L. Johannessen.

any Europeans except possibly the Norse had reached the Americas. These statues were strong evidence for the theory of diffusion that I had been working on for 40 or more years. I had come to accept that there was regular and ongoing interaction between the tropical and subtropical cultures on both hemispheres through the trade of mariners and ocean-going traders. The plants, animals, and diseases that I had traced across the tropical oceans in both directions had convinced me and a few other forward-thinking researchers that it was past time to completely rethink the paradigm of world history we were teaching. Needless to say, this was not well-received among the academic and professional organizations. Many of these researchers had a lot to lose if we showed that contact between the hemispheres was regular, ongoing, and began at least 9,000 years ago.

{Figure 43} On this trip, I was photographing the bas-relief statues on the supporting walls of these temples, showing the maize ears held in the hands of the dancing female and male god figures. These supporting walls were built in a very specific fashion that would make it nearly impossible to change the panels upon which the statues were carved once the many tons of stone roofs were completed on top of the walls. The Indian architects that designed these temples with a mortise and tenon structure to ensure the strength and stability of the temples, as every temple in the area has extremely heavy stone roofs. Some German anthropologist postulated that even in the face of the obvious architectural challenges of removing and changing the panels, this is what must have occurred since the early world did not have the ability to sail across the oceans. They further intimated that the hundreds of maize images in the bas-reliefs on a hundred temples were changed out intentionally to confuse modern researchers. This is simply unfortunate obstructionism from researchers who should have known better.

Now, in order to even take close-up photographs of the maize ears and the goddesses holding them, a person has to remove his shoes (in reverence of the temple grounds), climb a wooden ladder with one-inch dowel rungs to a height of eight feet, and then take the photograph of the corn representations; a process which caused my feet to hurt. I found a small board that allowed me to stand and balance myself on a flat surface. Interestingly, the board I found in the yard of our cafe at the temple housing unit was printed with the English words 'Bread and Jam.'

To return to the rat in our story; in the laboratory of field archaeological data relating to animals found in archaeological sites around the town of Tlaloc Mexico is a rat. At this location, under several layers of hard-packed soils under the series of floors of old housing, a rat skeleton was found and preserved. We have tried to have the skeleton dated but so far, it has been difficult to accomplish that task. The age of the rat bones would change the belief system about rats in Mexico and Europe before 1492 C.E. The rat's fleas are a carrier of the Bubonic Plague (Yersinia pestis), one of the diseases for which evidence of infection has been found in the Americas prior to 1492 C.E. The rats were carried to the Americas from China. This could account for the die-off of the Mayan culture in the 10th Century C.E. and would explain the loss of population in many Mayan archaeological sites. The plague, which also arrived in Europe from Asia after this time, was known as the Black Plague or the Black Death.

I took the experience with the rat in Halebid, India as a suggestion to me that I needed to do some more thinking about the obvious Ganesh I had seen earlier in the National Anthropological Museum in Mexico. I really should find out how there came to be a stone sculpture of an Olmec-aged Ganesh in a Mexican Museum. Ganesh is not supposed to have been involved in the first civilization in Mexico since it was an image normally associated with the Hindu religion and culture of India. However, I had seen the stone sculpture of what could be a Ganesh three years earlier on a visit to the Museum and I felt it was most probably a sculpture of an elephant head on top of a human body rather than a tiger head. The Museum staff had not known about Ganesh at all until I mentioned it and even after that they had trouble with the idea. That choice, elephant or tiger, was not one that they were willing to admit it was a choice at all. A tiger has been suggested and accepted as the likely representation in Olmec art by Beatriz de la Fuente, the recognized authority on Olmec history of sculpture. The puzzle of course gets more complex. Was it possible that the rat had been taken to Mexico with Ganesh's sculpture and in that way kept the philosophical–religious relationship as a unit, which was transported at the time of the arrival of the Ganesh? Or am I just being fanciful while I am here in India? Then, too, on the other hand, I guess it's possible the rat could have come into Mexico much later? Let's say, after the arrival of Columbus?

On my next visit to Mexico I tried to find the answers to those questions. One should always try to discover the truth before teaching material to students or the public on any subject. The education of youth and the adults in their lives needs to derive from the most factually based materials possible. It should be presented to them in a straightforward and factual manner rather than as part of a list of unsubstantiated theories, which they'd have to relearn later in life anyway. Whatever one wishes to teach, or show should be presented openly and candidly, and in a format that allows others to decide for themselves what is fact and what is fiction. In order to do that, I believe you have to know what you're talking about in the first place and make sure your theories are grounded in facts. That is what I am trying to do here.

With that in mind, I must admit that there are problems with the "sculptured Ganesh" that I saw in Mexico. For example, he is not sitting in a lotus position, as is the case with nearly all statues of Ganesh in Asia! He was sitting on his heels with his toes under his behind, a different and even older meditation position known in India as virasana or hero pose. Moreover, the Olmec civilization, in general, is supposed to have been significantly older than the origin of Ganesh in India.

When I arrived to check on the Olmec sculpture, I found that the authorities had decided that the head on top of the man was a tiger, not an elephant. If he had a long nose then the statue had been modified when they repaired the section with the trunk, which had been broken off. This made the statue look as if it had never had a trunk at all, and made the so-called tiger's nose too long, but, whatever. Obviously they failed to look very closely for if they had, they would have noticed the round spot on the tummy of the man in the sculpture. This spot, which is right where the trunk would have been, namely, it is at the end of the tiger-elephant's long nose, and thus it shows where the trunk had originally extended down the man's belly before it was broken off. If they had looked closely they would have noticed the change in the patina of the polished tummy where the trunk used to be. This difference in the patina is still visible (and always will be because it's a matter of exposure to the elements) and looks quite recently polished, probably in an attempt to make it match the patina of the rest of the statue. However, there remains this very visible small circle of lighter color on the man's belly. Of course they could not have a trunk there, because, after all everyone knows that artifacts sell better if they fit the belief system of the museums buying them and everyone has been led to believe that it is a tiger, just like Americans have been led to believe that Columbus discovered America.

Unfortunately, if the authorities in Mexico do not want to consider that the elephant is the animal most likely represented on the head of of Ganesh then all they have to do is tell us that the animal on his head is a tiger, even if the ears on this beast stick way out the side of the head rather than sticking up vertically, and the nose is twice to three times too long for a tiger, and even though it is in the correct location for a Ganesh's nose to have been placed (if it had been broken off). So with all of that in mind I say, "Rest in peace poor little misrepresented god."

CHAPTER 12: THE BLACK-BONED/BLACK-MEATED CHICKEN

The distribution of domesticated plants around the world offers very convincing evidence of contact between tropical civilizations across the entire world prior to the 15th Century C.E. The distribution of the Black-boned/Black-Meated Chicken (BBC) and other varieties of chickens, originating in Southeast Asia, offer incredibly rich sources of characteristics that indicate early transfer. Chickens have been domesticated, selected and modified for 6,000 or more years in Southeast Asia. Currently the melanotic chickens, chickens selected with black tissue on the outer layer of their bones and sometimes with black skin, and black breast meat are found in a vast area spreading out from southern Chile to northern Mexico (Fortaleza) and from the northeast coast of Peru to the southern coast of Brazil.

Around 1997, while George Carter and I were working together on a book about the history of the use of chickens, he pointed out that the names of chickens sometimes carried powerful pieces of evidence as to the history of the human transport of chickens around the world. Carter was updating his findings on chickens and crop plants, along with some other contributions included in this chapter. Carter pointed out to me that the name for BBC in India is *kukkutazavaka*. During the Hoysala Dynasty (950 C.E. – 1343 C.E.) well over a hundred significant temples were constructed for worship of Hindu, Jain, and Buddhist philosophies and their walls were studded with sculptures of people holding maize ears, annona, sunflowers and many other American plants. This powerful dynasty ruled the region of India known as Karnataka. George Carter noted that, Karnataka, is the basis for the name of the chicken among the Arawak tribes of the Amazon Basin. However, I have not found that name among the Maya Indians.

The study of melanotic chickens became a specialty of mine when I discovered them in Central America. The ritual uses were ascertained simply by asking questions of indigenous peoples out of curiosity as to the presence and use of melanotic chickens. No one had previously suggested that the BBC (BBC) of Latin America were used medicinally; this knowledge of the distribution of the BBC was not known to science before our report, as far as I can discern.

The whole set of rituals involving chickens from China and Southeast Asia that are found in the Mayan region of Central America are sufficient to force one into a diffusionist intellectual position. The first BBC's could not have come in on the Spanish Manila Galleons and spread throughout the Maya speaking peoples and only then into Middle America. The BBC is much more widely spread than the theory of galleon trading would have allowed. The chickens have been used by the Maya with greater specificity, and their use is more widespread than would be possible if they had only arrived at the time that the Spanish galleons arrived.

These claims follow from my observations in the field. These started out as a whimsy, with no real goal, other than following the trail suggested by my mentor, Carl O. Sauer. I continued my study of the BBC in his memory. Science is often presented as the testing of a hypothesis. Originally, the study of the BBC had no hypothesis. I simply developed a greater interest about their origin and dispersal after I had digested what Carl Sauer had said and then found examples of these chickens in a few Mayan backyards in Peru. I became convinced that whatever I found could be of interest to the scientific community in their pursuit of knowledge. It is fortuitous that my somewhat naive pursuit has led to a significant question. How could all these data be integrated into a meaningful story that would explain the evidence as discovered, that the BBC may have been imported to the Americas from South and East Asia prior to the 15th Century B.C.E.? Rituals using chickens and their sacrifice for the relief of stress and fears are widely found among aboriginal and highly traditional peoples in the tropical and subtropical world. If the same rituals were found in com-

Figure 44 - Black-boned Black-meated Chicken
Kekchi culture in Guatemala. Photo taken by Carl L. Johannessen.

127

mon in both the New and Old Worlds, they can be regarded as indicators of past cultural exchange of an extremely complex nature.

Our modern understanding of the function of the mind may account for some of the efficacy of folk cures in treating psychosomatic illnesses. When nutrition is involved in a 'cure', as when a patient is perhaps on a low protein diet and is made to consume cooked chicken meat despite normal taboos against that activity, the result may be life-enhancing in accordance with the modern concepts of human nutrition and healing. Whether we understand it or not, whether or not the phenomenon has a scientific basis, we need to learn about processes and distributions even when the beliefs in the supernatural effect cannot be found to have distinct, easily discoverable benefits (such as the more readily noticeable effects of nutritional benefits). When the rituals are elaborate yet do not have scientifically measurable benefits, then they cannot have been environmentally induced. In such cases, the argument that the ritual arose through 'independent invention' becomes difficult if not impossible to imagine. Diffusion is indicated when these ancient and modern, arbitrary rituals are virtually identical in both

Figure 45 - Black-boned/Black-Meated Chicken

Photo taken by Carl L. Johannessen.

hemispheres of Asia and America.

Carl Sauer was convinced that if it were possible to learn more about the BBC reported to have been donated by the Indians for the commodore's table on the flagship of the US Navy, the USS Frigate Brandywine, in Paita, Peru in 1828, it would lead to important information in the diffusion/parallel invention controversy. As far as I know, he had no specific idea about what might be found. He simply said, "See if you can find out anything about the BBC while you are in the field this summer." We graduate students and young professors would take off, skeptical but willing to try year after year; eventually it paid off. What we discovered was that when the aforementioned U.S. Frigate first landed off the coast of Chile with the admiral of the U.S. Pacific fleet on board, the chickens offered by the Indians were rejected by the sailors because they were afraid that the Indians were trying to hex them with "evil chickens."

My first field data for the study of the BBC came from observations made in Alta Verapaz, Guatemala. The study started with very few preconceptions about the specifics of what we would find. The presence of BBC in Middle America was first reported to me by a Guatemalan farmer, then by hacienda managers and government agents, but, frankly, since the BBC had not been discovered and documented by scientist's north of Chile and Peru, even I considered suggestions of these references suspect at first. It was as if, perhaps, they were telling me tales about it, when asked, just to keep me happy. They would say things like the BBC could be found after two days walk from the end of the road into the rainforest among the Mayan Indians in the woods.

We knew of the records of ordinary chickens from early Spanish explorers like Bernal Diaz del Castillo (1939) and others that they had been given chickens by the Indians in Mexico and elsewhere at the time of their initial contact with the Spaniards and Cortez in 1519.

Elsewhere in Chamil, a small town in Alta-Verapaz, Guatemala, there were hundreds of chickens of Asiatic origin with head featherings or top knots, or with naked necks, ear muffs, feathered tarsi, reversed feathers, half-naked bodies and/or taillessness – all traits which generally indicate non-European origin. Unfortunately, for the maintenance of genetic diversity, whenever disease kills off a significant number of the local Asian origin birds in the flocks of some villages, and the only replacement chickens come from mass incubators controlled by North American and European companies. These are chickens that have been hybridized from pure Mediterranean stock.

On Easter Island, the full range of Asian varieties of chickens was present in 1977 according to the many commercial chicken raisers. The naked necked, reverse feathered, feathered tarsi, earmuffs, top knots, and tailless melanotic chickens were all found mixing with the modern breeds from the United States and Europe. As Heyerdahl (1958) points out in support of the highly ritualistic use of chickens on Easter Island, the islands even had chickens that lacked gall bladders. This lack allowed the Islanders to roast and eat chickens in the dark, during nighttime ceremonies in caves, etc., without biting into the bitter gall in the livers.

I discovered that the BBCs are found from southern Chile to northern Mexico and from Peru to coastal Brazil at Fortaleza. Their ritual use in medical cures, as well as the ancillary beliefs in their protective powers, which are the features that vary most across these great expanses of countryside. This complex set of cultural traits allows researchers to predict the length of time these chickens have been in the Americas.

Chickens can barely fly across a barnyard, let alone over an ocean as several critics of my pre-15th Century Transoceanic Diffusion have suggested. They could not have migrated across the frozen high latitudes between Asia and America either. They would have been dependent on humans to provide their transportation from the Old World to the Americas. How did they get from their original regional home in Southeast Asia to the Americas? The rituals surrounding chickens also offer incredibly rich sources of characteristics that would indicate early transfer to and establishment in the Americas.

It is important to consider the breeds of many kinds of chickens. This can usually be ascertained by looking at the bird's physical characteristics such as coloration, shape, size, the kinds of feathers, combs, top knots, tails, feet, legs, necks, wattles and so forth. Once these have been recorded and the breed identified the chicken's ancestry can be traced, in many cases, to that particular chicken's original home in Asia. In addition, specific ritual uses are also labels that relate to named chicken types that ought not to be ignored. When the rituals are marvelously complex, and when they are performed with a specific variety of chicken, there is little chance that they could have been somehow independently created. It is obvious that they are evidence of diffusion.

The claim exists that a cock will crow at the first sign of the morning sun. Then cocks all over the world were excited by this idea and began crowing at the crack of dawn. Another claim is that cocks' crow every hour on the hour and, even though people know this is unlikely, they will still repeat this nonsense. Early farmers thought that the rooster's crowing cleared the morning of demons and specters that had been roaming the land by night, yet seemed to disappear at dawn. Specters of corpses were especially terrifying, and the villagers believed that the crowing paralyzed the specters who might otherwise be able to damage them.

The killing of chickens as sacrifices provided offerings to the gods in the Native American as well as the Indian and Chinese religious paradigms. However, the application of BBC blood as counteraction to fears of death and the unknown are widespread among the Amerindians. They used chicken blood on new tools and on new houses to emphasize the attitudes and beliefs of the local people toward the chicken. Blood was also applied to tools or houses that have not been touched for weeks at a time. Almost all these rituals in both China and America took place in the context of the consumption of alcoholic beverages, decoctions-for-odors, smokes, candles, incense, and special crackling sounds when tree resin, which was called *copal-pom*, or just *pom*, was burned in America, or firecrackers were set off in China. Prayers, and incantations, were directly comparable, as well. Feathers, young whole chickens, adult chickens, eggs, blood, organs, and meat all have special significance in rituals for counteracting the assumed black magic, hexes or devilish, spiritual attacks that an enemy, known or unknown, may have cast upon your house.

How did the chickens and their rituals get from Southeast Asia to the Americas? The whole set of rituals involving chickens from China and Southeast Asia are found, especially in the Mayan and Chilean region of Central America and southern Chile. They antedated Columbus probably by millennia. They couldn't fly or swim across the ocean. Asian sailors would have brought them on board their rafts or ships to absorb the evil spirits on board the crafts, although not for food. Neither traditional Asian nor traditional Central/South American cultures used the BBC for food except in times of emergency or major celebrations or anniversaries in life. The parts go together as follows: Rituals, using chickens and their sacrifice for the relief of stress and fears, are widely found among aboriginal and highly traditional peoples. If the same rituals are found in common in both the New and Old Worlds, they can be regarded as indicators of past cultural exchange of an extremely complex nature carried out by the tropical sailors. We will know better when bones of chickens of Central America and Mexico have been accurately dated and analyzed for their DNA such as has been carried out in Chile by Storey and her team in 2004. Of course, the opposition has criticized that research and their findings as well.

The simplest of the "uses" are the taboos against eating BBC as daily food. This taboo exists wherever I have found the BBC, with the exception of the modern, urban scene in the Peoples Republic of China (PRC). Every "socialist paradise" comes down hard on their ancient traditions; therefore, the lack of taboos on BBC can also be described as the official stifling of those taboos. In keeping with the political necessity of Chinese food production, the BBCs go indiscriminately into the stewpots of the government's dining facilities. On a recent trip to China, in response to our request, our cook saved an entire melanotic chicken for my partner and me. This was the first time I had eaten the BBC. Its flavor is essentially identical to the white-boned chickens (WBC), though some people claim the BBC is sweeter.

The Native tribes of Latin America have taboos against eating chickens in general. This may sound unbelievable, as the farmers are not as a class 'well off' and edible chickens abound, but it is nonetheless true. These taboos far antedate recorded history, and continue as a belief system among the most traditional tribes in the Americas. Their widespread existence is one indication of that feeling of respect for the chicken that exists here in the Americas. BBCs are kept around the house as pets, if possible, because it is believed that people who have them in their households will be protected from any and all evils. One question that puzzles us is that if only the melanotic chickens have healing rituals associated with them, why do the Latin American Indians avoid eating all Asiatic chickens? Since it is easier to pick up avoidance traits than the complex medical treatments, we can theorize that this behavior comes from early medical exchanges between the

Asians and Americans. The eggs are used in the households and the indigenous people may even sell the chickens and eggs to the people who are financially better off in the markets. The indigenous people of Guatemala with whom I became familiar recognized that when the chickens are sold they would surely be killed and eaten. This process is similar to the treatment of chickens in vegetarian Hindu India. In vegetarian Hindu India, if foreigners request chicken to eat, the worker is sent to the market and the chicken is taken from the seller to a different person at the markets who does the killing and cleaning of the bird. Once it is cleaned, the cook at the house can fry or roast the bird with apparent ease. It is interesting to note that the cooks know how to cook chicken although many Hindus of the Brahmin Class are vegetarians.

When the Iberian explorers arrived in the Americas, they brought with them their taste for chicken. This caused more chickens to be killed by non-indigenous peoples, who also ate the fowl. Currently in Latin America, anyone who eats chicken is able to buy them in the markets regardless of the desires and traditions of the indigenous populations. The chickens are sold while still alive to Ladinos in markets all over the region.

All of this ties in directly to the survey of traits in Latin America. The BBC in Chile, Bolivia, Peru, Guatemala, and Mexico is believed to absorb any hex or evil placed upon the house, tools or fields so long as the family can keep the chicken alive. It is another reason for the taboo on killing chickens, especially the BBC for simple consumption. The cocks are needed in the traditional segments of their societies to give peace of mind to these farmers.

One must remember that in the Andean and Mesoamerican aboriginal cultures, which I observed, most of the local country folk believe that if an illness or anything bad of any sort befalls one, it is the result of somebody's evil spell cast upon the family. This is deeply imbedded and has its counterpart in the Asiatic source region too. My experience with curing, in Guatemala, especially, reminds one of how thoroughly the Mayan rituals fit into the Chinese experience of old. The K'ekchi, with whom I carried out the most concentrated fieldwork, regularly use smoke and the snap-crackle-pop of copal-pom in those curing ceremonies just as they did in China, although in China they now use firecrackers rather than pitchy wood. They also have similar special sacrificial days. In addition, their practice of placing pine needles on the floor, and pine boughs over doorways perhaps has greater time-depth and significance than has ever been expected because of the similar record of the importance of this practice in Chinese society as well.

They heal in ways that have homologous tendencies between both the Maya and Chinese as well, although some differences are present too. The Chipayan, Mayan, and Chinese people, all would not consume a chicken after it had been sagitally split and applied as a compress, or a poultice to a

132

patient. After these applications, the cold chicken is taken out to either the forest. a river or a crossroads and left. Practitioners believe that the absorbed evil spirits will simply be unable to return to haunt the patient once this is done, and that the cooling effects of the forest or river locations, as the evil spirits take their leave, will reduce the fever in the patient.

In this section, we are discussing the many uses for chickens found mainly in aboriginal cultures in Middle America, and comparing them with the ways chickens have been utilized in Asia.

In this portion of the study we are basing our analysis of the living chickens on rituals and the reports both of which imply that the chickens and the rituals came from Asia long before the Spanish contact period. As for precise dating regarding the arrival of the chickens in the Americas, however, we will have to be content to wait for archaeological research, which has not yet been done, before we can set time depth limits on their presence here. The additional fact that these Asiatic-curing practices using BBCs are not present in many geographical regions has significance to our study, as well. It is of major importance to demonstrate which specific cultures had and still have the knowledge of how to use these chickens in curing practices, and which societies did not. But this, too, will have to wait for further research.

Chickens have been selected and modified in the domestication process for thousands of years in Southeast Asia according Barbara West and Ben-Xiong Zhou in 1988. The domestication process probably involved the killing of birds, which were not highly desirable, and were going to be used for medical treatments. They were either sold off or killed as sacrificial animals when young, thereby causing selective pressure to be exerted on the genetics of the species. In this way, the desired breeding stock is allowed to live. Black bones, skin, and meat, as well as all the other features of domestic chickens have been differentially allowed to exist in the farmyards. In general, the BBCs are not sacrificed or killed until a major threat to someone's life or a major anniversary occurs. To the Mapuches of Chile, when a giant ship like the Frigate USS Brandywine showed up in their port they brought the most revered chickens that they had as a gift for the person in charge of the United States Pacific fleet. Since the chickens were different, with black bones and some with black meat, the crew would not eat them and they were destroyed. If they had not done this, the BBCs would have been saved to have around the Mapuche house as pets, if at all possible, because it is believed that people who have them in their households will be protected from any and all evils.

Throughout Latin America in general, the BBC is normally very sparsely distributed. Its numbers increase among cultural groups who specifically revere the BBC as a protector of their household and health. Its widespread existence and taboos against its use as food, in a matrix of Asiatic chickens among the Amerind cultures in Latin America, indicate that the unusual taboo of the original probably came with Asian chickens and have existed for a very long time in the Americas too.

The Asiatic breeds in America are physically small in comparison to the European or Mediterranean breeds. The exception to this generality is in the fighting cocks that are currently being bred to include melanism and long legs. The Ladinos and Mestizos who submit cocks to the fighting rings select these melanotic genes from the BBC in preference to pure bred, white-boned, chicken cocks, because of the fear and awe induced by melanism in the gamblers who are wagering on the cockfights. The breeders feel that the addition of melanin (in the visible skin of the head and legs) indicates the cock will be a more vigorous fighter. I was told this both in Hawaii and in Peru.

It must be emphasized that probably the Mayan, Chipaya, Mapuche and other American Indian communities generally also maintained chickens as alarm clocks, for feather art, time markers, hex absorbers or hex inducers. They rarely, if ever, used them for food. Their status was somewhat similar to the East Indian sacred cow. Remember that the practitioners of Hinduism do not eat the meat of the cow nor do they eat other meat.

After I had acquired some knowledge of the healing systems relating to the use of the BBC in the K'eckchi culture, I was able to perform better interviews. The techniques that I was able to collect that were similar to those of Asia, included the application of cut chickens to the patient in specific ways, the use of an egg for diagnosing sick children by placing the cracked egg in a saucer of water to be read, the practice of reading the entrails of animals, especially chickens, to determine the future, and the practice of using blood to drive away spirits. Whenever the descriptions of the procedures by informants slowed, and especially after they had told me about the curing rites, more information was then frequently elicited by progressively asking more complex, open-ended questions. It occurred to me, during this process, that the more illogical the process would seem to be to the modern mind, the less likely it would be that any process, which matched that of the Old World so distinctly, could somehow be made up by these people independent of contact. The fact that the procedures are so similar, and in some cases precisely the same, flies in the face of the idea that the old paradigm of independent development might have value here. I think rather that it strongly suggests dispersal.

The data presented here should be viewed as somewhat preliminary; there is need for further fieldwork. At the time of this writing in 2015, my data is 30 years old and more current research really needs to be done. As soon as the political conditions indicate that it is logical and safe to do so, more fieldwork should be carried out in these Mayan language zones before acculturation, displacement, and die off of the conservative aboriginal population occurs. If we cannot act relatively soon, their curers, shaman, and older people, the ones who have this knowledge, may pass on and make such a study impossible. The chants of the extensively trained healers/curers may be lost if we do not get these five to ten- minute long prayers recorded in the original K'eckchi language, which may be different from other the current local languages of the various cultures. Since we have an indication of a Shang/Olmec connection, now, I predict that the long chants will be shown to be in ancient Shang-Chinese language. This oral history needs to be recorded soon. They can then be compared with the chants of Chinese healers in China. Wouldn't it be worth our funds to show this modern day remnant of an ancient culture, two or three and a half millennia old, which have been kept alive by chants memorized by the shamans? I suggest the town of Cahabon in Alta Vera Paz, Guatemala as the most likely location to find healers who still remember their ancient training. These predictions are most likely true from the evidence already assembled of Shang Dynasty influence on the east coast of Mexico near La Venta by Betty Meggers and later by H. Mike Xu.

Evidence on BBC and its uses in curing in the Indian subcontinent have been inadequately reported in the printed literature on the subject. I conducted field research on the pre- Columbian presence of maize in sculptures on temple walls in 1986-89 in India in Karnataka state with no abundant presence of the BBC being found. A return to India in 1991 allowed me to make a transect in Tamil Nadu, Goa, Maharashtra Pradesh and northern Karnataka. Only one BBC was found. Future research is needed in India in general and among the Hill tribes in particular (who also grow much maize), which could not be visited by us for local governmental political reasons during any of my early studies in India.

Chickens in China, especially Southern China, are said by Read (1931 to 1939) to be highly valuable and ritualistically significant. Unfortunately, Read's materials on the infirmities that can be cured with the BBC are mainly a list of the diseases, not a description of how the Asians treated the patients with the chicken. The length of his list indicates that the Chinese did think of the BBC as extremely important to healers/shaman; the Chinese still make medical tablets from dried BBC, especially for sale to women for "women's problems", and the pills are even sold in the United States.

The details of the applications of the BBC and their parts or blood to human patients contain a large number of highly arbitrary activities. These are listed below and were first, documented by Chinese literature translated by May Chen Fogg, and second, by direct observation and open-ended interviews of Chinese, which I conducted in China.

The most extensive writings on the BBC were recorded by Li Shih-Chen who lived from 1518 to 1593 A. D. He wrote "The BBC... (BBC) ...are the best chickens for medicinal use and are good for treating liver, kidney, and blood diseases. For these conditions men are to use hens and women are to use male BBC." In another passage, Li Shih-Chen says:

The BBC(BBC) is used for curing: 1) anemia; 2) diabetes; 3) possession by evil spirits; 4) shock from ghost-fright, all four conditions by smearing BBC blood on chest of the person; 5) problems with pregnancy and post-partum weakness by cooking BBC with herbal medicine. In order to make pills of the BBC, cook it until soft, grind the BBC bones and mix with medicine. The pills are good for: 6) menorrhagia and leucorrhea; 7) diarrhea, dysentery, and difficulty swallowing. 'BBC meat, when cooked, is 'warm food', neither hot nor cold; it is sweet, not poisonous. Because it is a 'warm food', it will cure arthritis if it is eaten.

Li Shih-Chen further wrote:

> 1) To obviate the consequences of sudden death by poison, put the blood from the BBC cock's comb on the face of the patient. Let it dry and blow into the nose of the patient to revive him. 2) If someone has hung himself, take the person down without cutting the rope, pierce the comb of the BBC and drip the blood into the mouth of the person in order to quiet the spirits of the person. Use cock's blood for women and hen's blood for men. 3) Put BBC blood on skin infections or insect and spider bites to cure the effect. 4) If an insect or worm is in the ear, drip BBC blood in the ear and the insect or worm will come out. 5) If the patient does not revive from convulsions, put the blood from a white-feathered BBC cock on the lips of the patient and the patient will wake up. 6) Blood from the comb of a BBC cures lactation problems, watering of the eyes by applying blood three times a day, and ghost-fright by applying to the patient's face.

Earlier, the Chinese uses of the chicken were recorded without reference to bone and meat color in the Chou li (Book of Rites of the post-Shang period, annotated by Hsuan Cheng, 127-200 A. D.): "1) Sacrifice chicken at the door or entrance of the village to avoid epidemic diseases. 2) In ceremony for completion of new house or new instruments (bells, drums, etc.) smear chicken blood on the door of the new house or on the instrument." In the book Feng su t'ung, Ying Shao (fl. 196 B.C.) wrote: "1) In ancient time one sacrificed chicken to avoid evil spirits by dismembering the chicken at the door of the house or entrance to the village, 2) Smear male black-boned chicken on the patient's chest, and throwing away the chicken when it is cold."

The annual sacrifice of a chicken to the house spirits that are buried in the center of the dirt floor of houses is found in Indonesia, Ecuador, Columbia according to G. Carter, and often in Guatemala, among the Maya.

136

The bones of those chickens should be discoverable in these archaeological sites if the researchers hunt for the bones at the center of the house.

Table B - Uses of BB/BM Chickens in Mesoamerica Physical and Psychological Medicinal Uses for BB/BMC

Type of malady	Guatemalan Informants	Chinese Informants
Pulmonary disease – divide live chicken. bind to patient's feet or rub over patient	X	X
Ojo possessing a small child – rub chick over patient	X	?
Ojo possessing adult – 5 organs and 2 pieces of meat rubbed over patient	X	X
Ojo – possessed ducks or chickens	X	X
Ojo – BB/BMC feet rubbed over patient	X	?
Headache – BB/BMC used	X	0
Fever – Hot liver of BB/BMC rubbed over patient; throw liver away in woods.	X	X
Almost any disease – BB/BMC blood is rubbed on the patient as *copal pom* incense is being burned	X	?
Almost any disease – BB/BMC used with cacao rite Vs. tea – bitters for the sick	X	?
Pregnancy pain and postpartum weakness – BB/BMC soup	X	X

Ojo – Evil Spirit or Demon

Other Relationships	Guatemalan Informants	Chinese Informants
Name	Bank	Wu ku chi
	Caxlan sao	Chi
Food Avoidance - BB/BMC and Mediterranean	X	X
Food Acceptance - BB/BMC pregnancy pains, postpartum weakness	X	X
Blood Painted in Coffin	X	X
Quaticinc and counteracting spooks	X	X red paint
Little divination with entrails – BM/BBC celebrations	X	X
Cock Crowing	X	X
Anniversary Celebrations – BB/BMC meat and soup	X	X
Cock fighting	X	X
Mountain Worship, as residence of the Gods	X	X
Maize/Rice Planting rituals	X	X
Maize, Peanut, Chile, amaranth cenopodium	X	X

Repeating- cyclic universe and reincarnation	X	X
Hot/Cold foods – yin-yang concept	X	X
Deer Antler veneration – long life and power	X	X
Ancestral worship	X	X
Cinnabar on bones	X	X
Cinnabar long life elixir	X	X
Compass	X	X
Cylindrical beehives under eaves	X	X
Incantations	X	X
23 eclipses/ 135 months	X	X

Cocks in general are used as a demon-expeller and, as a result, the custom in China forbade their being killed. Cocks of wood and paper were to be placed at entrances to their home and towns to keep evil away so that real ones did not have to be killed. Earthenware cocks have traditionally been formed and placed on top of the roof to serve as protective agents. Black cocks, presumably BBC, were considered able to cure disease in the heart or belly when the patient was rubbed with them. The early Chinese curer claimed that eight or nine out of ten patients were cured. The present method of rubbing with black cocks on those who are struck by evil, dates from Hia-heu Hung, according to J.J.M. de Groot. In addition, the cock bestows vitality as the symbol of universal source of life. In Koh Hung's old medical work we read, that "sudden death" can be cured when "blood obtained from an incision in the comb of a red cock is to be squirted by means of a tube into the patient's nose," Another recipe is to take the blood from a cock's comb and rub the patients face with it; and:

If anybody is hit by a specter's blow, blood should be drawn from the comb with a knife, and dropped into the mouth of a patient, so that he swallows it; and that same cock must be cut up, and the two halves folded over his breast below his heart, and when they have become cold, they must be thrown away on the roadside. If a black cock can be procured, the effect will be better.

For nightmare, likewise a spectral attack" the same author gives, among other recipes, this one: "Cut into the comb of a cock, and squirt the blood of it with a tube into the throat of the patient; this will have the best effect."

The study of melanotic chickens became a specialty of mine once I discovered them in Guatemala, Central America. The ritual uses were ascertained simply by asking questions out of curiosity as to their presence and use. Under the tutorship of Carl Sauer, I went to Guatemala for several years starting in 1976 primarily to study corn and was told various times that I could find the BBC out in the Indian communities in the distant forest terrain in Alta Vera Paz in northern Guatemala. I traveled from Copan to Chamil where they had developed the longest corn ears of the Kekchi

Mayan culture. I could not believe the directions given to me by the managers of the haciendas in which I was staying. I actually thought they were just teasing me, the Gringo, about the presence of the BBC. Then one day I asked the old mayor of the town, which is located over two hours hike from the end of the road at the town of Chamil, whether he had heard of the BBC and he said sure, "Mamma call the chickens" and her chickens came to get grain. Among them was one hen with her ear wattle-puffs, raised hackles, black comb, black legs, black wing bones (examined after we caught her) and black tongue. This was before anyone had really suggested that the BBC of Latin America existed anywhere north of Peru. No one had ever recognized that the BBCs were used medicinally either; this knowledge was new to science at the time. The National Geographic Foundation supplied sufficient funding for me to return the next year to expand the knowledge about the chickens in Guatemala.

The field data for the study of chickens, especially the BBC that I finally found were first discovered in Alta Verapaz, Guatemala. The presence of BBC in Middle America was, as I said first reported to me by Guatemalan farmers, but, frankly, since the BBC had not been discovered and documented by scientist's north of Chile and Peru, even I considered suggestions of these references suspect at first.

Most of the chickens gathered in typical flocking behavior in the area of the scattered maize grains just as M. Hartman had pointed out historically for European chickens. The previously non-flocking Asiatic chickens in the mix had long since been trained by the now abundant chickens from the United States and Europe to flock at feeding time. However, the BBC hen stayed on the outside of the group. She would pick up one grain and then walk into the maize patch of the garden before swallowing it. Then she returned to the edge of the group of chickens to take another maize seed. Other BBC have tended to behave this way in other villages as well, though some were more acculturated and would simply peck grain at the edge of the flock on the bare soil in front of the house and eat it there.

The strange sequel to the story of my recent village trip was that the main purpose of my revisiting Alta Vera Paz was to interview some of the Curers with whom I had talked 30 years before about the uses of the BBCs. I obtained a couple of taped interviews. One was from a man who lives another half day travel to the south. In order to translate his message, I went to the Capital for expert translators who could translate these interviews. When I was introduced it turned out that the person who was available in the K'eckchi Maya Language Center was Ramon's daughter, who was working, teaching K'eckchi to the city dwellers who wanted to be able to work in Alta Verapaz. She translated but the transcription was in K'eckchi and not in the ancient language of the curers. Sadly, I did not know that until I had returned to the United States.

Fortunately, Ramon had maintained contact for over a couple decades with Dr. Mike Wilson who had become a professor in Saskatchewan University at Saskatoon in Canada and the two of them had exchanged monthly stories in both K'ekchi' and Spanish. Mike kept up on both languages and he has a book of these short stories that he edited in English, Spanish, and K'ekchi and offered to the government. But I have not heard what became of Mike Wilson's writings which contain important learning tools for studying the K'eckchi language.

Since no other scientists had found BBCs on the terrain north of Chile and Peru, and since the descriptions of the BBC rituals in Chile and Peru had not been carried out, as far as I know, or recorded at the time of the discovery of BBCs in Guatemala in 1975, there was no basis for predicting which rituals would be found in Alta Verapaz, Guatemala. The interviewing technique used was asking open-ended questions that were posed in such a way that answers of 'yes' and 'no' were not reasonable. Instead such questions as "How do you use the BBC and the other types of chickens?" and "Please tell me more about that..." were asked. The lead of the interviewee was simply followed for as long as was possible for the interviewees to expand on their story. We really had no preconceived ideas of what we would learn at the beginning of the discovery process. Interviews were conducted in the language of the interviewee, frequently through translators who normally communicated with me in Spanish. When Spanish could be used directly, it was.

Some of the most detailed interviews were conducted with the man of the family, who was commonly a healer or shaman; other interviews were conducted with mothers or fathers of children cured by the shamans. We obtained responses with much more intricate detail when the shaman's wife or daughter was seated beside my translator or me. Usually, we sat on low stools or logs (in Guatemala) with the shaman in a hammock above and in front of us. That is the power location in the Mayan culture. Commonly a shaman would answer freely until he needed more information, at which time his wife (or daughter) would help by either giving him leads or by directly giving the information to my translator and me.

Following up on this earlier work, I visited China and the subcontinent of India to gain a few comparative insights from across the oceans on curing and husbandry practices in addition to the book information I had earlier obtained, but so far I have not been to any locations where data was readily available on the BBC. It took a couple of decades to find the evidence in America after all. Worse, the search in Asia has been ancillary to other pressing assignments. I predict that comparable rituals in curing medical ills and psychological problems and counter measures to hexes will be found in even greater detail when time can be devoted to the study in South Asia (India/Pakistan) and Southeast Asia. The reservoirs of knowledge are great in Asia as well as in eastern South America for the innovative student of the Social Sciences who has an interest and who can control the feelings of culture shock which are sure to arise. I urge the study to be conducted as soon as possible because modern Indians who think every good chicken is a roasted one are quickly eradicating these cultural features. The lead for the field person is, namely, when you get to a place where the inhabitants do not eat the meat or eggs of chickens because of religious beliefs, then the researchers should use their video to immediately start recording their activities; because, believe me, you are about to learn something. One cannot rely on the knowledge of the poultry specialists who are only concerned with animal nutrition and this only with regard to their economic value in poultry production. They generally have not seen the Asiatic chickens with which you will have filled your digital recordings, and, hopefully, photographs and notes.

One question that puzzled us is that if only the melanotic chickens have so many healing rituals associated with them, what creates the food avoidance practices that we discern with Asiatic chickens in general all over Latin America among the Indian cultures? Is it easier to pick up avoidance traits than the complex medical treatments?

As our research progressed, sometimes (for instance in Chile) it became necessary to demonstrate that we knew something about local ancillary magical or medical rituals practiced by shamans in order to gain sufficient acceptance to be able to elicit information on the BBC topic from these healers. In this situation, again the use of open-ended questions kept the interviewers from being tempted to steer the responses of the informant to some specific answer.

By traveling in long transects in which informants had no way of communicating with other shamans who had been interviewed; we felt we were obtaining reliable information when the same curing rituals were enumerated several times with different people. The interviewers gained confidence in the effectiveness of the open- ended question technique when it elicited these same highly esoteric treatments and similar rituals for the curing of the same specific maladies.

My greatest feeling of frustration comes from failing to have a tape recorder to capture some of the chants demonstrated to me by a few of the shamans. The K'eckchi Maya language proficiency of my translator, though he was a native speaker of K'eckchi, was insufficient to follow the memorized chants of some of the shamans. He said that the shaman had been required to memorize long and intricate chants in a strange language related somewhat to K'eckchi, but different from it, for them to graduate as a curer. Linguists would be needed to deduce the source language(s), and the meanings and ages of these chants. They must be gathered by the next researchers in Alta Verapaz, Bolivia, and Chile before these shamans die.

In 1976, anthropologist and acquisitions librarian Mary Chen Fogg, geographer Dr. Wayne Fogg, anthropologist Martha Burns, Professor Emeritus Ed Beal, and I received partial financial support from the National Geographic Society to study the larger region of Mexico and Central America and to continue the work from a year earlier in Guatemala when I was on my own. Mary Chen Fogg was the main Chinese translator for my research on Chinese language sources. We surveyed a transect through the east coast and southern central Mexico, much of Guatemala, and Belize. We asked healers and farmers whose chickens could be seen beside the road, what use they made of the BBCs (when they had them) in their flocks. The interviewing transect was made rapidly, although the interviews themselves were leisurely when the informants were willing and able to describe their belief systems relating to the efficacy of chickens, and the BBC in particular, in healing ceremonies. These people also had information on evil influences from 'black' magic, but no one would talk about it.

In 1977, the National Geographic Society and the University of Oregon together supported a trip to Hawaii, Samoa, Tahiti, Easter Island, southern Chile, the yungas of Bolivia and the altiplano of Bolivia and Peru. Several researchers worked with me in various combinations surveying a transect through Bolivia and Peru. In northern Peru, we searched both the coast and the highlands for chickens and their function in the matrix of curing processes utilizing animals of the region. We examined the uses of chickens in general and BBCs in particular as they related to rituals such as gambling on cockfights organized by the Ladinos. The BBC now play a new role as I already said in the breeding of fighting cocks in the modern scene. Black cocks capture the interests of Ladinos and Mestizos gambling on the fights.

Early on, I recognized that there were hallucinogenic plants habitually used by the curers. When they did not mention it, I raised the issue and let them know that I am a "curer" also and that we can discuss the experience that they have. I did not say enough to bias my informant into giving me some specific data of their specialty. In this situation, again the use of open-ended questions kept the interviewees from being tempted to steer the responses to some specific answer.

In 1977, interviewing the Maya seemed to be pivotal, because of their highly complex medicinal practices, to our understanding of rituals with BBC in the New World, the South American investigation was essential. People and shaman in the several cultures in southern Chile among the Mapuche, in Bolivia among the Chipaya, and other Amerinds on the Altiplano and the North Coast of Peru (mainly the curers) were interviewed about their relationship with BBC use.

When the BBCs were found, we tried to obtain permission and help from their owners to catch them and examine them in detail. The bird's mouth can be opened and checked for melanotic tongue. The wing bones with their visible black sheaths (around white bones) could be seen from the undersides of the wings, and the melanotic skin and dark breast meat were observed when the breast feathers were parted. When the naked necks of chickens (Salvadoran varieties so called) were also melanotic, their dark-colored head skin was visible from 50 meters. Any roseate coloration of the otherwise black face and comb commonly indicates non-homologous condition for the many genes controlling melanism. However, when the black head, skin, face, and comb are present, they obviate the need to catch and check whether the bird is a BBC. Sometimes only the bone sheaths are melanotic without the breast meat being dark, as many genes control various aspects of melanism.

The trip to Polynesia and South America was stimulated by the findings of Hamp and Olson, both linguists, that the Mapuche (Araucanian) Indians of southern Chile and the Chipaya Indians of the altiplano of southwestern Bolivia had language affinities with the modern Maya. Since by 1977, the Maya seemed to be pivotal to our understanding of rituals with BBC in the New World, the South American investigation was essential. So we interviewed people and shamans in several cultures in Chile. Among the cultures where we conducted these interviews were the Mapuche Indians in northern Chile, as well as some other tribes in southern Chile. We interviewed the Chipaya Indians in Bolivia, and on the Altiplano and on the north coast of Peru we interviewed the curers, but these latter were interviewed strictly as controls for the kinds of BBC use we found elsewhere. We interviewed each group until we had received many repetitions of answers in each region. We did this also with groups who did not know of any special BBC medicinal traits. In spite of this seemingly exhaustive research we feel that even more investigations into these rituals would be warranted.

Nowhere did we find Silkies (they are also melanotic) in local farmyards in Latin America. This suggests that there is need for more time in the field; surely, they are there. In the last hundred years, Silkies from the Orient, which frequently have melanotic bone sheaths and dark breast meat, combs, feet, tongues, etc., have been widely traded as exotics around the world to chicken specialists. We did not encounter these and, apparently, they have little influence on the BBCs under consideration here. The presence of Silkies in China-Towns in San Francisco and New York, for instance, may provide the Asian population in the large cities with the requisite BBCs for their required needs of healing and ceremonial activities, but this variety had not, as yet, been carried into the Latin American Indian communities that I saw. Silkies have been found on a worldwide basis only since the mid- 19th century according to Lewer (1912) and others (Anonymous, 1978).

White- or black-feathered Silkies have black skin, black meat, black tongues, combs, and wattles, etc. They may progressively lose some of these genetic features (especially silkiness) when swamped by out-crossing in the Amerind farmyards.

A political conflict, which is one manner of describing a government-led attack on the Guatemalan Amerinds, made it effectively impossible to gather similar data in the lands beyond the ends of roads in Guatemala in 1978. I was fortunate with the previous window in time and place that allowed me to get in there at all. Another hazard of the field, of course, is Third World thuggery. I didn't get a chance to return until 2004. Most of my contacts had passed away, and I can only hope they had died from natural causes. Sadly, this included my translator. I could find only one of my former curers in southern Alta Verapaz, but I made new friends who assisted. I interviewed two new curers that were interested. Their information is essentially the same as the information I obtained 30 years before, but the chants are now only in K'ekchi or Spanish. However, no one of the 'old school' who had a long memory and knew the ancient chants, was available to me. As I said earlier, new researchers in the field need to recognize that when they get to a place where the inhabitants do not eat the meat or eggs of chickens, then it's time to get out the cameras, notebooks and audio equipment.

In 2002, we were able to examine the avian bones in the collections of the Mexican Zoo-archaeological Offices in Mexico City and found no obviously ancient chicken bones. This survey found three bones of chickens from the surface of archaeological sites and can only claim that the sample was of a more limited area than desired. Thirty years ago, the problems were real throughout Tabasco. Now the threat to Amerinds is not so great. Perhaps research can be employed again in Latin America. During the dangerous times in Guatemala and Mexico, I left the Western Hemisphere and began to study and research topics on plant and animal diffusion in India, China and Southeast Asia.

Using chickens as our investigative tools, we believe we can link the Chipaya and Mapuche Indians of Bolivia and Chile and the ancient occupants of Easter Island. Easter Island is, at least politically, part of Chile today, but for a couple thousand years it was more of a Polynesian outpost. They probably had South American contacts because of the domesticated crops from the mainland that have been largely discounted in the last century of thinking by academia. That does not make the reticent academics correct, however, who discount the evidence. There are features of chicken management in the New World that may well demonstrate close ties between their cultures on Easter Island and those of the Chipaya. Both build chicken houses in somewhat homologous ways, the Chipaya use mud and adobe bricks. The Chipaya make complex clay, multi-storied structures to house their chickens. The Easter Islanders work with basalt stones, to construct simple structures over a meter high with cavities within, and arranged into structures that are more complex where they roost their chickens overnight. The fine grained basalt blocks are so placed that if anyone tries to steal chickens in the dark of night, the blocks are likely to fall, making a great deal of noise and allowing the farmer to catch the thief. There is a real similarity between the cultures in that they are both housing the chickens in "apartment housing" not in a room with poles or boards for roosting.

Whatever we can discover or read about the traits and behavior of these BBC chickens from ancient history, that are now being bred out of existence, we need to report it. Today's Agricultural Extension Agent' would think that they have little need for the curative or talismanic powers of BBCs. Agriculturalists of today are far more interested in egg production or pound yield than maintaining genetic diversity. Whenever disease kills off half of the flocks in any village, the only replacement for chickens come from incubators in North American and European companies and the U.S. AID Agency.

What are the possibilities that the BBC chickens were introduced to the Americas only after the Spaniards' contact in 1492 C.E.? How would Asian shamans who used BBCs as cures for black-magic hexes have arrived in the Mayan groups to teach them Chinese and south Asian traits and rituals for curing these hexes? Instead, consider what would have happened to the Spanish ship captain who brought a Chinese witch doctor and a flock of BBCs on board a Spanish ship in the 16th Century C.E. If the crew did not make him walk the plank out of fear of the Chinese and the BBC, the Spanish Inquisition would have burned him at the stake as a heretic. It was illegal to transport any non-Catholics into the New World and especially into New Spain (Mexico) at that time in history. They simply would not have been allowed until very late, perhaps after the Revolution, if then, to do that.

How would the Chinese witch doctor have communicated with the several Mayan language groups – K'eckchi, Chol, and Chorti, etc., who are at least contiguous? How would the same set of special treatments have been transferred to the Huasteca 800 km away that also use a Mayan language? How would this information drift down to influence the Chipaya and Mapuche in Bolivia and Chile in less than 500 years? No Spaniards were likely to have made any significant contact with curers in these Amerind groups. The traditional answer is that all of this occurred shortly after the contact between these three separate cultures and that the information spread extremely rapidly, catching on in traditional medical and religious ceremonies almost immediately. Given the complexity of the rituals, the known slow rate at which anything new is accepted into medical and religious processes, and the very fact that repeated introduction of non-Catholic Chinese shamans was profoundly unlikely, the suggestion from traditionalist specialists that the chickens and the curers entered in post Columbian times is really ridiculous.

Instead, we hypothesize an earlier contact in which people arrived during several developmental stages of American high civilizations, first to the Olmec. Initially they had some way of communicating, presumably in their own invading language, and that they carefully trained new recruits in the old ways of their Asian culture. The earliest and most likely chance was in early Olmec times, that the BBC entered probably along with the other Asiatic chickens (WBC). It was probably before the Huastecan peoples were split from their Mayan peers in the Veracruz- Yucatan-Guatemala-Chiapas-Honduras-axis. This time period is probably something in excess of 2,500 years (Wolf, 1959: 38; Coe 1966: 32; Thompson, 1966: 28; Johannessen 1986: 48).

Is it logical, as the opponents of my hypothesis would suggest with their colonial introduction, that the Chinese curers who taught the Native populations these cures would have gone only to the Maya linguistic groups now centered in Guatemala and that they would have known also to go to the Maya speaking Huastecan far to the north in Mexico, there to perpetuate the same Chinese rituals without teaching any other language grouping in between the distant Maya-speaking groups? The other cultures know of the BBCs existence and have the animals, but not the rituals! The separation of these two Mayan regions 2,000 to 2,500 years ago seems to me to indicate the regions had the BBC and the respective medical rituals prior to the separation of the Huastecans by the Toltec forces or some other Mexican military culture group.

CHAPTER 13: DISEASES OF THE EARLY WORLD TRAVELED

There is a great deal of archaeological and other evidence for the early diffusion and exchange of culture and cultural traits between the Old World and the Americas. This evidence includes radiocarbon dated finds in tombs, caves and other archaeological excavations; artistic representations of plants in temple complexes built by cultures across the oceans from where the plants originated; and identical, unusual practices among societies separated by oceans that surround the specifically transferred plants or animals. There are also many significant linguistic similarities among names and labels of plants and animals across cultures on other continents. Possibly the most interesting and persuasive evidence available in this interdisciplinary field of research is the presence of disease-causing microorganisms and pests in populations not living near where the diseases and parasites originated. Moreover, it is crucial to notice that several of the diseases are vector-borne. This means that the disease- causing organism requires one or more middle steps prior to re- infecting a human subject. The infectious agent (parasite or bacteria) must live part of its life in another species of animal or in certain types of soils before they are able to parasitize humans again. These vectors of transmission are very precise and without them, the disease cannot be transferred to another human. This is why countries in which malaria is widespread spend so much time and money destroying the places where mosquitoes breed. Malaria is a vector-borne disease that lives part of its lifecycle in the females of the Anopheles species of mosquito, and only that species of mosquito. By controlling or destroying the mosquito vector, governments have significantly reduced or eliminated the incidence and death rate of malaria in these areas.

Before getting into the actual evidence in this chapter, it would be helpful to spend a little time explaining paleo- pharmacology and paleopathology, as well as how researchers diagnose and discover diseases in people who are long dead. While it is true that many diseases do not leave behind traces of themselves or clues of their existence in a person's body after death, it is also true that many diseases do leave their evidence. Even with the diseases that do not leave direct traces there are often other clues that a person trained in medicine as well as archaeology can decipher. For example, some diseases affect the way muscles attach to bones thus altering bone appearance in a specific way. Others simply cause mutations and malformations that show on the bones directly or in the density or structure of the bone. Still others can be discovered while examining a mummy. A few, including all of the parasites, can also be discovered in the fossilized feces of the people in a region. Fossilized feces are called coprolites and to a trained researcher they contain a wealth of information about diets, illnesses, migration patterns, and more, of the people who were living in that place at that time. Finding coprolites that can definitively be shown to be human are rare so discoveries of this nature are very exciting. Since fecal material is so easily and often broken up and used by plants and certain animals as food, it is returned to the earth as nutrient-rich soil and little of it survived to become fossilized. Paleo-pharmacology is the specialty for researchers, both medical and historical, who are interested in the health of an ancient population group.

The very specific vector-borne nature of some of the parasites that have been discovered to have been transported across the oceans before 1492 C.E. undermines the opposing argument that all these diseases traveled across the continents during the earliest, crossing of the Bering Straits. (The idea that there never was a walking migration across the Bering Strait, either on ice or land, and that humans migrated to the Americas across the oceans by sailing near the ice shelves is the subject of a different book.) Our data also strengthens the argument that certain diseases were introduced to the Americas far earlier than traditionally accepted. The standard model argu-

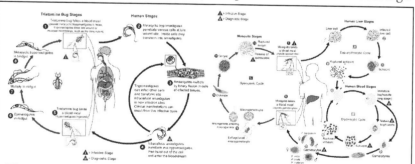

Figure 46 - Trypanosomiasis and Malaria Lifecycle.
Diagrams provided by the CDC.

ment that all these diseases and pests, 19 at current count, came to the Americas either during the various migrations across the Bering land bridge or were introduced by European explorers, does not square with either the archaeological evidence or the locations where the evidence was found by reputable archaeologists and epidemiologists worldwide. In this chapter, we are going to focus on the evidence available for seven of these diseases and parasites.

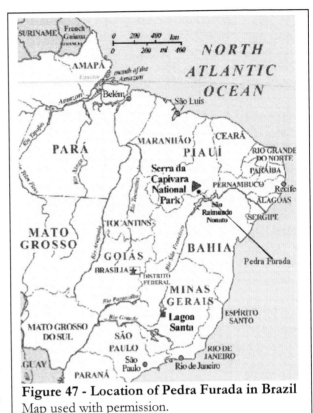

Figure 47 - Location of Pedra Furada in Brazil
Map used with permission.

The very first provable contact between the Americas and Southeast Asia is, oddly enough, the age of the eggs of two specific parasites. Since these parasites had to have been introduced by infected sailors from Asia, such as fishermen from Japan or explorers from China or Southeast Asia, it makes sense to look at the earliest discovered eggs of the parasites, and to examine how far they were from the coast, then from that evidence deduce the likely contact time when the infection first occurred. Verified remains of both the hookworm Necator americanus and the giant roundworm Ascaris lumbricoides, another parasite that found its way across the oceans from Asia, were discovered at Pedra Furada, Brazil. They were dated to about 5,400 B.C.E. Moreover, Pedra Furada was a large cave complex where people lived millennia ago. It is located some 400 miles inland from the coast of Brazil. Because of its inland location, the parasites were likely introduced to one or more coastal tribes quite some time before the infection was first introduced to the tribes living around Pedra Furada. It is also possible that the infection traveled across the Andes from the Pacific sites, down the mighty water highways of the Amazon rainforest, and infected the Pedra Furada population in that way. We simply have not yet found the oldest remains of infected people on the Pacific Ocean side. Until more evidence is discovered creating a path of dated remains, we will not be able to positively determine how the parasite got to these inland caves. We do know, however, that the Asian Necator parasites were in the caves about 7,300 years ago and the Ascarid parasites about 9,000 years ago based on human coprolite studies.

Although both of these hookworms are known to have originated in South Asia, both have been found in South American mummies of people who died long before any Europeans got to the Americas. It is even less believable that these European sailors sailed to Southeast Asia, became infected, and then returned to the Americas to accidentally infect local tribes in both Peru and Brazil. The mummies in which evidence of A. duodenale were found dated to 900 C.E. They were found in Tiahuanaco, a very unusual megalithic ruin in present day Bolivia near Lake Titicaca.

Tiahuanaco was the capital city of an important pre-Incan empire that lasted 500 years beginning in 300 C.E. Although the city became a capital at that time, there is significant evidence that it was a moral and philosophical center, a place to which people made pilgrimages and trips, by 300 B.C.E. or 600 years before it was the capital of this empire. Since the people of the empire had no known written language, it is difficult to know much more about them. A mummy from the same region and dating was found to have been infected with the hookworm, N. americanus. A. duodenale was also found in a different mummy that was discovered in coastal Peru. This mummy was dated to 900 B.C.E. It is possible that the first infections on the Pacific side of South America were among coastal tribes who carried the parasite inland as they traded with the various early civilizations and cultures in Peru, including the people of the Zaña Valley. It may well be that this hookworm was fairly widespread in the Pacific region around Peru and we have simply not found much evidence because we have not really been looking for it and that there is little availability of human coprolites in the archaeological sites. On the Atlantic side of South America, human coprolites, fossilized feces, were found in cave sites in Minas Gerais and Piaui, Brazil, that date between 1570 and 1490 B.C.E. Eggs of two types of ancylostomids (the biological family to which both of these species belong) were identified in the same mummy and one of these egg types was from the Necator parasite.

Although some researchers continue to assert that the parasites must have come over the Bering Strait route during human migrations while this area was connected either by a land bridge or by thick ice, the cold climate of the subarctic and arctic regions would have destroyed the natural lifecycle of both parasites. In fact, in several articles dating from between 1998 and 2003, Adauto Araújo, a specialist in paleoparasitology, indicated that these parasites have complex lifecycles that include human hosts, animal hosts and gestation in warm, moist soil. Given that the type of warm moist soil that is required for these parasites to spread and continue infecting other species does not exist in the northern regions of the Americas, it is impossible for the parasite to have infected the next generation of people walking into America across the Bering ice or land bridge. This means that the migrants moving from the Northern American regions, where they first settled before moving into sub-tropical and tropical America, would have been free from hookworms. In addition, no one has discovered any evidence of these two parasites existing in early North American tribal groups that were dispersed along the generally accepted routes from the Bering Strait to the Central and South American regions. So, either the parasite lay dormant in a human population until they had migrated far enough South for the inactive egg to sense that it was safe and then it entered the soil again (an event that has never been observed or recorded in the life cycle of this species of parasites by anyone), or they were introduced to the tropical and subtropical regions of the Americas through the arrival of different people, people who arrived directly in the tropics. If the first supposition is true, then the parasites would have had to remain dormant for multiple generations of the human population. This is simply not possible as the infection is only spread from the soil to a new host and not from a live host to another live host.

Since researchers and archaeologists have found definitive evidence of both A. duodenale and N. americanus infection in pre- Columbian South American human remains, including in their coprolites, it is most likely that both parasites were brought to the Americas by a route that does not include cold weather, cold soil, or unexpectedly intelligent parasite eggs. The only other way for the parasites to have been transferred into the subtropical and tropical regions of the Americas from the countries in Asia where A. duodenale and N. americanus were infecting the population millennia ago (i.e., in Japan, in China, in Southeast Asia, or on any of the tropical islands) is by crossing the ocean on a living host.

Hookworm eggs are also found in pre-European mummified bodies and coprolites in Peru. Therefore, it would seem to follow that transpacific migrants from Southern Asia must be one component of the ancient American population. Coprolites from coastal Peru show several other intestinal parasites that likely originated in Southeast Asia. These include tapeworms dating to around 2700 B.C.E., pinworms dating to approximately 2300 B.C.E., the whipworm dating to 2700 B.C.E., and the roundworm dating to 6,000 B.C.E.

The Egyptian mummy PUM II, dating to about 170 B.C.E. or the Ptolemaic Period, had eggs in its intestinal tissue that specialists agree were likely Ascaris lumbricoides, a large intestinal roundworm parasite. Some stated definitively that it was A. lumbricoides. Given that this is also the time period in which Dr. Balabanova found traces of metabolized cocaine and tobacco in Egyptian mummies as well as traces of metabolized cannabinoids from marijuana use by people who were later mummified from Peru, finding the same parasites in both locations strengthens the idea that these civilizations were in contact with one another. These same species had already been reported to be present in many Old World locations in antiquity, e.g., at Winchester, England. In Pre-Columbian Brazil, it has been discovered that, although the A. lumbricoides parasite was rarer in America than it was in Europe, it was definitely present. Daniela Leles and her associates showed that they could obtain evidence of the DNA of roundworm in human coprolites in Pre-Columbian dated Brazilian archaeological digs, even when the worm's eggs were not in the human coprolites, from its dispersed DNA. They indicate that the ascarid roundworm has been present in Brazil since at least 7000 B.C.E.

Piedra negra, also called Piedra ascospórica or Piedreaia hortia, is especially characteristic of inner South America, although found very rarely in North America. Professor Olimpio da Fonseco Filho is one of the founders of the scientific discipline paleoparasitology (the study of parasites in ancient populations). He studied in Brazil with some of the greatest minds of his day eventually becoming a professor of pre-med Botany at the University of Rio de Janeiro. He helped found the Oswald Cruz Institute where he taught and researched. In 1937, he became the Professor of Parasitology at the University. He was the field director for the Rockefeller Foundation and studied helminths. In his landmark 1970 book on parasitology, he cited such limited sources as existed when discussing the appearance of certain parasitic diseases in Brazil. "Separated from South America by the two great ocean barriers," this disease is in both hemispheres; [for] it is also in Southeast Asia—Thailand, Vietnam, Burma, Malaya, Indonesia. "In all these regions of Oceania and of Southeast Asia, Piedra ascospórica presents exactly the same clinical, epidemiological, and parasitological characteristics with which it appears on the American continent." He gives names for the disease in Guaraní and Tupí languages (lowland Amazonian). In previous works, he has concluded, and has justified the conclusion, that this disease was introduced to the Americas by pre-Columbian migrations and by natives of Oceania. He argues that since P. hortai is missing in those parts of northern Asia and in North America where populations would have been involved in the hypothesized walking migration across the Bering Strait, there is no possibility of the disease being transmitted in this way. None of the diseases related to this existed in Europe or Africa either.

Pediculus humanus capitis is the subspecies of human louse (Pediculus humanus) that only infests human heads (Pediculus humanus corporis or

Pediculus humanus- humanus is the subspecies that infests the human body other than the head). It is known to have originated in the Old World. In the early 1960s, Professor Fonseco studied a scalp from Peru that was dated from between 900 and 1300 C.E. In 2014, a team of researchers in Brazil was able to revisit the skull that Fonseco studied when concluding that the human lice (head and body) were introduced to the Americas before Columbus and they confirmed his initial findings of head lice nits and detritus in the hair. The new team, using very current microscopy methods and current computer applications, sampled the scalp and confirmed that the parasite on the hairs was definitively P. humanus capitis and that the infestation was from a time before Columbus got to the Americas. Although the team did not speculate as to how the lice got to the Americas, especially given the lack of lice in the Northern American region which precludes it coming across any northern land or ice bridge, it can be inferred that tribes in local Chile and Peru, that the lice likely traveled across the oceans attached to sailors and that the South American tribes were infected through their interaction with these infected sailors. This is especially true given the now verified widespread infection found in the 9th to 13th Century C.E. South American regions.

HTLV-1, the human T-cell lymphotrophic virus-1, is a retrovirus that has been implicated in causing a number of very serious diseases, including uveitis and Strongyloides stercoralis hyper- infection along with several lymphatic cancers. However, only about 5% of people infected with HTLV-1 end up with a related cancer in their lifetimes. When the AIDS scare first spread through the United States in the very early 1980s some prominent researchers proposed that the complex of symptoms that they were seeing was caused by HTLV-1. This was before anyone had found the actual retrovirus (HIV) that was actually responsible for the Acquired Immune Deficiency Syndrome (AIDS). Retroviruses like HIV are a special kind of virus which include a chemical called reverse transcriptase and either DNA or RNA all surrounded by a protective protein coat. The reverse transcriptase allows the virus's genetic material to be integrated into the cell's regular genetic material, making any infected cell into a virus factory. Regular virus's (adenoviruses') DNA cannot be integrated into the cell's genetic material as can those of retroviruses. This powerful ability makes retroviruses very useful in gene therapy and other medical research, but also makes them very dangerous as illnesses. The evidence for the diseases that HTLV-1 has been implicated in causing, such as HTLV-I-associated myelopathy, does show up in mummies and bones. This evidence includes changes to and/or alterations of the bones, unusual markings on the bones, changes in bone density, and/or nodules on the bones, etc.. This is the evidence that paleo-parasitologists are trained to find.

The route by which the human T-cell lymphotrophic (retro) virus

(HTLV-I) reached the Americas has been much and loudly discussed by medical researchers around the world. According to the research team that has asserted the idea that HTLV-1 arrived in the Americas before 1492 C.E., seroepidemiologic, genetic, virologic, molecular, anthropological, archaeological, and oceanographic data led them to the conclusion that this virus arrived not only from Africa (as has been previously suggested, via colonial-era slaves), but also from Kyushu Island in Japan. Moreover, it likely arrived from Japan more than 5000 years ago through direct voyaging. The subjects of this study, the Noanama people, were Amerindians from the high mountains of southwestern Colombia. Their geographical and social isolation reduces the chance of any contact with the slaves of African origin brought to Colombia by the Spaniards.

A comparative study made some years ago utilized thirteen genetic markers to distinguish racial groups of the world. The study yielded one very interesting result – the Noanama had very close relations with Samoans and Japanese – especially Ainu. This result suggests that HTLV-I was introduced to South America from the Far East thousands of years ago by sailing across a route other than the Bering Strait. Furthermore, recent genetic studies on native South Americans showed that their ancestors possessed genetic markers related to the histo-compatibility leukocyte antigen (HLA) like the Japanese of Kyushu. A direct voyaging contact from Japan to Colombia would explain this relationship, because populations of North and Central America are totally without the HLA markers. At a mitochondrial DNA level, study of the deletion 9 bp in the human genome has shown it to be Asiatic, especially being found in North American Indians and Polynesians. Yet, it is not present in the (Jomon-derived) Ainu, and the 9 bp deletion is also absent among the Noanama (as well as on the coasts of Chile and Peru a thousand years earlier). This suggests an intrusion of people from Japan. León, de León, and Ariza cite the archaeological findings of Meggers et al. for the intrusive Valdivia culture of Ecuador as confirming their position of contact with Japanese island's peoples.

Jaime Errazurriz, a respected Chilean architect and noted amateur historian, in his 2003 book, <u>Pacific Basin: 4,000 Years of Cultural Contact: Why Do Some Scholars See Macaws Where the Average Man Sees Elephants?</u>, discusses the voyage of a team of modern Japanese investigators who voyaged across the Pacific using the traditional North Pacific route to Colombia in vessels similar to the prehistoric sailing rafts used at that time in Ecuador, West Mexico, and Southeast Asia (especially among Taiwanese sailors). Errazurriz and Alvarado, after years of research on the Tomuco/la Tolita culture in Ecuador and Peru, assert that this was the route used anciently by these early Asian settlers in South America. The voyage undertaken by the modern Japanese team demonstrates that it was possible for early cultures to make such a voyage.

Evidence was found in a cave site in Minas Gerais State, Brazil, dated between 1490 B.C.E. and 1570 B.C.E., consisting of eggs of Trichuris trichiura, another whipworm, and Necator americanus. The same parasites (i.e., T. trichiura and N. americanus), found at Unai, Minas Gerais have now been identified in human coprolites from Boqueirão do Sitio da Pedra Furada, Piaui, Brazil, in a stratum radiocarbon-dated to around 7,400 years ago.

Although human plague (known historically as the Black Plague because of the black boils that appeared on an infected person's skin), or Yersinia pestis, is more commonly zoonotic in origin. It can be transmitted between people, with or without the agency of vector fleas, and humans can act as a reservoir of the disease thus resulting in tremendous die offs. Since the remains of a rat were discovered in an early archaeological site in Mexico dating from about 1,000 B.C.E., the odds are quite high that this particular rat had been infested with fleas, and very likely carried the Yersinia pestis bacteria. So we know that the disease was in the Americas at a rather early time.

Three forms of plague exist and they are differentiated ecologically. The two forms are Sylvatic and Domestic. The form experienced in Europe's urban population was the Domestic, or Urban Plague. Sylvatic plague, of course, is the plague which is found in wild animals, such as squirrels, ground hogs, prairie dogs, etc. The two are, of course, caused by the same Yersinia Pestis bacteria. The two often come together when domestic animals come into contact with and contract fleas from infected wild animals. In addition to these two types of plague, which are really the same infection, there are three different forms of plague which are differentiated by their pathology; (1) bubonic, (2) pneumonic, and (3) septicemic. All three are caused by the same Yersinia Pestis bacteria which is the same bacteria that infects both wild and domestic animals, but each type here infects a different system in the victim's body.

Bubonic plague infects and inflames the person's lymph system. It is by far the most common form of the plague. It can be transmitted by the bite of an infected flea, or by coming in contact with infected material, which has been in contact with an infected person. Its symptoms are swollen and tender lymph nodes (called the buboes, hence the name) and flu like symptoms (fever, chills, weakness and a headache). These symptoms usually appear 3 to 7 days after the person is exposed to the disease.

Pneumonic plague is more common in dry temperate zones. It is called pneumonic, because it attacks the respiratory system. It is the deadliest of the three types of plague because it settles quickly into the lungs and causes a fatal form of pneumonia. It, too, is passed to humans via flea bites, but in this case it can also be transmitted by a person coming in contact with particles of moisture emitted via a cough or sneeze. In other words, it is an airborne disease. Of course coming in contact with an infected person's artifacts can also be a way for one to contract the disease. Its symptoms are fever, coughing, sneezing, and shortness of breath. This form of the plague also appears much more quickly than the bubonic form. Symptoms can appear as early as one day after infection. It should also be noted that both bubonic and septicemic plague can develop into pneumonic plague if left untreated.

Septicemic plague, as the name implies, attacks and infects the person's blood. Septicemic plague is contracted in the same manner as the other two, but can also develop from either bubonic or pneumonic plague if they are not treated. Once the bacteria start multiplying in the blood stream a person begins to show signs of the disease right away. The symptoms are abdominal pain, fever, chills, shock, subdermal and internal bleeding and extreme weakness. The only good thing is that one's lymph nodes are not attacked.

Human fleas, Pulex irritans, can also spread the plague without the involvement of rats. Xenopsylla cheopis (the flea of Rattus rattus) can easily infect humans. Over 200 species of rodent, as well as other mammals in Western America, have been known to be carriers of the plague. Most domesticated and commensal rodents certainly are. The most compelling evidence in favor of pre-Columbian plague is the existence of several extensive sylvatic foci in both North and South America, with the largest being in western North America in ground squirrels and other rodents. It also has focal points in eastern Siberia and western Canada. This distribution suggests that plague is an ancient and widely distributed disease, and although many scientists believe that sylvatic plague is indigenous to the Americas, and there are lines of evidence that seem to support this conclusion, there are also several other lines of evidence that do not support it.

So far, I have found no direct link with the Scandinavian's diseases and the Amerinds in the northern latitudes. The consequence of these and other discoveries that we document here is that the paradigm has now shifted and those who wish to maintain, "no contact existed between the Old World cultures and those in the Americas" have to demonstrate that fact; they cannot prove it simply by making the claim! This allows major discoveries to be made in the Pre-1492 Trans-oceanic Diffusion Theory. The entire history of the American high civilizations had access to and gave input to cultures in the Old World especially in the tropical world around the earth.

SECTION 5: CULTURAL EVIDENCE FOR TRANS-OCEANIC DIFFUS BEFORE1492 C.E.

CHAPTER 14: ARTISTIC REPRESENTATION OF CROPS AND ANIMALS

When a plant or animal becomes endemic in a society, it will likely become a part of the art and literature of the same society because it has been part of the culture for a long time. Some of the plants, depending on how they were introduced or how they were perceived by the new society, may even make it into the religious art and iconography of the society into which the plant was earlier introduced. If we were to look at the paintings and sculptures of modern artists we would see many different plants and animal represented, both in the foreground as a primary element of the picture and in the background as a setting for the picture. We would find plants and animals from all over the world. If plants

Figure 48 - Maize Sculpture
Sculpture found on Hoysala Dynasty Temple in India. Photo by Carl L. Johannessen.

and animals were introduced across the oceans prior to 1492 C.E., and these plants became a natural and endemic part of the lives of the societies into which they were introduced, it would seem that we would see artistic representations of some of the species in the society's art. This would be especially true for those species that were given religious significance in the new society, such as corn or sunflower in India or the elephant in Mexico and Honduras.

Figure 49 - *Annona squamosa* Carving
Images found on the balustrade of the Bharhut Stupa in Mayha Pradesh, India. Photo by Carl L. Johannessen.

Figure 50 - Carving of Chili Peppers
These carvings of the plant at an ancient Javanese temple. Photo by Evelyn McConnaughey. Used with permission.

I have traveled around the world looking at artistic representations of plants in books, on bas-reliefs, and anywhere else that I can gain access to artwork, and have found numerous examples of plant representations

My research on ancient India, China, Indonesia, Assyria, and Turkey has provided artistic evidence that several indigenous American crop plants and animals were present in these countries between 600 and 2,000 years ago. We hypothesized that we could find art representations of these crops found in Asia, back in America. We reasoned that the people who received the new crops in Asia would have been interested in how they were grown, prepared, and how they were represented in Latin America and the iconography of their original owners. Little did we know that we would find evidence on the origin of maize in Southeast Asia in a very strange manner.

Upon visiting anthropological museums in Mexico in January and February of 2000, we found the remains of actual plants or their representations in sculptures, paintings, mosaics, and ceramics and we realized certain motifs were on both sides of the oceans. The plants we searched for in Asia included American: maize (corn), sunflower, pineapple, annona (chermoya), and annona (custard apples), chili pepper, guava (guayaba), peanut, moschata squash, lagenaria gourd, cashew, and others. The presence of these crops on both sides of the oceans in pre-Columbian times implies early sailing contacts on both sides of the oceans.

It is commonly accepted that the cultures in Mexico, Guatemala, and South America deified maize and represented ears of corn in their religious art. The Maize God headgear depicted both on bas- relief sculpture and in codex drawings from Mexico to Honduras emulates the shapes of ears of

Figure 51 - Mayan Madrid Codex Page.
The figure in the upper left panel of this Mayan book is the Glyph of maize ear bring held by Tlac, the 'long-nosed' rain god, who closely resemble a stylized elephant.

162

maize in the husk and clearly shows the silk in the form of a 'J.'

The Mexican National Museum of Anthropology in Mexico City was the first source for us to check. Unfortunately, lighting on the artifact exhibits in the Mexican museums regularly is limiting for taking photographs without a flash. Lagenaria gourds are displayed on both continents with no doubt about their identification. Lacking a digital camera, we had to forgo much photographic evidence of some of the better exhibits of the artifacts because of the low lighting and rules against using a flash. I, therefore, worked in the excellent library at the Museum. The library staff was extremely helpful, making available practical and useful reference books held at the Museum that facilitated several discoveries. This art material was found in several of the American Indian codices from approximately the period of contact with the Spaniards and they indicate that the religious imagery of several of these organisms that are displayed had already been transferred to or from Asia.

The nearly photographic correlation between Mayan glyphs and Sub-Continent Indian temple sculpture is especially apparent in the Mexican and Guatemalan codices of the pre- and immediately post-conquest period. In addition, in Mexico maize ears are carved on stone artifacts representing religious motifs both in bas-relief and in the round. The sculpture of maize in Mexico is usually simplistic, without showing the displacement of the kernels in the alternate pairs of rows, as occurs on live ears and often in Asia. Representations of maize ears also are found on ceramic idols, bowls and other useful utensils. Some of these ceramic objects in Mexico were made from the molded shapes of real maize ears created by pushing ears into fresh clay during the manufacturing process of ceramic molds. However, when maize ears were carved

Figure 52 - Close up of Glyph on Madrid Codex.
This figure closely resembles a highly stylized elephant.

by hand, in stone or clay, in Mesoamerica, they were usually represented schematically. The ears here have straight rows of kernels along the axis of the ear, and each lateral row is placed regularly so that the kernels line up in straight horizontal rows around the ear. Normally in nature, maize develops so that each two rows of kernels are displaced by half a kernel's thickness from the adjacent two rows (Nearly always in pairs of rows) as a two-kernel-per-cupule system. The cupule is the location on the cob from which two kernels grow as a pair.

Maize ears are sculpted so simplistically in the New World that they were carved easily and fast. I interpret this to mean that in Mesoamerica the artists considered that there would be no doubt that maize was being represented, and therefore, they did not have to make the ears look particularly realistic. In India, maize was frequently represented in stone sculpture in almost photographic detail. I presume that this is because the artists recognized that, at the time of the stone carvings, the maize crop plant might not be commonly known in India. The "J" representing silk strands on the side of the husk is the religious signature of maize in the codices.

The relevant sketches in the codices from the New World indicate a cavalier attitude about the need for accuracy within the paper record of Aztec culture. The fascinating aspects of these maize representations are that the symbols for a maize deity in the codices frequently are sketched as elliptical maize ears, 'in the husk'; with a maize-silk curl hanging from the upper tip of the ear. The symbol for the curl on the ear on the husk is also carved in stone in the same setting as the ears of maize held in the hands of the Goddesses/royal female assistants in the sculptures of a hundred Shiva Temples of Karnataka Pradesh, India. In Mexico, these curls on the husks of the ears of maize are used both in Aztec literature and in the records of the Mayan culture, whether carved or written, to signify that maize is being depicted. The curl signifies that corn is inside the husk, it is 'short-hand' for the Maize God, or the God of fertility. This may not be so strange, but when we also found the chicken image in the calendar diagrams, we easily infer the recorded images of the early presence of chicken.

The most revolutionizing artifact at the Mexican National Museum of Anthropology is the elephant- headed sculpture of a pot-bellied man sitting in a kneeling position with his hands on his knees. I found this figure in the Olmec Room of the Museum. This is very similar to the elephant-headed god, Ganesh, from the Hindu religion. Beatrice de la Fuente, the author of the definitive work on Olmec giant sculptures (and other sculptural studies), credited the head to be of either an elephant or a tiger. Since real tigers do not have that long a nose and elephants do, the decision must be made in favor of an elephant head on top of this sculpted human figure. When asked to identify the statue was of, other passing visitors to the Museum (who happen to have been from Germany) called it an elephant headed figure. This was without any coaching from me. This sculpture has no ears of the tiger rising from the top of its head, so the head can easily be identified as that of an elephant.

This Olmec sculpture closely resembles statuary in India of Ganesh, the elephant-headed god of prosperity and good fortune in Hinduism. This statue was found in the Americas and is housed in the Anthropological Museum in Mexico City. It dates to long before Columbus, as the Olmec civilization was long dead by that time.

In a 1977 peer-reviewed article, Dr. Fuente said that this sculpture is the strangest of the Olmec sculptures, but she never considered that Ganesh was being represented. In fact, no scientist with whom I talked in the various museums in Mexico had thought of the Ganesh resemblance they do not compare pre-1492 C.E. religious art with other pre-1492 C.E. religious art from across the oceans. Excepting the lack of a crown on the Mexico statue, one can see very similar images of

Figure 53 - Sculpture of Olmec Ganesh
This Olmec sculpture clowely resembles statuary in India of Ganesh, the elephant-headed god of prosperity and good fortune in Hinduism. This statue was found in the Americas and is housed in the Anthropological Museum in Mexico City. It dates to long before Columbus, as the Olmec civilization was long dead by that time. Photo by Carl L. Johannessen.

Ganesh in the rickshaws and all over southern India today. In fact, it is more common to see a Ganesh without headgear in these more casual locations in India. Each time the Ganesh image is depicted without headgear it has a flat-topped head with a ridge at the, back edge, very much like the Mexico statue. The ridge has a priestly symbol of a 'v,' cut as a notch in its middle, as you can see in the photo from India. The presence of a Ganesh statue in Olmec Mexican art is significant because it is the most abundantly distributed image of the Hindu religion. This implies that there may have been Hindus in the Americas who created the idol for the prayers for assistance from the Hindu's Compassionate God, Ganesh, while living in the Olmec culture. It is the essential mark of the functioning Hindu culture. The problem with the statue at the Archaeological Museum is that the nose of Ganesh was broken and the burred end polished. But, the patina of age on its nose

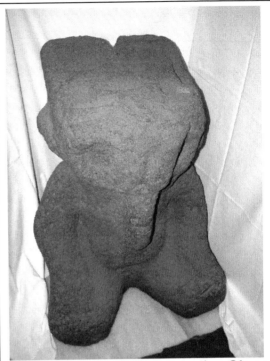

Figure 54 - 'V' Notch on the Olmec Ganesh Statue.
Note also, that the statue is in a very traditional yoga pose or asana. Photo by Carl L. Johannessen.

has new stone color shining through at the trunk's lower end where the curl of the trunk was broken off and polished, leaving a circular remnant for evidence. It is also possible to interpret the statue as not having a trunk curled outwards and broken off, but rather that the trunk extends down the chest and belly of the human body terminating just above the pelvic girdle. Moreover, one can see the strong representation of elephant ears on the upper sides of the statue, extending up to form a very standard elephant profile.

Greg Howard, a former geography student at University of Oregon, found evidence of elephants portrayed in religious art. When I discovered that he was going to Copan, before he left on his trip I suggested that he might find representations of elephants there. There were six elephant heads on the margins of the first step of the ball court (or placed in the Copan City Museum); these represent the elephant-headed Rain-god, Chac. Their noses are shaped quite differently from the bill of the macaw; to which they have traditionally been compared by professional American archaeologists who have not wanted to consider the presence of elephant carvings in the New World

Stela B at the Mayan ruins of Copan (shown on the book cover) became notorious for the two elephants on its upper two front corners at this religious site with Smith's (1924) Elephants and Ethnologists. It provided in great detail, I think, definitive proof for elephants having been sculpted in Central America. Originally, Stela B even had mahouts mounted on top of the elephants, who wore easily identifiable turbans on their heads at the time of their discovery. Dr. John Barr Thompkins, Librarian at Bancroft Library, studied the plaster casts of Stela B at the British Museum, London, while writing his Ph. D. in Anthropology. At that time, one could see the mahouts clearly on this cast.

Figure 55 - Elephant Noses in Copan. These distinct architectural features are at the corners of the Ball court at Mayan ruins of Copan in Honduras. Photo by Carl L. Johannessen.

They have now been broken off the original Stela in Copan, but the vandals did not know about the photographic evidence in the British Museum of the mahouts with their turbans. Unfortunately, when I was in London several years ago, the British Museum was unable to find the casts of Stela B in their storage facilities. Recently, however, I discovered that the British National Museum's Photographic Archives had the original glass plates of Alfred P. Maudslay's photographs of Stela B. These photographs were taken prior to the Stela being completely defaced by vandals and fortune hunters. The Curator, Harry Persaud, was kind enough to take time to find the plates in the vaults and make high quality scanned copies for me to use in my future work.

Figure 56 - 1880's Photos of Stela B
Photos originally taken by A.P. Maudslay on glass plates. Note the mahout on the top left is not yet broken off. Courtesy of the British National Library Photo Archives.

Alfred Percival Maudslay was a British colonial diplomat, archaeologist, and explorer who was among the first people to study the Mayan ruins. Maudslay was born in England in 1850 to a wealthy engineering family. He attended Trinity College, Cambridge and after graduation, he went to medical school briefly. He dropped out due to acute bronchitis. Maudslay moved to Trinidad where he started working in the Governor's office. For the next several years, Maudslay worked in the British Foreign Service in the Pacific. In 1880, he resigned the service to pursue his own interests. Maudslay returned to Guatemala and was one of the earliest explorers of many important Mayan archaeological sites, including Copan in Honduras and Tikal,

Figure 57 - Stela B and The Great Stupa
Comparison of the elephants sculpted on Stela B (left) with the elephants carves at the Great Stupa at Sanchi in India (right). Note the many similarities between the two works. Photo on the left taken by Carl L. Johannessen. Photo on the right taken by J. Lochtefeld. Used with permission.

Quirigua, and Yaxchilán in Guatemala. During his many years as a researcher and field archaeologist Maudslay developed many of the methods of careful field research still used by archaeologists today, including plaster casting, careful illustrations, and in place photography of major sites and artifacts. He took hundreds of pictures of the various archaeological sites. These early photographs allow current researchers to know exactly what the buildings and artifacts looked like just after the site was discovered. Many of these photographs have either never been published or were published over 100 years ago in Maudslay's 5-volume report. Many of these glass plates are archived at the Library Collections of the British Museum. Maudslay died in 1931.

Figure 58 - Detail on Temples at Uxmal.

This Mayan ruin on the Yucatan Peninsual, Mexico, sports many decorative elephant trunks. Photo taken by Carl L. Johannessen.

It is wrong to claim these corner sculptures on Stela B are macaws. The artists (or their instructors) certainly demonstrated that they had experience with elephants during the time of the sculpturing of Stela B because the mahouts had mallets for guiding the elephant and the mahouts in the Stela have mallets. Also, note that the trunk length, curling tusk, and spirals on cheek are typical of Indian representation of large joints, such as the elephant's jawbone). However, in the recent book on the Maya (Stuart and

Figure 59 - Macaw Compared to Stela B.

This photo compares the beak of the Macaw to the elephant carving on Stela B. Photos by Carl L. Johannessen.

Stuart, 1993:105) the face on Stela B is shown with the elephant exposed without their saying a word about the implications of the sculpture to the National Geographic Society who published the book. It, obviously, is unrecognized and the professionals wish to ignore the elephant message.

This Mayan ruin on the Yucatan Peninsula, Mexico, sports many decorative elephant trunks. Photo taken by Carl L. Johannessen. The elephants' curved, raised, and recurved trunks in the 'Nunnery,' at the Mayan archaeological site of Uxmal, for instance, could only have been sculpted by someone who was intimately knowledgeable about the elephant's trunks. In 2015, my son observed that the top trunk had been broken off. One of these representations of an elephant head with elephant-like recurving trunk has been transported from Uxmal, Yucatan, to the National Mexican Museum of Anthropology in Mexico City. There, the official designation for the elephant carvings from Uxmal is that they represent the rain-god Chac. This symbols from India to the Americas may well be factual, but the currently posed hypothesis that they were carved from the image of the head of a macaw or turtle (Figure 59)is pure avoidance of a changing paradigm.

The Codex Tro-Cortesianos (Codex Madrid) is one of only three pre-colonial Mayan books to have survived the purge of the Mayan libraries and universities by the conquistadors and dates to the early post- Classical Period (900 - 1521 C.E.). Many scholars tend to date it to around 1100 C.E. and place it as being from Petén. There are many stylistic similarities to the stone carved writings at Chichen Itza, another important location in this story of early diffusion, and the Codex. It is housed at the Museo de América in Madrid and is considered to

Figure 60 - Ganesh Holding an Ear of Corn.
This statue dates to the early 11th Century C.E. It is located in Karnataka Pradesh, India. Photo taken by Carl L. Johannessen.

be the most important piece in their collection. It shows half a dozen long-nosed gods in its printed illustrations. Though I do not have a current translation of this Mayan codex, the fact that these long-nosed images appear in association with maize, and the Maize God (in sketches, planting corn, and cooking

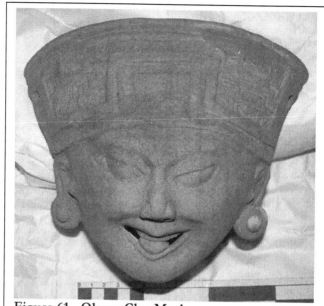

Figure 61 - Olmec Clay Mask
This mask is an Olmec artifact with distinctly Asian facial features. It is displayed in the Museum of Archaeology in Jalapa, Vera Cruz, Mexico. Photo taken by Carl L. Johannessen.

it) appears to show that the Long-nosed God, Chac, was well integrated into the Mayan culture. Does the elephant in the Hindu iconography relate to weather? Yes, through Indra.

Another interesting association of Ganesh with American maize can be found in Coondapur, on the coast north of Mangalore, Karnataka, India, where a Ganesh figure holds an ear of corn instead of the more traditional bowl of sweets. This sculpture is built into the walls of a Shiva Temple that is in excess of 1,000 years old. It is not the common image for Ganesh to hold maize, but there are other examples of him with maize in his hand.

In support of the "Ganesh among the Olmec's" hypothesis, it should be remembered that the Hindus of the 3rd Century B.C.E. to the 9th Century C.E. were in an expansionistic mode expanding from India to Indonesia, to Angkor Wat in Cambodia (not built by Buddhists), and to the Philippines. It is logical to postulate that they also traveled to the Americas and must have done so during the Olmec Era.

The Museum of Archaeology in Jalapa, Vera Cruz, Mexico, is focused on Olmec cultural relics. One can see in the Museum a modeled ceramic Chinese person with a conical Chinese 'straw hat,' tied in the traditional

Chinese manner under the chin. The figure the model depicts has a 'pig tail' hair dress and his eyes have epicanthic folds (See Figure 68). We have no context within which to place this image, so far, other than from the Olmec time period. However, throughout the Olmec exhibits of the Mexican Gulf Coastal region in Jalapa, Santiago Tuxla, Palenque, etc., there are a few small Chinese-like ceramic figurines or sculpted stone human figures. Each have epicanthic eye folds and Chinese-like appearances. The abundant use of jade in the artistry of the Olmec's casts a Chinese glow on this artwork too, as does subsequent Mayan art (See Figure 64 for an example). Jade was mined in the lowland Matagua River valley of Guatemala. Although the only known mines that sourced pre-colonial jade were lost with the collapse of the Mayan society, most researchers agree that this region of Guatemala is the most likely source. I also see Egyptian elements among the archaeological remains of this culture. Perhaps the Egyptians were the source of the people who were the models for the giant Olmec Negroid heads that we find all over the region of the Olmec in the isthmus of Tehuantepec, Mexico. At Santuario de los Guerreros Águila, other Olmec sculptures have headdresses that flare out on each side of the head at about the ears that appear African. As discussed earlier we know that the Egyptians had contact with the Americas because the chemical signatures of both coca (cocaine) and tobacco (nicotine) have been found in the mummified bodies of Egyptian royalty (1070 B.C.-A.D. 395). Those mummies even had tobacco embalmed with them. Another, very striking symbol of the Egyptians is the excessively weathered and worn recurving cobra head on the front of the headdress of the rain-god Tlaloc in the Museo del Templo Mayor in Mexico City. Tlaloc also wears the flying headdress in this case,

Figure 62 - Small Stelae with Chinese Writing
These small stelae are on display at the Anthropological Museum in Mexico City. There are distinct Chinese characters carved on the stelae and the heads of the people are Oriental in appearance. Photo by Carl. L. Johannessen.

which is typically seen where the temperatures in which one has to work are high, as in Egypt, or in some places in Mexico.

Professor Mike Xu, remember, claims that the inscriptions in a display at the Mexican National Museum of Anthropology from the Olmec culture are written with the symbols of the Shang Dynasty. All of the epigraphic marks on the small stelae (See Figures 76 and 77) are found in the gazetteers of Shang-era writing, Xu says. These Shang writings were also carved on their oracle bones in China originally. Xu claims that many other examples in the epigraphy of the Olmec's are also Shang in origin. Professor Winters however, claims that the same writing-glyph system that are on the bricks at Comalcalco dating from the Olmec period is an example of the writing of the Mande culture from western Africa. Winters also records that he translated the messages of the little Ol-

Figure 63 - Olmec Figure With Chinese Characters
This figure had the appearance of a Chinese person. Note the Chinese writing on the body. Located in the National Anthropological Museum in Mexico City. This is an Olmec piece. Photo by Carl L. Johannessen.

mec stelae from the Museum in Mexico City. The stelae are perforce pre-Columbian in creation by a culture from across the oceans regardless whether the diffusing culture was from the East or the West. My impression is that the writing on the miniature stelae in Mexico relates to the Chinese glyphs rather than the African writing.

We do have evidence for the movement of humans across the oceans in the distant past. The artistic symbols that have been used to represent plants and animals demonstrate that the contacts were significant. The ancient people left sculptures, especially of maize, sunflowers, annonas, cashew, etc. in India in religious motifs that had to have been carefully taught by Olmec's or Mayas. These plants and the imagery of elephants and chickens that are present from across the sea are the signatures of these travels. If more proof is needed, one can accept the appearance of sculptures of humans incorporated into Olmec history as being African and Asian, which should clinch the fact that we need to change the paradigm extant in the American Social Sciences.

CHAPTER 15: MORE CULTURAL TRAIT DISTRIBUTIONS

Across the globe, throughout the various ancient cultures of the tropical world, there are cultural traits and practices that are identical to other traits on the other hemisphere of the world. Some of these traits are important for the survival of the local population, but many others bear little weight for functional necessity in the new dispersal area. Many cultural anthropologists seem to consider these traits, whether necessary for survival or simply interesting, as always independently invented even though there are significant similarities. Their reasoning is that since the human mind works in exactly the same way for everyone, it makes sense to them that we would all come up with identical ways of doing things, whether or not our survival depends on the trait. This idea is known as "parallel evolution," or "parallel invention."

There seem to be several difficulties with this idea. Taken to its logical conclusion, this would indicate that all populations should have come up with human sacrifice to keep the sun coming up in the morning as the Aztecs did, or mummification for eternal safety as the Egyptians did, or a snake living at the base of your spine as the Pre-Hindu Indians did. The truth is that populations often came up with very different ways of solving similar problems, depending on their locations, environment, available resources, previous experiences, and needs of the moment. Occasionally, these cultural traits would overlap and show similarities which to diffusionists means that the new culture had been carefully taught on contact.

However, what if the cultural traits are identical in two remotely separated populations? If the populations were close together and were known to have contact with each other, we would conclude that the trait was likely passed between the two populations rather than independently discovered.

Rather than looking at the possibility that the distant populations, especially those separated by the tropical oceans, did have some interaction which would explain the identical nature of the trait, many researchers and scholars suddenly revert to the parallel evolution idea. It is true that some traits may have been independently discovered by populations both in need of solving the same type of problem. However, when it comes to traits that are not necessary for the survival of the population, this is less logical. It assumes that all populations across the world would have similar histories, stories, ideas, religions, social pastimes, etc. This is simply not accurate as scientists have studied cultures far away from each other.

In the previous sections of this book we looked at the evidence for early transoceanic contact between the tropical and subtropical cultures around the world. It is interesting that many of the populations in which we find similar or identical cultural traits are also populations that seem to have shown early interaction with different populations where these traits had been developed previously. From the medicinal use of the BBC to carvings of elephants, to depictions of maize and sunflowers among others we see cultural traits that logic would indicate were brought by travelers and traders that interacted across the tropical and subtropical oceans beginning at least 9,800 years ago. We believe this had to have happened in order for these cultural traits to have been shared in this manner. In this chapter we will spend some time looking at some of the other cultural traits that we believe were most likely transported across the oceans by sailors and traders.

WEAVING

Ikat (Ikkat or Resist Dye Thread) refers to a special form of cloth dyeing technique where the fibers or threads are dyed with the intended pattern before the cloth is woven. This is done using a resist dyeing process where the fibers or threads are bundled together and then tightly bound with a cord so that when the bundle is dyed one color the tightly bound area is not dyed. The dyers can then change the bindings and dye the threads different colors. This allows for a vibrant pattern that is identical on both sides of the cloth. Ikat is a complicated process that requires very accurate patterns and knowledge to properly dye the threads. Weaving with ikat-dyed fibers is done in one of three manners. In the first weaving technique, the fibers of the warp (the threads that are held in tension by the loom) are ikat dyed and the weft (the threads that are passed back and forth across the weft to weave the fabric together) is not. In the second technique, the weft is dyed while the warp remains undyed. In a complex and difficult third technique, one that requires extremely high skill levels, both the warp and the weft are dyed. This last technique is known as double ikat and the resulting cloth is quite costly. This dye technique is found in Indonesia, Cambodia, India, Yemen, Uzbekistan, Japan, Thailand, Mexico, Guatemala, Peru, and other

Central and South American countries.

There is no clear agreement as to where ikat originated, since cloth usually only lasts a few thousand years at the very best. However, the word "ikat" itself comes from the Malaysian word mengikat, meaning "to tie or to bind," referring to the practice of binding the pre-woven fibers with wax-coated cotton thread to determine where dyes will hold in the threads. This process has spread across the world both west and east from its likely starting point in Southeast Asia around what is now Malaysia.

Figure 64 - Ikat Pattern Example, India

From there it likely spread across China through the Silk Road to Uzbekistan and Yemen. Spreading to the East happened through trade and exploration by Malaysian sailors as well as by trade with sailors from the various island groups that fill the China Sea and South Pacific Ocean. Given the information already shown about the various plants and animals that were transported across the oceans from the South and Southeast Asian areas long prior to Columbus, it is not hard to imagine ikat dyeing and weaving techniques also being spread at the same time. It is important to remember that cotton is one of the plants shown to have been spread across the oceans by early sailors. When woven on a

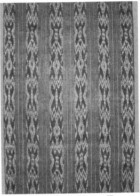

Figure 65 - Ikat Pattern Example, Phillipines

Figure 66 - Ikat Pattern Example, Guatemala

belt loom, the woven product is limited in the same way regardless of its geographical location. When the locations of alleged "cultural hearths" (places of origin of an idea or artifact) are separated by continents and oceans, it usually takes more than a mere 'appearance' of "similarity" to convince most professional scholars, especially those with training in concepts of diffusion, that they are looking at something other than independent invention. The apparent vigor of their need for control in such matters leads them to a false sense of security whenever they are confronted by such evidence. They think that their ideas are safe and stable. However, the belief that independent innovation or invention of identical traits found in distant areas is the "only" concept to be considered is simply misguided. Most people who recognize the difficulties involved in "independent invention" realize that really new ideas are extremely rare and having them rejected is the norm. Our experience suggests that it is so much easier to copy and alter a known idea than it is to come up with a new one, especially when that idea or concept consists of very complex features, and when all of the causes of selection of those features have been shown to be unnecessary to the ideas success and acceptance. The odds, in our opinion, of a complex procedure such as 'ikat' tie dyeing being simultaneously and independently "invented" are zero to none.

Let us consider the fact that "Ikat" thread produced for the weaving of the recognized skirt patterns of both Guatemalan and Indonesian women, which, by the way, are distinct in each village, could only have happened after the development of very specifically designed, tie-dyed thread. The dyeing of the thread, with the use of specific sequences of tying, results in special and unique patterns which are dependent upon the varying tying procedures. They are distinctly different for each village, but yet each village's "theme" remains consistent. Accomplishing this requires a very specific and complex skill set. One immediately recognizes that the weaving loom has to be constructed in a specific and identical way in each village as well, and that all looms in the village must follow that same design. Other villages would have a different pattern, but it, too, would be consistent throughout the village.

The pattern of the weave develops from the placement of threads of given colors and dying sequences in a specific way when stringing the loom. The creation of the threads through tie-dying and the manner in which they are loaded onto the loom is what makes each village's skirt pattern unique. Now, what are the odds that a similar methodology could have been developed in distant Malaya, Sumatra, Borneo and sections of Cambodia? Because of the complexity of this process it would seem to me that the odds against "independent invention" would be astronomically high given there was supposedly no contact across the seas. The women in these two distant culture regions who dyed and wove these beautiful skirts and huipiles (blouses) had to have learned this process via the sharing of ideas among the peoples of the New World and the Old. This, of course, could only have happened if there had been social intercourse across the oceans, most probably carried by traders or weavers in sailing vessels.

BARKCLOTH

Barkcloth is a material made from beating the soaked bark of certain trees with a specialized beater until they fuse into flexible sheets that can be used to make clothes, mattresses, bedding, etc. It was a common material in India, Africa, the Malay Peninsula, and Central America. Many people feel that this technique reached its height in Polynesia and Central America long before 1492 C.E.

As a young student of Geography, I recognized that barkcloth was used to make clothing, paper, art objects, blankets and mattresses and yet the barkcloth is usual-ly not seen in western cultures except for Polyne-sian Tapa cloth art objects which might be brought back by people who have visited some South Sea Island. Barkcloth is a versatile and flexible material made from the inner bark of the

Figure 67 - Traditional Bark Beater
This example is from Costa Rica. It is held in the Carl Johannessen Private Collection. Photo taken By Jerrid Wolflick. Used with permission.

tropical fig trees by a process known as felting, that is by pounding the moist inner bark of the tree until it adheres and becomes a single piece of material. Beaver or rabbit fur is often used to make felt for hats in the modern world. As I was exposed to the tropical cultures, I found the widespread use of barkcloth to be truly fascinating. As I observed the ubiquitous use of this product that has been a part of tropical cultures for ages, and yet has been ignored by most western cultures, the impact on me was fierce.

Paul Tolstoy is one of the writers I read early in my exposure to Geography. His thinking and theories, as well as those of my mentor, Carl Sauer, dominated my understanding of the diffusion of cultural traits in the early stages of the history of civilization in general. Tolstoy's writings were an effective power in stimulating my search for other alternatives to the erroneous hypothesis put forth by Historical Anthropologists and Archaeologists that nearly all cultural traits that seem to develop in more than one society, especially those separated by oceans, were developed independently without any possible contact between the cultures. The fact that people of tropical cultures around the world pounded the bark of species of tropical 'fig-like' trees to obtain a cloth or "canvass" demonstrates the fact of contact and development between the cultures by sailors having crossed the oceans. I felt that Tolstoy's definitive evidence had proven his case. Anthropologists around the world just shrugged and felt it was too much of a stretch of logic to accept his evidence of sailing across the oceans. A lot has changed since that was written 59 years ago.

While I was in Costa Rica on my first research trip from the University of Oregon in 1963, I was given a heavy mattress-like sheet of brown, fibrous material that was made to provide a comfortable sleeping situation. The Bribri Indian people in southern Costa Rica were adept at making this mattress material as well as the thinner materials used for clothing. When I arrived in Costa Rica among the Bribri people, some of the women were wearing this felted cloth around their torsos and waist. This thinner cloth made from felted bark material was the normal clothing for the women. The men of the Bribri preferred the modern woven cloth shirts and pants of European cultural origin. I recognized what was involved in this tropical indigenous culture in Costa Rica. It verified what Tolstoy and other authors had said was involved, namely that since it first arrived here in about 3000 B.C.E., it would have to have been a transfer from Asian cultures who are known to have used this cloth and process before that time. This verification confirmed my belief that studying barkcloth and its manufacture was important for creating major support for the theory of trans-oceanic diffusion of cultural traits long before Columbus.

Over the years, as I traveled extensively for various research projects and lived in aboriginal homes in the tropical heat of the lowlands in Latin America, in Polynesia, and in India, etc. I continued to look for evidence surrounding barkcloth utilization. Wherever I asked about the barkcloth and the process for making the cloth I was shown the old wooden beaters and the anvil logs or timbers used to pound out the felt of the layers of the inner bark next to the cambium into a paper cloth. The grooved cuts in the beaters that I repeatedly saw around the world gradually began to make sense. On one side of the 50 cm long piece of hard wood beaters used to create the felted bark were a series of crossways or long grooves on the beaters. I realized that the grooves improved the felting process. This process went as follows: 1) the soft inner bark is pried away from the hard outer, harder bark after soaking in fresh water; 2) this tender bark fiber was soaked in water and crushed together in the felting process using the long, hardwood beaters that were used to pound the wet fiber; 3) the fibers form a cohesive mass and plant glues are added to the mixture, creating the felted material; 4) the felted material of the many strips of fiber are then dried in the sun. Once the drying is complete the fibers in the material remain stuck together no matter whether the cloth is to be used as clothing, mattresses, or ornamental paper for painting designs for decoration. The people wearing the barkcloth do not worry about the felted cloth coming apart while it is covering their skin.

The first family in Bribri culture in Costa Rica that I made friends with was back in 1963. They gave me a mattress sheet of the barkcloth to use at night; I still have it to this day. I am still grateful for their kindness. The trail into their village was far enough away from the Pan-American Highway that I was advised to rent a horse on the highway and ride up their little narrow trail beyond the side of the hill that provided the start of the trail. The ride to the village was quite exciting and thanks only to the athletic ability of the rented horse was I able to navigate to the village. At one point the horse was able to pull itself back up onto the trail when his rear legs slid off and down a 30-degree slope. Happily, we did not tumble down the side of the mountain. As my guide and I entered the village an hour or so later, we rode through a place on the trail that had been so severely worn and eroded that we had to tuck

Figure 68 - Barkcloth Blanket from Baguio, Philippines

This is an example of a barkcloth piece from the Philippines. Photo by Raymond McCartney Used with permission.

our legs up under the horse to keep from hitting the dirt on each side of the trail. This was just as we were getting to the first houses. The clay soils in the tropical rainforest area are a slippery, sticky mass upon which everything tries to slide off and away. The erosion of the trail itself was made by the pounding of animal hooves. It was so bad that where the horses had been traveling and loosening the soil the trail was more a ditch than an ordinary trail down the hill.

The friendly folk of the village were kind and gentle toward this Gringo who was brand new at this kind of independent research living. They showed me what was required to clear brush and cut non-fruit-bearing trees, where and when they were about to plant crops and dibble in holes for planting of maize seed. Other kinds of holes were dug for slipping in

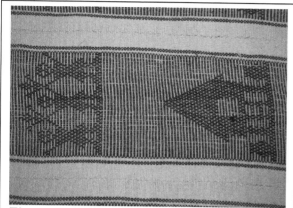

Figure 69 - Detail of barkcloth Blanket from Baguio, Philippines
Photo by Raymond McCartney
Used with permission.

shoots of manioc and other vegetatively planted root crops like sugar cane. We ate corn, manioc, plantains and beans daily with the occasional chicken eggs for me. I shared my canned sardines, rice, and catsup with them. They provided my first exposure to barkcloth. It was a very heavy-duty material, 3-4 mm thick, and brown like an old organic material. The cloth had no decoration on its surface. According to the public records in Central America and Mexico, and as mentioned earlier, the use of this material goes back to at least 3,000 B.C.E. It has been found in archaeological digs to be in their homes and I assume that the thin barkcloth, as thin as a cotton shirt, would also have been present. The women probably would have worn pieces of the thinner barkcloth wrapped around their waist with a belt to hold it, much as they do now. Today, the men of the village no longer wear the tradition barkcloth shirts. In its stead they wear cotton clothing that I presume has been purchased at the country store. There seems to have been some status increase in wearing Mestizo (cotton) clothing. Perhaps because it indicated that those wearing it were the people were well off enough to go to town to do their shopping.

As this habit of the village men showed, the ancient use of barkcloth is quickly disappearing. The process for making it has not been mechanized and the traditional method requires the intense manual labor of incessant pounding for its manufacture. The production process has become almost totally "women's work." The women used to come together and pound on the inner fiber of the bark in the felting process while exchanging the local chitchat of the community. It seems that there is simply less of this kind of cooperative work anymore. In the old days, pieces of barkcloth were anywhere from the size of a sheet of paper to over ten feet wide and up to 50 feet long, which showed that the village was producing something to honor the region's elite. I have seen pictures in Hawaii illustrating these extremely large cloth sizes. The men of the village traditionally prepared the dyes used in decorating the cloth, but as use decreases the men who used to prepare the dyes to stain the barkcloth are becoming less available and the intricate decoration of the cloth, seen in many museum exhibits, is decreasing or disappearing in areas where it used to be prevalent. At least the truly intricate designs once created have been lost to, or are not easily discovered by modern field observers.

According to William T. Brigham (Botanist and geologist), Wendy Arbelt (cloth design specialist), Simon Kooijman (anthropology), and Roger Neich and Mick Pendergrast (ethnography researchers), the skills needed for bark cloth making and decoration of any sort is fast disappearing. Their books detail the intricate designs once found on barkcloth. These beautiful and intricate designs are lost to us because we are losing the skills and knowledge of the intricate methods of the application of the many different dyes, each with its own applicator and application requirements, which were reasonably colorfast and did not wash off when the skirts became soiled.

If you study the museum pieces, the largest collection being at the Bernice Pauahi Bishop Museum in Honolulu, pictured in their books you begin to get a sense of how much detail and care that the ancient peoples put into their barkcloth creations. The specialists in aboriginal art of the Pacific mentioned above have stated that in the modern world the only regular use at present of barkcloth is as slices of stationary, often for sale to tourists or as exports to developed world markets. When I left the Bribri village in Costa Rica, they gave me an old bark beater and a significantly large piece of mattress barkcloth, which I appreciate still because it has allowed me to show my students what was involved in the old ways of life in southern Costa Rica and elsewhere in the tropics. In the 1990s, the use of barkcloth and the barkcloth itself had largely disappeared almost everywhere I went.

Across the ancient tropical world, barkcloth was more than a simple utilitarian device. It was also rare and beautiful art. In some ways, barkcloth can be seen in the same light as pottery. Although the purpose of pottery is simply to store things, the various peoples and societies turned these simple containers into some of the most beautiful art in history: utility and beauty, something for which people seem to strive. In the Hawaiian Islands, the indigenous inhabitants of 500 years ago were using elaborately decorated cloth festooned with several colors of dyes and many complex and beautiful designs. Their use of barkcloth was in the full range of simple cloth as decorated honorific ornamentation. At the present, these peoples, just as those throughout the tropical islands of the Pacific Ocean, are using woven material like we in the developed world use: woven cotton, wool, and plastics.

In Polynesia, the regional barkcloth was historically called different local names, such as Kapa. Currently the tourist trade calls the barkcloth created for this industry tapa. This wonderful, thin, and delicate paper is currently a type of stationery paper for writing letters and notes by tourists. At European contact, however, the Polynesians used the barkcloth in the same way that woven clothing is now used. The Polynesians did not use weaving at the time.

The tree used for the fiber material from which barkcloth was made in other tropical lands farther to the west into Asia, such as in Orissa, India, is Symplocos racemosa. Its common name in Orissa is the Kumbhi tree. The inner part of the bark that is in contact with the cambium is the source of the barkcloth fiber that is pulled free from the harder outer bark. In the present time, the only people really using barkcloth are the traditional religious holy men who live very isolated lives and feel they must use this type of cloth for religious reasons.

Another group of people who used to wear barkcloth is the Baganda of Uganda. Specialists used to make the village's barkcloth that gave them prestige in the area. The trees from which the Baganda made their cloth were grown in their gardens. It was a very easy process, simply shoving a six-foot long branch into the ground. The resulting tree roots itself and is said to have produced a 30-40 feet tall trunk in only three years. They could then start harvesting branches from which they planned to skin the bark. The tree trunk itself can then be harvested merely two years after planting. The trees live for decades, but the bark is harvested for twenty to thirty years. In Africa, strips of fiber roughly six feet long are removed from the trees to start the manufacturing process. The bark is cut laterally at the base of the tree and again at the length they need. Once the branch is cut and soaked in running fresh water for a few days the bark can quickly be stripped off the stem down to the bare cambium. The outer "dry" bark of the strip is separated from the softer part of the inner bark, which is then put in water to keep it more pliable for later utilization.

Before the introduction of steel needles, fish bones were crafted into needles for sewing the barkcloth into usable clothing. The final material was created out of as many sheets as needed for the kind of wear it was going to get. Color and design were added as desired. This was before the modern industrial materials were available, which changes the size and frequency of the threads in the weaving process. Prior to the introduction of the loom and the weaving process by European missionaries, barkcloth was one of the only ways to create clothing and paper in the tropics where animal skins are too warm for clothing.

In Polynesia, the color and designs in the modern museums show that art was especially perfected into highly specialized decorations for high society's intricate clothing development. We see complex creations of kapa (pronounced as tapa) from Japan, Indonesia, and across the Indian Ocean to Madagascar; they were connected culturally to the Polynesians genetically and linguistically and kapa was obviously in use. The tropical Latin American barkcloth has most of the complexity of barkcloth in Polynesia. The barkcloth patterns were designed in a similar (nearly identical) way to the finest cloth in Polynesia.

Several kinds of trees provided the fibers for this manufacture of kapa but the most normally used tree was called Paper Mulberry in English. The paper mulberry stems need the close tending care that produces many moderately elongated stems that have branches plucked off early in their growth to allow the fibers under the bark to be straight and not separated. Captain Cook's Journals, written between 1768 and 1779, suggest that in the Hawaiian Islands the people also used the bark of the breadfruit tree as a source of fiber for some of their barkcloth. He also recognized that they made use of the paper mulberry from China. Cook's Journal indicates that the fiber used for the finest, thinnest cloth was made from the breadfruit trees. However, he was told that the women do most of the fine work on the tapa from other trees as well.

In his 2008 article, and the parent study, Paul Tolstoy exhaustively lists 418 distinct cultural characteristics of the 177 methods used to manufacture barkcloth around the world. His reasoning was that a tool used in the biological sciences, namely, cladistics, could be used in the social sciences as well. Cladistics is the process of creating trees of related species so we can follow their development back and forth in their evolutionary progression. These tree diagrams, also known as cladograms, show how various species are related, how they connect, and other related information. Tolstoy felt that these cladograms could be put to use comparing cultural events and processes around the world. After listing every possible characteristic for the creation and manufacture of barkcloth, Tolstoy developed very precise cladograms which show that barkcloth manufacturing first came into being in Fiji and the nearby islands of Polynesia. Tolstoy then constructs cladograms that allow him to show how the technology was spread across the world by sailors. He showed that by using cladistics, the science behind creating cladograms, in social sciences where there are often many complex characteristics across a wide set of populations, one could see how ideas traveled across space and time. Although Tolstoy did come to any definitive conclusions about the spread of barkcloth by diffusion, his data and cladograms indicate that it was widespread across the Pacific long before Columbus, therefore strengthening the evidence for early diffusion of cultural traits along with the plants, animals, and diseases that we have already discussed.

A short list of scientific names for several of these fiber sources from different locations of barkcloth manufacturing on the Hawaiian Islands follows.

- Chinese paper mulberry or Broussonetia papyrifera,
- Bread-fruit tree (Sitodium) or Artocarpus incisa,
- Wild fig of West Indies or Ficus prolixa, which produces fibers, that

resembles the other fibers.

The first item on this list is the most desired, since it produces the whitest cloth and most elegant of fibers and accepts colored dyes quite well. These dyes are applied to it for the most elite people in the Hawaiian Islands. The other sources provide fewer white fibers, therefore, are used by the lower class peoples on the islands. The dyeing of the whitest barkcloth from this tree species was specially provided for the most elite people in the Hawaiian Islands at the time of discovery by Europeans.

In 1943, my friend and colleague, W. W. Borah expanded his 1940 Doctoral Dissertation into a very powerful book that explored the very early Spanish Colonial creation of the 'Chinese' silk industry in Mexico under Cortés. Hernándo Cortés de Monroy y Pizarro arrived in the New World in 1504 and was soon part of the conquest of Hispaniola and Cuba during which he was awarded large estates. In 1518, he was appointed by the Governor of Cuba to be the commander of an invasion force to the mainland of Mexico and by 1523 he had conquered the Aztec Empire. Also by 1523 he had usurped all Mulberry trees to be used in the production of silk (remember that they are the trees that silkworms use for food and nesting) and he likely forbad the destruction of these trees for any barkcloth production. Making this change would have been very profitable as getting silk from Mexico to Europe was far easier and cheaper than getting it from China to Europe.

When the European and Middle Eastern missionaries, especially those of the Christian and Muslim faiths, arrived in these remote places of the world, they discovered societies that logically maintained semi-nudity or near total nudity as their style of dress given the heat and humidity of these regions. The missionaries found this lack of modesty repellent and morally wrong, especially for the females (given the sin of Eve), and they began enforcing their Judeo-Christian/Muslim values on the people. Women were required to have their breasts and pubic region modestly covered with cloth and the missionaries worked hard to enforce these restrictions throughout the world. Moreover, they worked very hard to embed these moral shames into the fabric of these indigenous societies themselves.

The commercial weavers of the world spent a lot of time, money, and energy to entice people everywhere to wear woven clothing for covering their bodies. Once the industrial revolution was in full swing, they were able to effectively hire people to work at low wages and in this manner rapidly stimulated the weaving industry. This was seen as more efficient than were the ancient methods and so the industrialized weaving industry won the battle. The manufacture of cloth shifted in the last two to hundred years from the pounding of plant fiber, which was previously one of the village women's main activities, to mechanized weaving. The original weaving industry and mat-making industry located in these countries has transformed itself into the communal rug making and weaving industry and is solely done for the purposes of having get- togethers. Now, however the felt pounding activities are mainly left to the older women and the weaving and knot tying are primarily assigned to the younger women, because their small fingers are better suited to the tying of small knots. Child labor is certainly alive and well during these village folk activities.

The earlier spread of barkcloth technology with all its intricacies and biological elements, including the idea that it was the men's job to create the dyes from the natural world, indicate that this was passed across the oceans by traders, artisans, and sailors.. The barkcloth manufacture was ancient enough to have developed 418 identified traits within the 177 adequately described procedures for making the cloth. The uses and techniques involved in the production of barkcloth or kapa/tapa were definitely sufficiently similar all over the tropical world, including the complex and intricate dying techniques, to indicate that they were transferred across the tropical oceans from one early society or culture by sailors to other distant ones.

To summarize, today, examples of ancient barkcloth showing all its complexity can only be found in the museums, especially the Bernice Pauahi Bishop Museum in Honolulu. The museum displays show that the systems were highly similar throughout the entire tropical and subtropical world and that essentially the same plants and dyes were used across cultures. This seems to indicate that the use of barkcloth was carried by someone, probably by sailing traders or weavers as there does not seem to be any other possibility, around the world as diffused traits.

BLOWGUN

The blowgun is a weapon that has an origin lost in the mists of time. It is thought that the early Stone Age people used these weapons, if not an even earlier people. The blowgun exists in some form on every continent except Antarctica and has been in these locales for centuries (e.g. Europe and Africa), or in some cases for millennia (e.g. North, Central, and South America; Polynesia, Borneo, India, and Japan, among others). (Figure 68} Some researchers believe that since the blowgun is so simple to make that it was independently invented where it was discovered. Others feel that the extreme lack of variation of form around the world indicates that the blowgun is evidence of early tropical interaction between Southeastern Asia, the Pacific Islands, and the Americas long before 1492 C.E. For example, both Sumatra and Guatemala, countries on opposite shores of the Pacific, have developed the same method of making a certain variety of hardwood blowgun, and since their technique is very unusual and requires very similar and related technologies, it is very hard to continue insisting that each of these items was developed independently. It is also noteworthy that both of these cultures have the same weaving technology as well, yet another indicator supporting the idea that cultural traits were shared by early travelers from these cultures across the tropical oceans.

Also of import is the fact that the manner of holding their particular brand of blowgun was very specific and unusual as well. In both cultures it had to be held with both hands placed near the mouthpiece, which itself was unique and special, is an indicator that very careful training by the source people had taken place. Then there are the sighting knobs on the blowgun which have similar forms in both locations as well.

All of these traits point to the fact that the blowgun was not developed independently in Guatemala and Sumatra.

Methods Of Construction

The fact that various modes of construction of blowguns all seem to have been developed in similar ways on both sides of the ocean is also fascinating. There are three different blowgun construction techniques found around the world. The first two are similar but require different tools and woodworking techniques. The third technique requires advanced tools, training, and knowledge and is unique to Sumatra and Guatemala.

In the first technique, the builder finds an appropriate length and girth of bamboo or

Figure 70 - Traditional Blowgun
This example was collected from Costa Rica. Held in the Carl L. Johannessen Private Collection. Photo by Jerrid Wolflick. Used with permission.

other mostly hollow reed tube. He then splits it to remove the various internal barriers, polishes the interior, then puts the two pieces back together using twine, glue, or another kind of wrapping material, Once the glue is dry, he polishes the interior again to ensure that there are no burrs or rough spots, and then fashions the mouthpiece and exterior sights (if they have them). The second technique uses much the same process as the first except that the original material is a straight piece of wood. The wood is split and then hollowed out with woodworking tools. The rest of the process is the same as the first technique. The third technique is the one that is unique and would have needed to be taught, both the process itself and the use of the specialized tools. In this technique, the builder finds an appropriate solid piece of hardwood, such as palm trunks of the appropriate length. Using water soaking and fire, the branch, tree, or pole is straightened until it is nearly perfectly straight. The builder then lashes the pole to a tall tree and builds a platform above the top. With special forked guides, the builder drops a triangular-bladed drill bit attached to a slender pole onto the center of the end of the pole. The builder repeats this process of dropping and turning, keeping the bit carefully centered using the guides and an assistant, until the pole is hollowed out. During the process the assistant regularly pours water into the bore hole, both to float the drilling debris up and out of the hole and to cool and soften the wood. Once the tube is completed, the builder smooths the inside using the same techniques as the other processes and the external sights are placed on the blowguns in the same manner. Given the complexity and unusual method of the third technique, and that it is found only in Sumatra and Guatemala, it is clear that this process had to have been brought to Guatemala from the Sumatran people.

Figure 71 - Close-up of Aiming Structure
This is the aiming sights on the tip of the traditional Blowgun. Carl L. Johannessen private collection. Photo by Jerrid Wolflick. Used with permission.

To a certain extent, we come back to the plants involved in diffusion with one of the kinds of woods that was involved in the creation of blowguns. The bamboo stalks that were frequently used to construct blowguns have very long internodes (the space between the joints) and the blowgun is fashioned by searching for the bamboo species with the longest internodes in the area. Some bamboo has significantly long internodes and these are preferred. Were any of these species of bamboo carried, as growing plants on board ship crossing the ocean for trade that could have allowed this use also? Jim Parsons, one of my geography professors and a colleague of Carl Sauer's, was convinced that the giant bamboo used for construction purposes in the American tropics was transported in this way. Giant bamboo clumps are certainly now in abundance in the American tropics. To my knowledge there has been no DNA analysis of bamboo. Having such could certainly help determine the origin of the bamboo used in construction in the Americas. It is certainly possible that the sailors who came from blowgun-using cultures may have brought the hollow tube plants that were sometimes used on the most ancient blowguns; or they could have brought the construction bamboo for rafts or structures. Since bamboo blooms very infrequently, sometimes up to thirty years after planting, it is very difficult to get DNA sources from the flower.

HUMAN SKULL MODIFICATION - THE CLEFT NOTCHING OF SKULLS

Another interesting cultural trait that is most easily explained through interaction and trade is the fact that human head shape modification in the Olmec civilization and on Easter Island both show a distinct cleft that has no analogue in the real world

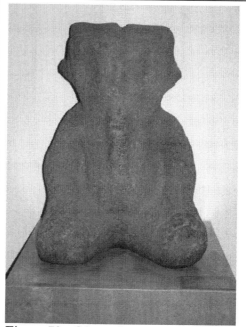

Figure 72 - Olmec Statue of Ganesh
This Olmed Statuer, housed in the Anthropolgical Museum in Mexico City, seems to be a definitive elephant figure. It is likely that it is representation of Ganesh. Photo by Carl L. Johannessen.

189

of either culture. This cleft head epigraphy further ties the two sites together and also strengthens the idea of ocean sailing technology and cultural interaction. Since there is no causative relation between the cleft head representation and a functioning person, it makes more sense that the cultures interacted and shared this trait, as well as plants and animals, across the ocean. The notched skulls must have had some religious or class significance that showed up in their art and sculpture as well. Cleft heads may well have been represented in small ceramic figures and statues that were carried all across the Pacific and Atlantic oceans where archaeologists later found them. We have to acknowledge that religious symbolism of this kind found in separate and distant places, especially when those places were separated by large bodies of water, indicate transference by some means, and probably by sailing vessels and sailors either carrying passengers or trade goods. These kinds of similarities raise real doubts about any claims that some kind of independent innovation has been involved.

BOARD GAMES AND OTHER GAMES

Patolli/Pachisi

Anthropologist E. Adamson Hoebel (1966) said the Aztec patolli derives from the East Indian game of pachisi, but R. Barry Lewis, University of Illinois anthropologist, countered with an article written in 1988 claiming the similarity between the two games is due to the limitations of a board game, meaning to him that the two games were independently derived. This is not logical given the huge

Figure 73 -Patolli Board Rendition in Aztec Art.
Photo used with permission

Figure 74 - Pachisi Board, near *Diwan-I-Aam*.
Photo used with permission

amount of particulars in the two games that are alike or more than just similar. The idea that there is a limited number or possibilities for layouts of board games is absurd. One need only visit a major toy store to see the fallacy of that idea. Also, when juxtaposed with the amount of plant, animal, and disease transfer we have already shown, it makes more sense that it was transferred by sailors or trader. {Figure 71 and 72}

Wheeled Toy Wagons In Mexico

It is generally accepted that the great civilizations in Mexico, Central America, and South America did not use the wheel for any meaningful work application. Some writers have concluded that this indicates that they did not know about the wheel. However, in archaeological sites throughout the Aztec, Mayan, and Incan Empires we find many examples of children's toys with wheels on the base (much like modern children's toys). These toys date to far before the European contact with the Ameri-

Figure 75 - Mesoamerican Wheeled Children's Toy.
This Pre-Columbian child's toy shows that the cultures of the Americas understood the concept and usage of the wheel. Photo taken by Carl L. Johannessen.

cas. There is no doubt that these great civilizations knew about and made some use of the wheel. Why, then, is there no evidence of these cultures using the wheel in their work days for pulling, hauling crops, products, immense stones, and the like around the land? There are a couple of different ideas as to why this was the case. According to many scholars, none of these cultures lived in environments that were conducive to the use of the wheel. The Incas lived in high, steep, and Rocky Mountains where wide roads for wheeled vehicles would not have been safe or logical. The Maya lived in a type of forested terrain that was too variable and rough for easy building of roads. The Aztecs home and main city was located on a small island so again not a location suited to the wheel. Moreover, none of these cultures ever domesticated large work animals for hauling and dragging.

Another idea, in line with the regular and common contact we have shown between the Chinese and the Americas, looks to the religious beliefs of the people. Although we are uncertain as to all the religious beliefs of the great cultures of the Americas thanks to the massive destruction and burning of Mayan libraries and books by the Spanish conquistadors in Merida and Yucatan at the time of contact with Mexico. We do know that the Taoist beliefs in China date to around 2700 B.C.E. and the philosophical ideas extant at that time. One example of such a belief was the Taoist ideal, which stated that when working, a person was not to use animals or other people to pull, haul, or carry anything, but rather had to use his or her own muscle and power for that work. We think it highly likely that it was the transfer of this idea to the Americas that led them to reject the wheel for working purposes. So we do not find it a great stretch of the imagination, since there was a lot of interaction between the Chinese and the ancient Americans early on, that this Taoist ideal made its way into the thinking of the peoples of the Americas (de Groot, 1901).

CHAPTER 16: THE 260 DAY SOLAR YEAR

Many years ago, one of my graduate students, Falkan Forshaw, brought an interesting and revolutionary idea to my attention relating to a religious calendar system that exists in the area around the Izapa site in Chiapas, Guatemala. It piqued my curiosity, but at the time, I was very busy with another research topic in the area of pre-Columbian plant and animal diffusion across the oceans. Falkan went on to complete his Doctoral degree and went into his own career. He and I, however, maintained regular contact and continued discussing this calendar idea; the new idea that there might be a South American connection. I mentioned it to the seminar class at the University of Oregon and we all got a kick out of the possibility of this. For whatever reason, we just left the idea as a fascinating concept and put it firmly on the back burner. He continued doing his personal research on the subject. After John

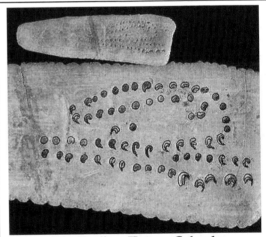

Figure 76 - Earliest Known Calendar.
Dated to around 40,000 years ago among the Aurignacian peoples, this calendar seems to represent a date-keeping system for the hunters.

Photo in the public domain

Sorenson and I completed our academic book, World Trade and Biological Exchanges Before 1492 C.E., laying out the evidence for regular and sustained interactions between tropical and subtropical cultures across both the Pacific and Atlantic Oceans I decided to focus more of my research time on the cultural traits that could also have been transferred by these early mariners. In speaking with Falkan soon after the book was published, I recognized the potential importance of this particular calendar dating in exploring the transfer of cultural traits around the world.

{Figure 77} Calendars have interested and fascinated scholars for ages. When did humans first come to the realization that the seasons were cyclical and could be predicted using the position and size of the moon, position of the sun, and the positions of both the fixed stars and the planets (planetai asteres or wandering stars). Since written history is quite young, and notoriously incomplete, researchers have had to rely on archaeological discoveries to define the earliest calendars. From the research, we know that the earliest calendars were lunar rather than solar. The earliest archaeological remains that are thought to be calendric date from 40,000 years ago. They are attributed to the Aurignacian culture flourishing in Southern Europe at that time. In Scotland, hunter-gathers also created a calendar system using variable sized pits aligned on hills to follow the moons size. This was dated to 10,000 years ago. In the Americas, the earliest calendar seems to date from around 4,200 years ago, found in a temple in the ruins of Buena Vista about an hour north of Lima, Peru. Oddly this calendar is a solar calendar marking the date of the winter solstice. It is likely that the many and varied forms of calendars in the Western Hemisphere started with this one. The calendar system of the Olmec seems to date significantly before 32 B.C.E. in Veracruz, Mexico (Probably because of an inscribed complete date on Stela C at Tres Zapotes on Latitude 18°N). This date is fully articulated in the written Mayan dating system so we can decipher it using the complex Mayan calendric system, which allows us to infer that the calendar, which later became the Mayan calendar, had been perfected long before it was adopted by them. This calendar includes the 260-day religious dating system, which depends upon the solar zenith at 14° 42' N., and/or the zenith at 14° 42' S. At these locations the sun's zenith occurs twice a year. If you count 260 days from the zenith in the fall you will arrive at the second, or spring zenith. Then you will have a period of 105 days until the fall zenith comes around again. These dates are not   to   be confused with the equinoxes.

There are calendric timelines related to the use of a 260/105-day solar year, like the one which was used by the Maya at Izapa, Mexico and the one used by the Inca at Nazca, Peru, the two major Pre-Columbian cultures in North and South America. In fact, this calendar was used by all Meso-American cultures before Columbus, but these two cities are the only ones that provide us with locales that are both at 14° 42' latitude, although they are in opposite hemispheres. This means any solar observations of the sun made in either city would have been, from the Earth's point of view, the same, just offset by six months as the earth's orbit takes the sun from north to south and back again.

Figure 77 - Mayan Calendar.
Note the 19 characters surrounding the central carving.
Photo in Public Domain

This calendar system, best known as the Mayan Calendar, was used by the Mayan political and religious classes. It is among the most fascinating of calendar systems created by any peoples on Earth. It consists of solar and lunar reckonings along with dating astronomical structures taking into account the movement of all five planets that are regularly visible with the naked eye. From the 989- day cycle through the religious 260-day cycle, this Mayan total calendar system is among the most complex in the world. The following summary is adapted directly from Floyd Lounsbury's Maya Numeration, Computation, and Calendrical Astronomy, (1978, p. 760) which is still the most comprehensive study of its kind to date.

- Maya numeration was and is vigesimal, base-20, meaning that there are twenty symbols used to write numbers. In the enumeration of days, it was modified to accommodate a 360- day Mayan Tun or "chronological year with five or six days left over for dancing and celebrating at the end of the year."
- The chronology of the Mayan calendar was kept through a continuous day count, which was reckoned from a hypothetical zero-day some three millennia B.C.E., or over 5,000 years ago.
- Basic calendrical cycles were a cycle of thirteen months, the vientena of 20 days each, the "sacred almanac" (or tzolkin) of 260 days (the product of the thirteen months and the vientena), the "calendar year" or Haab, of 365 days, and the "calendar round" of 52 calendar years or 18980 days (the lowest common multiple of the sacred almanac and the calendar year). Others were of 9

days, 819 days, and 4 x 819.

- A concurrent lunar calendar characterized days according to the current moon-age, moon-number in lunar half years, and moon duration of 29 or 30 days.

- The principal lunar cycle, for the warning of solar eclipse possibilities, was 405 lunation's (11960 days = 46 tzolkin), in three divisions of 135 lunation's each, with further subdivisions into nine series of 6-month and 5-month eclipse half years. The saros was a station in this cycle (the end of the fifth series) but was not recognized as a basic cycle.

- Venus cycles were the mean synodic Venus year of 584 days, an intermediate cycle of 2,920 days (the lowest common multiple of the calendar year and the Venus year, equal to 8 of the former and 5 of the latter), and a "great cycle" of 37960 days (the lowest common multiple of the tzolkin, the calendar year and the Venus year, equal to 104 calendar years or 2 calendar rounds). Reckonings with the periods of the other planets are more difficult to establish.

- The calendar year was allowed to drift through the tropical year, the complete circuit requiring 29 calendar rounds (1,508 calendar years, 1,507 tropical years). Corrective devices were applied by using the Venus and eclipse calendars to compensate for long term accumulations of error owing to small discrepancies between canonical and true mean values of the respective periods. For numerology, canonical values were accepted at face value.

As I said, it is very complex and filled with a lot of fascinating information. I am going to focus specifically on the 260-day cycle as it relates to places on the Earth where this cycle is also involved in the various solar events. I am looking specifically at the Earth locations built at about 14° 42'N latitude and 14° 42'S latitude. The 260-day calendar is a special religious calendar that would have to have been created in some society that flourished along either 14°42'N or 14°42'S latitude as these are the only latitudes wherein the cycle of the vertical sun is expressed in this number of days. The Aztec culture came into the area from the North and likely adopted this calendar from the Olmec or Epi-Olmec people around Veracruz. We are not sure where the proto-Mayan people came from but we do know that they did adopt the Olmec calendar for their society.

There are many sites built around the world near these same latitudes. We are going to focus on the ruins of both Izapa, Guatemala (the coastline nearby in Chiapas, Mexico) & Copan, Honduras (14°42'N latitude) as well as the Nazca Plains of Peru (14°42'S latitude). At both of these latitudes, North and South, the sun provides a complex cycle per year that shows when the 260- day year starts with the zenith sun at that specific latitude.

The cycle in Izapa begins at the end of summer when the sun is vertical at high noon in the sky and exactly 260 days later this event happens again after the Spring Equinox and before the Summer Solstice. There is then a 105-

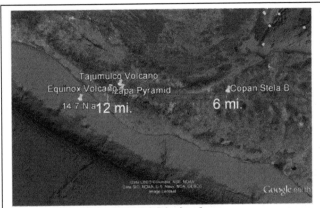

Figure 78 - Map 14°42' N latitude.
This map is of Central America and includes landmarks discussed in the chapter. The map was generated by Jerrid Wolflick using Google maps. Used with permission.

day period until the sun returns to vertical again in late August at latitude 14°42'N. This is the likely reason that the Mayan calendar has a 260-day religious element in its complex system. According to Vincent Malmstrom, Professor Emeritus of Geography from Dartmouth College, the origins of this calendar system can be placed on modern dating August 13, 1358 B.C.E.

This date was even more significant to the Zoque priests living in the region where Izapa would later be built because not only did the sun start its 260-day zenithal interval, but also that Venus rose directly over Volcán Tajumulco, the highest mountain in Central America. We know from studying later peoples of the area, that the heliacal rising of Venus was an event surrounded by great awe so it would make sense that the calendar would begin on that date. Dating was made easy because the sunrise over certain pyramids would indicate the day of the start of that calendar year.

As cultural Geographers, if we assess a relationship between two locations on the Earth that show similar specific cultural uses in their calendrical counting of their relative location, then we need to explore possible locational similarities that may account for the cultural ones. For example, we know that this solar cycle happens on exactly the same cycle every year at 14°42'N latitude so we need to look and see if there are other sites around the world where the same sequence occurs with similar uses arrayed along those latitude lines. We also need to look at the matching Southern latitude locations to see if there are potential sites there where diffusion of these simple uses of such a calendar might show that contact had been established between people using these ideas. It is a marvelous search and it will pay off. Looking first to 14°42'S latitude, we find the southern side on the famed Nazca Plains in Peru. Even more importantly, we find markings on the plain at almost exactly the same latitude as Izapa in the north that indicates that the people responsible for the many mysterious glyphs scattered across the Nazca Plain were also aware of the 260-day interval of the zenithal passage. They created a series of intersecting lines that intersect at 14°42'S latitude and may show that the Nazca people may not have been given credit for their recognition of the corollaries with the zenith passage of the sun in the Southern Hemisphere. The starting point of some of these multiple radiating lines is positioned on the East-West lines at Latitude 14°42'S. When these relations are found together, they tend to cause us to search for more relationships that are the result of diffusion across the oceans. According to the first serious researcher on the topic of the Nazca Plains, Professor Paul Kosok (later of the Chair of the Department of History at Long Island University), "While* investigating this region in 1941, I was suddenly struck with the thought that these remains could have had some connection with early calendrical and astronomical observations." (p.6) in Mexico.

In 1966 Professor Kosok noted that these lines were relevant to the rising and setting of the sun on certain days but failed to put them together with other sites located on the same latitude lines around the world: "A number of lines and roads were found to have solstitial directions: A few with equinoctial direction could also be identified. Moreover, various alignments were found to be repeated in many different places" (p. 54). It is quite possible that Professor Kosok did not know enough about the other sites to make the connection.

Figure 79 - Map of 14°42'S latitude.
This map focuses on teh Nazca Plains where the figures cross 14°42'S latitude. Note the ray-armed formation very near the parallel.

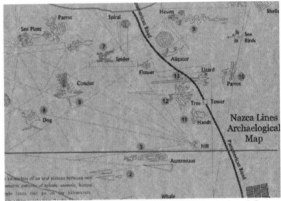

Figure 80 - Archaeological Map of the Nazca Plains.
This map is given out by one of the tourist services in Peru to people visiting the Nazca Plains.

The Toltec of Mexico seem to also have had a 52-year and 260-day calendar that they used before they conquered either the Aztec or later the Mayan cultures. We can speculate on where this calendar originated as it has many similarities to the other Mesoamerican calendars and it is close to an older calendar in India. We have not yet found the origin of the Hindu 261-day calendar that is shown in the altar tiles of various Indian temples. Although it might be reasonable to infer that all of these cultures got their calendars from a single origin, likely centered at Izapa, in reality our search is just beginning, so it would be premature at best to draw any conclusions regarding the origin of these calendars. When looking for similar calendars in the future, however, we will be broadening our day count to include any calendars that at least come close to the 260-day count.

It has also been pointed out that since a tribe, such as the Kalapuya of Oregon, may have been forced to migrate northward it may have taken its 260-day calendar with it and kept it even though the sun no longer reached a true zenith at the new location. There is one group in the northern hemisphere that deserves further investigation, because it, too, according to the records we've seen, operated on a rough 260/105-day rotation (3 moons each of fall, winter & spring, then 3 moons of summer) even though they lived roughly between the 45th and 46th parallels. This information begs the question, "Where did they come from and how did they end up with this calendar?"

The mountain peaks around Izapa, Mexico are positioned in such a way that the priests could observe the first dawn light of the equinoctial sunrise from the temple at the site. The sun rose directly over the tallest mountain as observed from the pyramid temple on that day, allowing the priests to determine the start of the new religious year. They would then be able to maintain a continuing observation, one that would allow them to correct their complex calendar system every 1508 years, or so. Similarly, the arrangement of a temple location could be found with the mountains being used as markers for solstice and equinox dating, a relationship that could also hold true for the Peruvian location as well as the Izapa, Mexico and the Honduras sites, such as Copan. At the archaeological site of Izapa on the border between Chiapas, Mexico and Guatemala, near the Pacific Ocean, one finds a large basaltic rock sculpted in the form However, it was also the place where the sun could be observed to achieve its zenith on the 260th day of their calendar year. Once they had made their measurements and determined the placement necessary for their temple in order for them to be able to observe both solar phenomenon on the same day, they simply moved their religious site to that location. Once the temple was built they could regularly predict the dates of this spectacular solar event and in this manner maintain their spiritual leadership and the awe of the uninitiated populace.

The temple at Izapa is of a modest size and is not more than a few meters high. The stonework is not tremendously high but it has a moderately extensive area in front and has significant native platforms of rock that apparently served as a sacrificial location to the side of a large stone sculpture of a sailing canoe with a mast in its center and waves sculpted on the sides of the 'craft'. From there one can see the dawn sunrise over the critical volcano peak (*Volcan Tujamulcho*). One could see the sunrise over the tallest volcano in Central America to mark the day that will have a vertical sun at high noon. The fact that the sun was directly overhead on this late summer's day after the temple had been set on the line at the equinox and was already set in its East- West latitudinal axis meant that the 260-day solar year had started. Having the sun rise over the crest of the volcano assisted the priest on the morning of the zenith passage to know that it would return to being directly overhead 260 days later after the Spring Equinox!

I have begun to search across the globe for other cultures that use some form of a 260-day calendar. It does not have to have religious

Figure 81 – Photo of Izapa Archaeological Site
Photo by Carl L. Johannessen.

significance; just have the 260-day/105-day cycle. Wherever these cycles show up, we need to trace back the society in which they were used to locate the spots on the appropriate Latitude Line (north or south) from which the cycle was found. I suspect that we will find sacred sites in these areas related to measuring the solar zenithal passage on the respective dates.

I find that one can easily see that India, which used a 261-day division in their calendar, among other things, has a belief system similar to that found in the cultures of the Americas. When one reads the publications of many scholars on this topic, he will find many bits of evidence for the diffusion of ideas across the Pre- Columbian oceans. Unfortunately, many of these scholars, by the way, have been discredited and demoted because of their findings, and their refusal to accept the dogma of "No Pre-Columbian contact across the oceans." Some of their findings which we think indicate early diffusion are listed here.

- The use of stone thrones for the seat of the king or ruler, sometimes carved as a Mexican Lion or a Lotus Flower.
- The Parasol was seen as a sign of royalty in the Inca, Maya, Aztec, and Indian cultures.
- Incan and Indian caste systems were quite similar Both Peruvians and the people of India worshiped invisible and supreme beings above the worship of lesser deities, i.e. 'practiced a form of monotheism.'
- There is a Lotus motif in both Amaravarti, India and Chichen Itza, Mexico. These were originally recorded by Heine-Gelder and Eckholm.
- Both Mayan and Indian/Muslim/Arabic mathematicians used the concept of Zero.
- The Inca and Indians both plied the seas in rafts and catamarans. In Tamil catu means 'to tie' and maranu means 'wood or plank', a reference to their own sailing on rafts.
- There are carvings of maize in the hands of male and female figures adorning the temple walls in Karnataka, India which date to the Hoysala Dynasty (10th to 14th Centuries C.E.).
- Both used vestal virgins in court temples.
- The Indian and ancient Mexican peoples all played a similar game. In India, it was called pachisi and in Mexico it was patolli.
- Both baked tortillas and chipotle in the same way, using maize.

The next feature of the 'magical' sites is that they both, perforce, have a magical number of days of the passage of the vertical sun at high noon, (and to the completion of the solar religious year). In the case of the Nazca site, so many additional points on the horizon are present with all their endpoints as extensions of the center viewpoints. They extend to the horizon. As I stated earlier, some of these points are on the ridgeline at Nazca to the northeast of this ground center point. Most are not known and there is little in the way of written remains, just Quipus, a knotted string system of the Incas. Scholars know that the Quipus were used for numerical recordkeeping and accounting, but some scholars believe that the quipus could entail an entire written language system, one we have not decoded. (For instance, the Jewish writers used the same symbols for both the letters of their alphabet and their number system, as did the ancient peoples of Peru).

The latitudinal relationship of 14°42' S latitude has apparently not been pointed out in any previous work. As I mentioned earlier, it should be noted that the places on the Nazca plain that I refer to which were at 14°42' S latitude had exactly the same relationship to the sun as those at 14°42' in the northern hemisphere, only the date of the sun's achieving its zenith would be six months removed. It is known now, that this was also knowledge that the people of Meso-America had. In fact, all Meso-American cultures had the same or a similar calendar and religion and there was constant communication among the various culture centers as well. This fact helps us realize why the trading rafts that were being used to exchange products at the time of Pizarro's invasion of Peru were noted to have cargo on board that was headed for the northern hemisphere. Contact and the exchange of products and ideas was obviously a common occurrence among the American Indian priesthood. As we will see in a later chapter, not only ideas and products moved among the civilizations of Meso-America in Pre-Columbian times, but also architecture and urban design.

Figure 82 – Copan Ball Court and Altar L.
The Great Plaza is located behind the tree in the upper left-hand corner of the photo and Stela B, the artifact with the Indian elephants carved on it, is located just beyond that. Photo by Carl L. Johannessen.

In India, the Vedic priesthood had a 261-day solar year that had religious significance to them, and perhaps a 260-day cycle as well. We need to explore the rest of the world, especially Africa and Southeast Asia, to see if this calendar might have been used elsewhere along the 14th parallel. In India, this would take us considerably north of Bangalore and Mangalore in the province of Madras. Perhaps when we search for archaeological sites in the region of the following cities wherever we could find archeological sites, near Horihor, Dhormavoram, Davangere, Nellore or Guddapah, all very close to 14°42' N, we may be able to suggest applicable locations to test our hypothesis. I think that Goa would have been an interesting site, but it is a half a degree too far north and Hellore on the west coast is too far south by half a degree of latitude as well. These fail to meet our requirement of the 14°42'N location of the site.

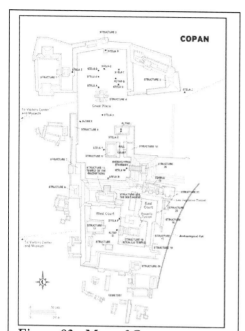

Figure 83 - Map of Copan.
This map shows the location of all of the major points of interest Provided by the Copan Tourist authority.

Nellore, however, on the east coast is right on the mark and does have a huge Siva Temple complex that might be worth looking into.

In the Middle East, Yemen is the only country through which this latitude line runs. It would be an ideal location to test our hypothesis because it is on the proper latitude line and it is known to be the home of ancient advanced cultures including the Kingdom of Saba and several megalithic and tumuli prehistoric locations. However, an archaeological investigation in this area is still quite new and there is much yet to learn. The repeated unrest and war in the region, especially the civil war, makes this very difficult. In Northern Africa, we would be searching across Senegal, Mauritania, Mali, Niger, Chad, the Sudan, and Eritrea at 14°42'N. Again, these are sites of known ancient cultures. Senegal is of especial interest as Dakar is exactly on 14°42'N. In Asia, we would be searching across lands in which some of the most ancient cultures in the world came to power. We would look across central India, Burma, Thailand, Vietnam, and Laos and off into the ocean through the center of the Philippines just north of Manila Bay. Coming back to the Western Hemisphere, we have started looking heavily at the southernmost point of Mexico and into Guatemala. We have also found it in Honduras, at Copan, but still need to look further at Copan, Honduras. We also should study at the tip of Nicaragua across which our latitude line lies. This may have been missed in the past because most scientists thought that it was insignificant to conduct solar studies at this latitude.

When we look across the world at 14°42'S we cross some very remote and unexplored lands in southern Africa. In these Southern Hemisphere countries, we need to hunt for archaeological locations that astronomer/priests may have built at 14°42'S. We need to search across Angola, Zambia, Zimbabwe, Mozambique, Malawi, and Madagascar for temples or ruins that would show the location of sun worshipers with a devotion to the

205

260-day solar year. There are fewer landmasses on the southern line because the earth has less land in the Southern Hemisphere. After looking across Africa, we will have to examine the northern edge of Australia, likely close to where the first sailors came ashore at least 60,000 years ago. In the Western Hemisphere, we have examined the surfaces in Peru, but would need to look across the Andes in Bolivia and Brazil as well.

We have found that a 260-day cycle calendar was in use in the northern hemisphere at both Izapa and Copan, which was likely brought into the Olmec and later the Maya civilizations, culminating in the intricate and complex Mayan Calendar. At Copan, we also see other signs that there was contact across the oceans prior to the Europeans, especially the elephant figures on Stela B. The writing and publication of Elephants and Ethnologists by Grafton E. Smith has brought about a threat to the author's life and scholarly position. He completely lost his standing in the scientific world with the publication of his discovery of the elephants on Stela B, etc. The authorities at the British Museum at the time simply could not accept the idea that oceanic trade had taken place, or that elephant figurines from India might have been used as the basis of sculptures in Mayan temples.

To the South, in Peru, we again see markings on the Nazca Plains that indicate that the people who created these massive markings across the entire length and breadth of the high plateau also recognized that there was a 260-day solar cycle. Further inland in Peru, we see a stone marker lined up with an unusual line of stone construction in a field beside the railway. There are unused rows of stone which look like they could have been terrace boundaries. However, the lines of stone are not level so they could not have been irrigated. These occur along this same Latitudinal line adjacent to the railroad line south of Santa Ana, Peru. I noted them on my trip to Cusco, Peru. If one looks to the horizon across the flat plain from this strange construction site along our latitudinal line, one would be able to see a lone standing stone structure that looks like it could be a marker indicating its line of latitude. This stone structure is visible form the rail car as well.

It is likely there are other places in the world, all along the 14°42' North and South latitudes where we will find monuments, temples, or other indications that people looked up and recognized this 260- day zenith solar cycle. It is highly likely that the Hindus also would have noticed and memorialized this cycle along the 14°42' N latitude line that runs across the center of the subcontinental peninsula. Since half of all the plants transferred to the Old World from the Americas were taken to India, it is likely that we will discover that the 261-day calendric cycle may also have been a cultural transfer between these peoples. Remember that many cultural features are the same in both the cultures of India and the cultures of Mesoamerica.

CHAPTER 17: THE IMAGES OF ELEPHANTS AND OTHER ANIMALS THAT WERE DIFFUSED TO THE MAYAN CIVILIZATION

If there is one animal that we think of as associated with exotic, old world lands, it is the elephant. We think of them as huge beasts and carriers of huge burdens in Asia. A different species of elephant lives in Africa. Elephants in Southeast and South Asia were used for moving logs, transporting maharajahs, etc. Placing their images mentally in Central America and Mexico takes a modification of ideas of history. However, prehistoric Mayan artists were occasionally making sculptures of the elephants within their religious sites. The Olmec & Maya, among others, were worshipping the idea of the elephant, although the elephant was not supposed to have been in America; so an image of elephants must have arrived in the America's long ago in the form of small statuary carried by sailors Sculptures of elephant heads, especially their faces, trunks, and bodies are present in Middle America from Olmec & Mayan times. We have had evidence in academia of this image since at least 1924, when G. Elliot Smith published his book Elephants and Ethnologists: Asiatic Origins of the Maya Ruins. The book is about the symbolism of the Elephant in America. At the time it was published, the book was made fun of, ignored or dismissed. Nevertheless, it's been 90 years and we can re-examine this evidence without harming the careers of his detractors because Smith was ultimately correct.

{Figure 85} The Asian elephants had a certain meaning and hagiography by the time the images (models or drawings) or ideas were introduced to the Americas. Throughout the regions in South and Southeast Asia it is seen as a god of rain, which makes a lot of sense if you think of what happens when an elephant fills its trunks with water and them blows it up into the air; rain comes back down. The faces on the sculptures having the giant trunks have been interpreted as macaw bills; however, this explanation has been an unsatisfying compromise by archaeologists and zoologists. This giant parrot's bill does not regularly fit all the shapes of elephant trunks shown in the Mayan sculptures; the 'lower bill' of the macaw is never present in their hypothesis. It is a bit like drawing a mustache on an old picture to convince yourself that it's really your uncle.

In our book, World Trade and Biological Exchanges Before 1492 C.E., Revised and Expanded Edition, John Sorenson and I delineate the evidence from both the Old World (South and Southeast Asia primarily) and the Americas showing and reinforcing the paradigm that there was regular and sustained transoceanic trade between these cultures of the tropical world long before Columbus's voyages. The sculptural evidence of the images of the elephant being present in the Olmec (1400 B.C.E. – 400 B.C.E.) and Mayan (2000 B.C.E. – 1500 C.E.) cultures, long before European contact with these peoples, also strengthen this position. Uxmal, in Mexico's Yucatan state, is a ruin of a Mayan City. The Mexican government, mindful of tourist dollars, is trying to top that, and they have constructed two hotels and a museum there. Some of the decaying architecture has been restored. Moreover, it is possible to look at a slice of Mayan life throughout the ancient site.

Figure 84 - Chichan Itza Elephant Trunks at Ball Court.
Photo by Carl L. Johannessen.

The Mayan rain god, Chac, or the Aztec rain God, Tlaloc, is illustrated by an elephant-shaped God-Head in the east wall of what is now called, the Nunnery at Uxmal. The similar Chac's are found on the front of the Governor's Palace and elsewhere. In 2001 Henri Steirlin, a Swiss art historian who was made a Knight of the Legion of Honor in 2004, wrote, "At Uxmal, the image of Chac, with its curved nasal appendage – which the …European visitors, when asked by me, took the sculptures to be the head and trunk of elephant – is treated in a schematic way" (p. 140-1). This location is just north of the largest Pyramid, called the Magician, at Uxmal. The defining features of these smaller sculptures are the elephantine noses. The giant faces of Tlaloc/Chac with their long, recurving trunks, their broad face and deep-set eyes illustrate the elephant. Essentially, the nose of the elephant is proposed as the indication of the image representing the "long-nosed" rain-god, as it is labeled by the anthropologists/archaeologists.

Examples of the Chac's nose curve up as if the elephant had raised its trunk to near verticality. In other examples, the trunk hangs down and then curves up as if begging for fruit. Essentially, the same set of elephantine faces are found at all the major Mayan archaeological sites at Chichen Itza (Figure 92), Laban, Uxmal (Figure 93), etc. in the Yucatan or Xunantunich in Belize, and other locations. The Rain-Gods of the Maya all have recurving and, potentially, water-giving trunks (as if the elephant has just filled his nose with water). It may curve up and then down or down and then up with

Figure 85 - Stela B Photos by A.P. Maudseley 1880's.
Used with permission Henry Presaud, British National Library Curator.

the tip sometimes curling under at the end of the trunk. No macaw's bills have all those shapes, even without the macaw's lower bill, yet some archaeologists have, for their own reasons, assigned that giant parrot's head and its beak to these sculptural interpretations. I see these noses as elephant's trunks and sometimes they have a point or coil of the elephant's tusks represented beside them.

If there were any doubt about the fixation of the Maya on the Long Nosed Rain God you can see it in their temple architecture in the Yucatan area. Henri Steirlin, in a second article published in 2002, said that you can see it "on the façade of the Place of Masks, or 'Cods Poop of Kabah' (Yucatan), the stylized masks of the rain god have an obsessive quality. Its protruding eyes, long shaped nose and rigorous frontal symmetry cover the whole building" all indicate elephant" (p. 31). Most of the trunks begin by descending toward the ground. (Unfortunately, most of the trunks have been broken so that only stubs frequently remain, now.)

The elephant was not considered to be the model for these giant sculptures because that elephant would have illustrated contact with South Asia (or Africa), and the Spaniards would not have wanted ever to accept this pre-Columbian contact across the oceans! The public is not as firmly indoctrinated as academics are (who tend to be in charge of even the modern tour groups). In our experience, the random tourist identifies the facial shapes as elephantoid instead of being similar to the macaws of the academicians. I know this; I asked them nothing more than, "What does this image look like?" They would invariably respond, "Elephants" even when they were looking at the disfigured Huastecan Ganesh, the elephant-headed god of India, in the archaeological museum (in the Olmec room) in Mexico.

The "Long-nosed God" is more easily accepted as the homologue representing the elephant than some of the social scientists claim. Giant curves of the elephant trunks are found at the front of Temple 21 of the Copan

Figure 86 - Sanchi, India and Stela B, Copan Honduras.
Comparison of Elephant carvings from similar times. Photo of Sanchi taken by J. Lochtefeld and the Photo of Stela B taken by Carl L. Johannessen. Photo of Sanchi used with permission.

Ruins, just above the ball court. These elephant trunks at the front of the temple at the top of the hill are the largest that I have seen in America.

The most certain figures of the elephant images in Middle America are on two upper front corners of Stela B at the Ruins of Copan, Honduras. Remember, G. Elliot Smith in his 1924 book caught the wrath of archaeologists over 90 years ago by pointing out this similarity to elephants. Not only was there an elephant on the two front corners at the top of Stela B, but on top of the elephant necks were the two turban-wearing mahouts. (The mahout images have since been smashed off. Maybe harvested is the better verb for what the thieves did to the mahouts.) The mahouts were the kind of evidence that was just too much for certain people, who could not stand for such beautiful examples of diffusion to exist in their native state. They also ignored the two passengers on the elephants' saddle. When you see the photo taken in the 1890s then there is much less doubt about the elephants. Harry Persaud, Curator, Library Collections, The British Museum, Department of Africa, Oceania and the Americas, kindly scanned and sent me these photos from available glass negatives in their collection. This photograph clearly shows the Stela when one of the mahouts was still on it. That mahout is clearly riding the elephant's neck.

The thieves had not counted upon the fact that plaster casts had been made of the originals by Maudslay and those casts had been shipped back to the British Museum, London at the times of their discoveries. When I checked on the plaster casts fifteen years ago, they had been lost; but they may yet be found; we can hope so. We need a deeper and more complete search for these missing parts of Stela B. The late Anthropologist/Librarian, Dr. John Barr Tompkins, at the Bancroft Library, University of California, Berkeley studied at the British Museum in London in the late 1930s and was assigned office space where he could look at these plaster casts of Stela B. I was a graduate student, had a desk at Bancroft Library in the 1950s, and had long talks with Tompkins. He had seen the Indian mahouts, on these plaster casts. The mahouts had earplugs, pendants, bracelets, anklets, etc. as do the mahouts in India. The returning British military officers, who had served the Raj in India, could even identify the exact source location of the mahouts based on the turbans and garb worn by the mahouts. It was easy for them to recognize the significance from the imagery of Stela B.

Figure 87 - Top Half of Stela B (1880's)
Note that the Mahout on the top corner is not yet broken off in this much older picture of the Stela (See Figure 92 for comparison). Photo taken by Arthur Maudslay. Used by permission of the British National Library.

Author, architect, and gifted amateur archaeologist Graeme R. Kersley has described the arrangement of the elephant heads on Stela B as very similar, in shape and attitude to the elephants, to the calendrical iconography at the Great Stupa at Sanchi in North Central India. He further notes that during the 19th Century Stela B was commonly referred to as the Elephant-stela. Note that the last Maudslay photo including the mahout was taken in 1890 and that by a 1902 photo, the mahout had been broken off. Although the mahouts have been broken off by thieves, treasure hunters, or vandals and the plaster castings have been apparently lost in the archives of the British Museum, it is clear that the top section of the Stela shows elephants. This is a creature that the Maya had not seen and therefore were carving from statuary arriving with mariners or traders from India and Asia or from descriptions of the elephant by people who had seen the elephant or the Indian and Buddhist statuary. The fact that two riders on the middle of the elephants above the "Indian Ruler" are seated in a side saddle position; the seated humans give a scale to the elephant part of the sculpture as was pointed out to me by the Guatemalan artist, Lucy Drimany. The humans are small by comparison to the elephant, which is itself small (and totally out of scale) in relation to the "Indian Ruler" below, with his turban which dominates Stela B. The elephant's trunks are properly scaled by these little men, each headed in the opposite direction as risers on the elephants' square- carved saddle blankets. It should also be pointed out that the two corn (maize) plants that rise alongside of our "Indian Ruler," reach to the height of the elephants "finger" at the bottom end of the elephant's trunk on both sides of the front of the Stela and both elephants can touch their own maize leaf. The maize plant has a sculpture of the maize god carved on the side of the maize stem statue near the elephant's trunk. In addition, under the two human passengers there is a typical rectangular saddle blanket under their saddle. The central figure, the large human who dominates the center of the Stela, appears to have Asian or sub-continent Indian features and the turban the figure in the center is wearing is typical of "Sikh turbans" in India even today. There are nine (once ten) smaller human figures around the perimeter of the Stela, on the first sketches (and photographs) of the Stela B (blue in the illustration). Four of these individuals are wearing similar turbans and are likely mahouts or elephant guides; one on either top corner of the Stela. The two passengers with their legs bent up in the saddle are dressed with similar headdress – turbans as the four mahouts on the side of the Stela B, who have turbans, and three who have elephant goads or rods for directing the elephants.

The main mahout on the Stela B's south or right-hand top corner was removed by thieves or vandals soon after several glass plate photographs were taken by Alfred Maudslay in the early 1890s. This south mahout, with his elongated turban-like headdress [or just wrapped hair decoration] on top of his Asian baby face with giant ears, was elaborately arranged. The headdress is distinctively organized. It looks as if it had been used as a model for the design of some pottery vases available in markets in Mexico in recent times. These vases look similar to the turbans of the mahouts on the Stela. Note that there are four more mahouts on the front of the Stela. Other carvings of the Corn God are also present in the Copan ruins and depict the deity with the same headdress as the one carved on the maize stem as seen in the Maudslay photographs.

Stela M, another sculptural work at Copan, has apparently had its entire, long elephantine-nose broken off. It might simply have been broken by a souvenir hunter, but the thief left the two giant elephant ears in place along

 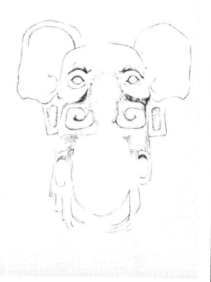

Figure 88 - Stela M at Copan
This stela is bound at the Copan ruins in Honduras. The draw detail on the right is by Paul Shao. This carving shoiws a typical headdress worn by Mayan ptiests. The headdresses were of animal/god forms. This one is clearly and elephant head. Used with permission.

with the two tusks that were carved as a curl beside the stump of the trunk on the elephant face. Patrick Ferryn, a photographer, author, editor of the journal Kadath, Croniques des civilizations disparues, among others, studied this and wrote a piece for New England Antiquities Research Association (NEARA). His article further validates the hypothesis that the idea of the elephant as a religious symbol was known in America and placed in Copan.

Decorations of elephants were sculpted on the ends of the roof tiles in Mexico in the best of tradition have been found by Neil Steede, a Latin Americanist Archaeologist, but I have not seen them.

Decorative impressions of bas-relief/etchings, on a ceramic platter in Ecuador suggest evidence for the diffusionary activity known as the "long nosed god". There was surely enough trade and other modes of contact between Maya population and the mainland of South America that we can state that this kind of sailing contact was likely with the people of Ecuador and can be entertained without having to sharpen Occam's razor excessively. Once one starts to look critically at cultural traits of the Amerinds in Mexico and Central America and the Andes, in comparison to those of the Old World, one is motivated to consider many more traits than just elephants. We humbly submit that students can gain a great enthusiasm for their studies of ethnology if they are allowed to be scientific and look at alternative hypotheses such as transoceanic sailing and trade to explain the presence of these hundreds of other cultural traits.

If we look at Smith's (1916) list of cultural traits found in the Americas, we get some marvelously stimulating ideas for research. All of the ancient, pre-Colombian behaviors and rituals listed below have been found in both the New and the Old Worlds.

- mummification as a cult
- megalithic monuments
- worship of the sun
- circumcision
- tattooing
- massage
- piercing and distending of the earlobes
- skull deformation
- trepanning
- dental mutilation
- use of ocean shellfish for purple dyes used to dye thread and cloth
- conch-shell trumpets
- pearl worship
- metallurgical techniques
- phallic worship
- agricultural terracing
- the boomerang
- divine origin of God-king
- incestuous union of the kings with their sisters for reproduction
- Ikat tie dyeing and weaving

The weight of the concept of 'coincidence,' or of the 'independent invention' of these esoteric traits requires less necessity for anguish now that we have shown that the plants that arrive in Asia before Columbus could not have been transported without contact across the oceans and that this is especially so when we are talking about highly complex plants and cultural practices. When these domesticated plants are necessary for subsistence, the

214

odds of their spread by contact diffusion increases in any event. The actual transfer may not have come from the farthest cultural existence, but the odds are very high that the ideas were exchanged with intermediaries along the routes of the sailors to and from their homeports. We should try to stimulate interest in research among students, and citizens in general, so that they can expand our horizons of knowledge and provide the joy of discovery to more people. We may then spread credit to the tropical sailors of the ancient world, Arabs and Africans, as well as Asians, who traveled, discovered, traded, and even missionized the entire tropical world long before the Europeans began to colonize.

One can argue that sailors carried many cultural traits on these voyages which brought about the ultimate civilizing of the world's peoples, starting as long as 50,000 years ago. If this sounds crazy, remember that scientists have proven that Homo sapiens traveled to Australia from Indonesia and New Guinea. In addition, there is even evidence of Homo erectus sailing to islands 200 miles beyond New Guinea before that, which proves that they must have known about the art of sailing very early on.

CHAPTER 18: BUILDING WITH STONE BLOCKS

It is fascinating to note, with relation to our hypothesis, the very similar techniques and, to a lesser extent, architectural forms that were employed by the high civilizations around the world during ancient times in the construction of massive stone structures. These structures were created by the heavy and prolonged labor of a worker class that was subservient to an elite class, the latter belonging to the often religiously based, power structure. The cultures that produced the structures had developed sufficiently beyond the struggle for simple subsistence needs to have available a large pool of excess labor. Most structures were built as symbols of the power of the ruling, religious elite, and their purposes were tied to religious practices and keeping a large army busy on a job for when it might be needed by the leaders of their culture. Perhaps some, like the Great Wall of China, were built not primarily for defensive purposes, but still, their impressive presence across a long landscape was clearly a statement of power. What is most interesting to our hypothesis is the similar technique of building with polymorphic blocks of stone was found in many of these early structures from different cultures of both New and Old World with stones cut into similar shapes.

The stone block palaces and pyramids of the Maya, who appear to be the cultural derivatives of the Olmec, remain as reflections of the religious power exercised by that culture's leadership. These Maya and Aztec and Central American megalithic structures may also echo the power politics in China. Southeast Asia, e.g. in the Khmer dynasty's dominance during slightly earlier periods, where tremendous structures that were also erected, using cheap labor, for the aggrandizement of the ruling class. These concepts spread with the ideas of terracing for agricultural and irrigation around Peru and Southeast Asia. The Greeks, who also produced stone blocks of a regular size and shape in a mass production style at the quarries, did use them for magnificent construction. Do they compare or exceed the engineering done by the cultures immediately prior to the arrival of the Incas in Peru, who expanded on the demands made on the labor of the subservient subjects? Most assuredly, for we have observed that polymorphic stone block structures exist which would indicate that those civilizations must have had contact with the older cultures of the world.

The stone structures that come down to us from the Inca realm seem to have had a direct connection to the building techniques used by the subcontinental Indian and Mediterranean cultures. The Inca developed these techniques to such an expert level, that polymorphic building blocks interlocked, especially at their corners, so as to produce long walls that were very resistant to earthquakes. They had walls that all sloped a little bit to the center of the room and were, therefore, internally braced. They have continued to stand without steel re-bar or mortar to bind them for centuries. Another powerful feature of these massive stones in both the Mediterranean and Mesoamerican regions is the precision with which they were hewn. The joints are unbelievably tight and smooth having been cut so precisely that one could not find a single spot where the thinnest of razor blades could be forced between the joints of these 15 ton stones. Another interesting feature of these huge stones is that they are not all cut at 90 degree angles, or square. This feature gave the walls extra strength and allowed the walls to be built higher than would have been the case with straight stacks of stones. In addition to the precision of the cuts on the tops, bottoms and sides of the blocks where they were cut to fit precisely with adjoining blocks no matter the angle, the builders created an aesthetically pleasing wall by rounding the sides and corners of each block. This feature catches the eye of both engineers and artists alike. If one were to wish to view this for himself, there is an excellent example of this remarkable precision stone cutting on display at the archaeological site of

Figure 89 - Building Blocks
Note the knobs near the bottoms of some of these stones. Could these have been used to raise and lower the stones into place and even to facilitate grinding of the stones to fit.
Photo in the Public Domain.

Sacsayhuaman just north of Cuzco, Peru.

These blocks obviously took tremendous amounts of time to shape so perfectly. They were evidently shaped in place on the building wall. The nearly vertical surfaces of the end blocks were ground to fit with a sliding motion. They were probably hung from a giant 'A' frame with rope and ground against the adjacent blocks in the wall under construction until they fit. The molecular make-up of the stones involved made them well suited for such a procedure. The proof of this methodology is that the top or bottom surface of the blocks is commonly slightly arced, as I found when I measured the horizontal surfaces on the tops and bottoms of the blocks. The top of each block has a slightly concave arc and the bottom of the same block is slightly convex. This would have occurred because the trajectory of the swinging stone would have been a curve as in swung horizontally from the A-Frame. The ends of the stones would have remained straight, because the arc of the stone swinging from an A-frame would not affect the horizontal movement, only the vertical.

Because of the shapes of the original stones that were quarried, there may often have been protuberances that had to be smoothed into a parallelogram or some other shape so that it would fit with the adjacent block. The segments of this polygon would have been more or less normally vertical straight-line segments, when cutting on the vertical plane. It is believed that the vertical segments making up the ends of each block would probably have been ground at the same time that the tops and bottoms were being ground. This would have sped up the process and assured a tight fit for all three stones involved. In order to keep the ropes holding the huge stones as they hung and swung from the A-frame, they had to cut huge notches in the bottoms and sides of the stones, wherein the ropes would fit and would be kept from the grinding surfaces. The evidence of this is still apparent in the stone blocks today. One can see the 'lumps' left after the stone was ground down to the level of the inserted ropes. There are four of these 'lumps' on each stone's sides and bottoms.

Evidence for their mode of construction still remains on the blocks in the form of knobs sticking out on the front and rear bottoms of the stones. If the block is to be held and ground on a long arc of a rope, then the rope must not get ground off and cut. To accomplish this, the masons left knobs on the vertical sides of the blocks, normally four protuberances per block (See figure 93) around which the rope could be looped to suspend the stone from the A-frame. The bottoms of the extending knobs are flat and would have held the rope in place as it looped over the top of the block to the other side. This suspension method was used for carrying the blocks from place to place as well. You can clearly see what's left of the knobs in the photograph above.

There have been many other theories put forth by archaeologists, engineers and scientists over the years since the stones' discovery as to how the Incas and others managed to move and cut these stones. Some have speculated that the rocks were somehow softened and then reformed at the construction site. Others have suggested that they were cut and formed at the quarries and then transported and lifted into place by means of sheer manpower and/or the use of pulleys and rollers. Some have suggested that they were brought to the building sites and then carved in place. All of these speculative methods have one major problem, especially as regards the stone blocks of Peru, and that is the sheer size of the stones in question. The smaller stones and even some of the medium sized ones could have easily been handled in just about any manner, but how do you handle a stone that is 30 meters (100 feet) tall and which weighs 500 tons. To put this into perspective, two comparable items in modernity that approach this weight would be a Boeing 787 (509 tons), and a Carnival Cruise ship with 400 rooms and 200 passengers on board (500 tons). There is no possible crane or A-frame even today that could handle such tremendous tonnage. Nevertheless, the stones are there and the fact remains that similar construction methods were used in all of these places. Take for example the ancient builders' solution for keeping corners of non-mortared blocks in place. In all locations around the world where such construction occurred, a similar locking mechanism was designed and employed to solve this problem.

All the corners of all the walls have a locking mechanism that consists of a wedge, staple, or butterfly shaped insert so that the corners were always held together as long as the insert was in place. These were not all made of the same materials, however. Some were made of iron, some gold or silver, and some even of wood. Where they were made of iron, they have mostly rusted out. In places where they were made of silver or gold they were extracted by fortune hunters and so those buildings tend to be in ruins. This can be attributed to the looting of the conquering and marauding conquistadors in Peru, for example and greedy looters elsewhere. When the wedges at the corner were of wood, they, of course rotted out and have long since deteriorated and nothing is left but a powdery wood residue, and crumbling buildings. It is to be noted, however, that all of these forms are present regularly in all places where such building took place. From the Sumer and the eastern Mediterranean, to the coasts to Morocco, India, the Maldives, Tenerife, Easter Island, Peru and Mexico. The conclusion that one has to draw from this is that these methodologies were diffused from one original location. Since we know that contact was active among these various places, it is logical to conclude that the technology was transferred by sea and that potentially the routes of such diffusion can be deduced on the basis of the age of these structures, at least where and when such dating is possible.

I once asked the stonemasons in India, what they would do if they did not have steel stone-chisels to carve in these mineralogical hard rocks, such as the granite that exists in Peruvian buildings such as at Cuzco. They said simply, "We could not do it." They were emphatic when pressured for some other answer that could be applied by me to Peru and their cutting of architectural stone walls and fences. I am left with the conclusion that the stonemasons of the Inca and pre-Inca had iron chisels. Maybe it is not totally far-fetched to hold that view despite the prevailing view that no worked iron was available in the in the Americas at the time when they were carving these mineralogical hard stones. When the director of the excavations at the site of the cave temples of Ajanta, India was asked about this, he claimed that in the archaeological excavations they have made in the debris from the excavated temples at Ajanta and Alura, India, they find no chisels, yet they know that they had them.

CHAPTER 19: THE DIFFUSION OF PYRAMIDS THE ORIGIN AND DISPERSAL OF PYRAMIDS

Probably one of the more compelling pieces of evidence for the existence of pre-Columbian transoceanic travel is that regarding the history of the evolution and dispersal of pyramids across the globe. It is pretty well established that the idea for pyramids came from the Biblical land of Ur, or Sumeria, the earliest known Semitic civilization. The famous story of the Tower of Babel (Babylonia) comes from this region of the world as well, and indeed the famed tower seems to have been a pyramid. Sumeria is where the Ziggurats, the precursors to the pyramids first make their appearance in the world. The Sumerians are also known for their system of writing (Cuneiform), and their being the first known developers of sails and sailing in the world in addition to being the builders of the aforementioned, Ziggurats. These latter were com-

Figure 90 - The Reconstructed Neo-Sumerian Great Ziggurat of Ur of Chaldea near Nasiriya, Iraq Photo in Public Domain

plex structures built of stone blocks of the sort we discussed in the previous section of this chapter. The earliest known Ziggurat is thought to have been built around 3900 BCE, or 6000 years ago, in what is now Iran. The Ziggurat was a rectangular shaped structure that was An elevated platform upon which other buildings such as temples and palaces were built generally in stair-stepped tiers like the terraces of China. They were religious structures to start with and later the Egyptian Pharaohs borrowed the idea for their tombs. The first real pyramid, not a Ziggurat, was the pyramid at Djoser built by emperor Imhotep. It was built in 2667 BCE. This date is interesting because it is very similar to the date of the erection of the first pyramid structure in the Americas at Caral, Peru. The dates for the culture that built this pyramid run from 2600 BCE to 500 BCE. There are six pyramidal structures that were built during this period in Caral, the largest of which is 60 feet high and 450 x 500 feet in area. If it were built near the start of this culture's existence, it would have been contemporary to Imhotep's pyramid at Djoser.

Interestingly, there is a Sumerian manuscript which tells of a journey they made across the great oceans to a mountainous land by the sea and to a city by a great

Figure 91 - Ruins at Caral built around 2550 - 2600 BCE. UNESCO World Heritage Site Photo in Public Domain

lake. The description of this place matches that of Caral's location. If that is not intriguing enough, remember that there is evidence that they were a seafaring people like the Phoenicians after them. They certainly would have been capable of such a journey since their records show that they traveled the entirety of the Mediterranean Sea and the Persian Gulf. Circumstantial evidence you say, well, yes, but consider this. There is also a linguistic link. The name Ur is a Semitic word which has several meanings. It is used for mankind, for things of origin, for original man, for example, and we find this root word in many Sumerian compound words as well, such as 'essuru,' or 'rooster,' or 'colorful bird.' Now let's take a look at the Guarani language spoken in Peru and the surrounding areas of South America. They claim, by the way, to be descendants of a people who came across the oceans, and, interestingly their word for bird 'uru' is the very same root word used in Ur for 'essuru' a colorful bird. Now we know the word 'essuru' made it to 'Greece' in the form of 'ornis,' or bird (or => ur, and nis => ess), but to find it as far away as Peru is interesting indeed. Now, do linguists think it likely that the same word for the same animal would just pop up in two separate locations 12,000 miles apart at exactly the same time? Hardly. So that's one example. Now for another before continuing our story of pyramids. The country of Uruguay is a Guarani word borrowed by the Spaniards given to this land and people located on a major river in South America. Many locals claim the name means 'The river of colorful birds.' This would, of course, fit with the Sumerian meaning of the name, and since the meanings are exactly the same we could simply stop there, However, since most native peoples did not name rivers, it is unlikely that this was the meaning. What First Nation peoples did do, however, was call themselves 'The People.' There are many tribes on record that even called themselves 'The Original People,' 'The Real People,' and so on. So it would not be out of the ordinary for 'Original Man' to be the meaning of this word, and in fact this meaning also fits with the original meaning of the word in Ur and in other Semitic languages. "Ur' was also used to mean 'Original' or 'Original Man.' The rest of the word is Guarani in derivation and means 'of the river.' So 'The Original People of the River' fits. Now Paraguay, on the other hand, a similar construction, does not mean that. It just means 'big river.' It was also not uncommon for First Nation peoples to refer to rivers in this way. The Kalapuya, for example, referred to the Columbia River as 'Antsala uapal' or 'big river.'

When you look at the picture above of the pyramid at Caral, Peru, you see that it very much resembles the Ziggurats in Mesopotamia. It is low slung compared to other pyramids and longer than it is wide or tall. It would not be a stretch at all to say that it might be a copy, and probably is, of the Ziggurats of Iran and Iraq.

So it would appear, and I doubt we would get any argument, that the idea of the stair stepped pyramid structure spread from Sumer (Ur) into

Figure 92 - The Great Xian Pyramid
Built in about 240 CE. Photo in Public Domain

Babylon and then Egypt. This was followed later by another diffusion into Sudan, Nigeria and perhaps Tenerife, and then even later into Italy, Bosnia and other places in Europe, not the least of which was the UK. What will be controversial is my contention here that it also spread from Sumer into Peru and then into the rest of South America and from there into Polynesia and Indonesia, all of which would have needed transoceanic travel to have occurred.

Another diffusion that we have not discussed is that of the pyramid's being taken to China. In about 300 BCE the Han Dynasty in China constructed the now famous Silk Road in order to establish and maintain trade with countries in the Middle East. The Chin (Xian) Dynasty followed this up by improving the road and building the Great Wall in order to protect travelers on the road from marauders from the northern plains. Chin (Jian or Xian), the emperor who gave China its name, also brought the idea of a pyramid for his final resting place from Egypt in about 240 BCE. A number of pyramids were built in China during his reign, but, of course, the largest was to become his final resting place. To make sure he would be protected throughout eternity, he also had the now renowned Terra Cotta Soldiers created to follow his exploits into the heavenly realms. Not to be outdone, his main pyramid at Xian, China is considered to be one of the tallest

Figure 93 - Pyramid in Tahiti was described in Captain Cook's journal of his early voyages to the Pacific. This drawing comes from the 1799 book The Voyage of McDuff.

Figure 94 - Pyramid in Korea Near the city of Soktapri, Andong, South Korea. It is only about 12 feet tall and is approximately 30 feet wide and 40 feet long. Photo is in Public Domain

pyramids ever built. It stands an amazing 1000 feet tall. The only taller pyramid is the Fire Pyramid in Mexico which is over 1200 feet tall.

From China it is believed that the idea and the construction of pyramids followed a continuous path eastward across the Pacific to Japan, Mexico and the United States. Pyramids were constructed in Korea, Japan and Mexico, which followed the general shape and size of the Ziggurats and stair-stepped pyramids of Mesopotamia. There are also pyramids in Indonesia and Tahiti, but it is unclear whether these were diffused from China or from South America as it is known that the Polynesians and hence the Southeast Asians traveled to South America on many occasions after the Sumerians brought the pyramids there. From its rectangular shape and stair stepped construction, however, I would deduce that it was more likely a transplant from Peru rather than from China. This theory does not really hold any real weight, however, in light of the style of pyramids which were built by the Koreans. They were all rectangular in shape and stair-stepped as well.

Figure 95 - Woodhenge at Cahokia, IL
Built by the mound builders of the southeastern U.S. Crystalinks Photo

It is also not known whether the pyramids which were built late in Mexico got their influence from the Meso American pyramid builders or from China, but again the shape of the pyramids and the timing makes the latter more plausible. You can see from its shape that it more closely resembles the Xian pyramid than it does those of Peru and Meso America. Then again the appearance recently of the Aztec Fire God atop the pyramid tends to lend credence to a Meso American origin. The rituals known to have surrounded this pyramid and the internal passages, however, more closely resemble those of the pyramids in Egypt and China and are a definite hint that their origin was other than Meso American. The carving of the god could have been introduced later on. However, its exact place of origin is of little consequence as our intention here is to show that from their place of origin in Sumeria (Ur), pyramids have traveled far and wide and they could only have done this if there were pre Columbian transoceanic travel. This seems by now to be well established by this author, in this book as well as in many other books on the topic written by competent and reliable researchers in the fields of anthropology, archaeology and geography.

The final leg of the pyramid's journey did not require oceanic travel. It was the use of the Ziggurat style pyramid by the people of Cahokia, Illinois in the US. What does show travel across an ocean there, however, is the henge that was constructed there, which is believed to be a calendar just like the Stone henge in the UK. But that is grist for another mill and we will not discuss it here other than to mention that the idea for it could only have come there, because of its date at 1100 CE, from the Salisbury people. Its date of construction is definitely pre-Columbian.

Figure 96 - The Pyramid at Teoti-huacan in Mexico
Creative Commons Attribution 4.0 International license

SECTION 6: SUMMARIZING THE EVIDENCE FOR TRANSOCEANIC DIFFUSION BEFORE 1492 C.E.

CHAPTER 20: PUTTING IT ALL TOGETHER THE PHILOSOPHY OF DIFFUSION

TRANSOCEANIC TRAVEL

Recent evidence that humans have been traveling across the open oceans for at least the last 60,000 years is gradually being recognized. We are proposing that it is time to significantly reevaluate the long-held hypothesis of cultural historians and other scholars who believe that there was no significant dispersal of cultural traits across the oceans before the Spaniards and Portuguese sailors began transporting them after 1492 C.E. Researchers have tended to accept that a few Viking ships may have gotten to the Northern American region early. A great deal of good evidence that supports earlier movements has been either ignored or discounted. The belief of many academics in the independent development of common cultural traits on both sides of the major oceans has been so strong that negation of any other hypothesis, even with accompanied evidence, has been automatic by traditional scholars. Traditional scholars who have rejected one by one the evidence of the presence of cultural traits and species proposed to have been the result of diffusion, because accepting these proposals, despite compelling data, would contradict their existing paradigm that held that there was no contact. We recognize that long-held scientific beliefs are subject to change. During the Dark Ages, for example, European cultures were wrenched from the view that the earth was in the center of the universe by the discoveries of Copernicus and others. During the lifetimes of many of us living today, scientists have had to accept that the continents have been shifting their locations on the surface of the earth (Plate Tectonic Theory, first proposed in the late 1940s and early 1950s and not generally accepted until the mid-1960s), and that evolution has normally been very slow over the long run of history with a few major rapid die offs due to cataclysmic consequences, then rapid evolution took place after the die-offs. Eventual acceptance of continental drift has helped to explain why mountains and plains assume the shapes they do with predicted regularity. The acceptance of the understanding that the slow evolutionary process has been punctuated from time to time by catastrophes, such as giant meteors striking the earth's surface south west of New Zealand, which has also helped explain previously misunderstood observations. These have helped to explain why up to 95% of the earth's species suddenly died off at the end of the Permian-Triassic boundary that ended the Paleozoic period of geology after the large meteor hit the earth near Antarctica and New Zealand.

Just such an impact event occurred north of the Yucatan Peninsula at the end of the Cretaceous geologic era and caused changes in the earth's atmosphere so severe that most of the world's dinosaurs died for lack of food and conditions necessary for their eggs to hatch. Perhaps fire storms touched off by the heat of the impact devastated much of the Earth's vegetation. The co- occurrence of the gradual drift of continents that was taking place 50–60 million years ago, about the time of this particular catastrophe, accounts for the continental-scale landforms on the surface of the earth observed today as well as the newer climatic zones that produce evolving biologic developments. Most of the flowering plants currently in existence were not present when the dinosaurs died off and have evolved since then because of the changed habitats and ecological voids created by the consequences of the meteor's impact.

FLORAL EVIDENCE

When we begin to find significant numbers of plants that were taken over seas from their continent of origin there is the need to remind us that a species of plants can only evolve or be selected from the wild origin on one hemisphere. The same species does not evolve in earth's biological history in more than one place. This biological phenomenon is well documented by the geneticists of Science, such as Steven J. Gould, among many others, and can be ruled a fact of science. The world's habitat is just too variable for evolution to have developed identical DNA over again especially if you do not have the wild plant of origin existent on the continent of development. The shifting continental Plates separated 50 millions of years ago before the flowering plants had evolved on Earth to any extent; so that hypothesis of similar wild plants on the earth's hemispheres is invalid as well.

Living organisms provided on the earth's two major hemispheres are the most powerful kind of evidence to invalidate those earlier belief systems which were based primarily on environmental determinism of the original traits. Biologists are generally agreed that all domesticated crop plants evolved only once from one wild species in one area of the world, unless the species was put in contact with another member of the same genus at another location where hybridization had occurred via natural or human selection and centuries of cultivation. Each species has a genetic source specific to it. No crop plant or weed can evolve on another hemisphere independent of its wild source. It is, therefore, only necessary to demonstrate the dispersal of one major crop plant from the Old World to the New World, or vice versa, to invalidate the long-held and widely believed view that "No pre-Columbian transoceanic contact could have occurred." Worldwide biological inventories now available have expanded the number of crop plants that meet the evidential threshold for showing definite diffusion across the oceans to 100 plants and 28 animals. In addition, there are at least 27 other plants and 28 animals which partially meet the criterion, but which are in need of further research before we can definitively claim transference. But just because sufficient evidence, in our opinion, is not there does not mean that the idea of diffusion can be summarily discarded.

Peanuts, for example, whose wild ancestors are all from South America cannot be claimed to be of Chinese origin just because peanuts have been found in the Neolithic strata of Chinese archaeological sites which seem to indicate they have been there for 5,000 years. Agave, or century plant, which is known to have originally evolved in the Americas, cannot be claimed to have evolved independently in Africa just because its fiber has been found mixed with pine pitch used to caulk an ocean-going ship found at the bottom of the Mediterranean Sea just north of Cyprus.

When we add to the single extremely well documented species maize the over 128 organisms that were carried by sail across major oceans before Columbus, the independent invention hypothesis and Bering Strait paradigm must shift. These living organisms make the evidence incontrovertible and therefore invalidate the independent invention hypothesis of cultures. With 129 plants, animals, and diseases, however they are counted, which have been confirmed to have thrived on both sides of the major oceans from early times, the evidence for diffusion is overwhelming. The age of forbidden fruit to science is just opening as we learn about what was transported by early mariners. What will be found for the milder stimulants, like chocolate, coffee, cava, etc.? When were these plants actually first transferred to new continental homes?

In the North and South Americas, Asian Peoples have, for 4- 9,000 years, been cultivating gourds, squashes, beans, corn, and chili's, all first domesticated in America and then supplied to sailors who took them to the other side of the oceans to India and Oceania. Recent data shows that the genes of the wild Teosinte (Zea) species of corn, for example, is present in every variety of maize, making the Americas the only likely point of origin for maize. This includes the primitive popcorns and other small-eared primitive varieties of maize. Given the presence of these small-eared primitive varieties throughout Asia and India, I have hypothesized that corn was first transferred to Asia 9 to 10 thousand years ago by sailors who had contact with the Balsas River culture in Mexico.

It is possible to show that the ancestors of today's various dark- skinned peoples gave us coffee (in east Africa), bananas, sugar cane, tea, rice, pigs, chickens, (in Southeast Asia and Indonesia). For 5-7 millennia in the Americas, other Tanned Skinned Peoples have been cultivating gourds, squashes, beans and corn (maize) and the Europeans make use of these as their food but they did not originate them. The results of the domestication of these crops, domesticated in America, were relatively new products taken to Southeast Asia and South Asia (India) at least 2,000 - 10,000 years ago, and certainly hundreds of years before Columbus. However, the diet of the Europeans benefited from these works of the early American populations. Virtually all the domesticated crops used in Northern Europe came from somewhere else on earth. They only changed lettuce, tulips, rutabaga, and a few others in their domestication activities. Amusingly, according to experiments by Charles Darwin and others, these are the very plants that have been suggested as being able to actually float across the oceans (as the naysayers opine about how many of the plants we have discussed got across) and yet not one of them was found to have floated across the ocean independently.

So European countries were not the origin of most of their food crops. Even the turnip, rutabaga, and lettuce came from somewhere else and then had to be changed by the Europeans for it to be useful to them, and, as great as these crops may be for nutrition they certainly did not provide a highly varied diet. We could say that perhaps rye and oats could be considered to have self-domesticated in Western Europe from a rye or oat seed that was originally treated as a weed in Middle Eastern grain fields, but when the Europeans tried to grow wheat and barley in northern Europe, its cold damp climate killed the wheat and barley seedlings and 'weed grasses' of oats and rye grew instead.

We have found new, well-researched, and documented evidence indicating that at least 129 organisms were carried in early times by sailing ships and rafts across oceans. These have been confirmed by at least 2 reported pieces of biological evidence as having definitely been dispersed before the time of Columbus. Furthermore, the observed distributions are extensive enough to indicate significant time depth to their movements to the new environments so that no serious opposition can be made. These findings are especially true for crop plants, their respective weeds, derivative drug plants, and medicines that have been transported across the oceans. In addition to this there are presently at least 50 more organisms that are substantiated by only a single solid piece of evidence showing their antiquity in a non-native home.

DIFFUSION OF WEEDS

In addition to defining the term 'weed' as any plant not developed for agricultural use, we also discussed how these plants may have made their way across the seas in early times. They could have been inadvertently mixed in with other seeds, or have stowed away on fruit or vegetables used on board ships. No matter how they arrived in places distant from their place of origin, it is a fact that they did arrive there.

We saw that common reeds got from Peru to Easter Island, and that Purslane and Carpetweed have been found in archaeological digs in the Southeast of the United States. Since these weeds originated in Southeast Asia they must have begun their journey long ago to have been present in places like Kentucky and Louisiana 2700-3000 years ago. One of the plants found in the South-eastern U.S. has also been shown to have been used as a food crop in ancient Rome and Greece. The French missionaries to Canada and the present day U.S. found these plants growing among the First Nations' maize crops, and wondered that the natives here did not use them for food. All of this would certainly indicate, however, that these plants traveled far and wide from their place of origin in Southeast Asia long before Columbus.

Going in the other direction, i.e. from the so called New World to the old, we find the Phasey Bean, which is known to have originated in Peru, but then found its way to India, also long before Columbus.

The only way for the Totora Reed, Purslane, Carpetweed and the Phasey Bean to have got from their native soils to places far across the seas would, of course, have been by transoceanic transference, and this movement had to have occurred long before Columbus made his infamous journey.

TOBACCO, COCA AND CANNABIS

Breakdown chemicals known to be both specific to certain drugs, such as hashish, tobacco and cocaine, and the product of physiological processes in humans, have been found in the mummies of Egyptian pharaohs. The tobacco plant and the coca bush, from which two of these drugs come, are native to Central or South America. The Egyptian kings apparently consumed such products, along with hashish – the concentrated resins of a plant of Middle Eastern origin – during the 1500-years of reigning pharaohs. Hashish has also been found in early Peruvian mummies. This seems to indicate that there was a robust, extensive, and worldwide trade in mind-altering substances (what we, today, would call drugs) during pre-Columbian times. This is further supported by the discovery of a Chinese mummy showing evidence of tobacco use in its forensic signature. Because the chemical signatures for coca and tobacco found in the mummy remains definitively indicate ingestion, and not, as is the contention by traditional scholars, that the drugs found in these mummies resulted from contamination of the cadavers (e.g., by cigarette ash) during the centuries after their discovery in storage lockers in the museum.

THE CASE OF BRITISH/AMERICAN BREAKFASTS

Have you ever considered where your breakfast food came from? I know that I never had until I began studying early transoceanic diffusion. The typical breakfast in the U.S. or England is likely to include a couple of chicken eggs from chickens that were originally domesticated in Southeast Asia or Southern China. Often we add a couple of pieces of toast, whole wheat if you are healthy. The wheat was domesticated in the upper slopes of Turkish Peninsula or Iran. If you insist on more carbohydrates, you can add hash browns. Potatoes were domesticated in the Andes of South America. Of course, a couple strips of bacon add that nice salty flavor we all love. Pigs, of course, were tamed and changed genetically in Southeast Asia in a domestication process applied to animals that were about a tenth the size of the giant pigs in the modern pig farms today of the United States, Canada, and Europe. Some people also like a little heat with their eggs so add a dash of chili pepper. Chilies originated in the Americas. If you have an omelet, you will be eating ingredients from the Americas, India, and Southeast Asia. Jam is a mainstay of many delicious meals. The sugar was first produced from sugar cane that was originally domesticated in Southeast Asia. If you like coffee with your breakfast, it originated and was domesticated in Ethiopia. If coffee is not your thing, a nice glass of tea often fills the bill. Of course, we all know that tea has its origins in China or India. Overall, we have looked at a nice and hearty American or British breakfast. It is interesting that nearly all the foods we eat for what we consider a very traditional breakfast are plants and animals that were transported back and forth across the oceans long before the 15th century. Our traditional European breakfast is actually very compelling evidence of the idea that humans have sailed across the oceans between the tropical and sub-tropical areas of the world for at least 10,000 years.

The black, East-Africans, for example, who had spread to Southeast Asia, 70,000 years ago, domesticated bananas, plantains, sugar cane, white yams, coconut, pigs, chickens, tea, rice, and peas and took all except the last three to the Americas thousands of years before 1492 C.E.

The Northwest Europeans make use of all of these crops currently for breakfast, but they did not originate them. These domesticated crops were new products from America and were introduced from Southeast Asia, South Asia (India), and the Mediterranean into Northwest Europe over several thousand years ago, many hundreds of years before Columbus was able to sail west to America. We know this because of written records and archaeology conducted often mainly by Asian archaeologists. No doubt is left about the collected evidence; it is real and has been published in our book, World Trade and Biological Exchanges Before 1492, Revised and Expanded Edition by Professor Emeritus John L. Sorenson and Professor Emeritus Carl L. Johannessen.

PESTS, PARASITES & DISEASES

With respect to certain parasites and diseases we have shown, that the travels of Southeast Asian mariners to South America in ancient times were certainly the causal factor for the presence of specific Asiatic diseases and parasites in tribes that lived in the interior of Brazil 8,000 years ago. The archaeological artefacts of four diseases are found in the interior of Brazil. Those same artefacts are not found anywhere in North America dating from the same or earlier times. This means that these diseases were not walked into the Americas from the north over 8,000+ years ago. These four diseases are specific to people and not to any other animals or plants; therefore, they had to have come from early sailors.

Those mariners may also have transported from Euro-Asia- Africa, knowingly or unknowingly, nearly 20 human parasites and diseases to the Americas where they landed or where they had been based. We have discussed the evidence for the dispersal of diseases across the oceans starting at least 7,300 - 9,800 years ago, with the arrival of parasites on the shores of the Americas.

These sailors would have had to have had contact with Southeast Asia as is shown by the fact that they had been parasitized by the whipworm, the ascarid roundworm, and two species of hookworm, which science again has shown originated in Southeast Asia and thus had to have been carried to South America by humans. These sailors must have traveled to Peru and Brazil and left their diseases there, where the parasites' eggs, and worms were later discovered in the dated Peruvian mummies' intestines and Brazilian coprolites (found in the Pedra Furada Caves in interior Brazil and dated at 7800 B.C.E.) It is also likely that the Ascaris roundworm was present at the Pedra Furada Caves 9,800 years ago as well. This shows that sailors definitely traveled to these locations very early, as the parasites cannot swim or travel by other animals and they were not present in North America by the time of contact with the Spaniards. They were and are still are only found in South American people who live in close contact with the soil. This is because an integral part of the life cycle of the worm is in the warm, moist soil.

We do not know and could only guess how long it took for those diseases to have been transmitted across the continent from their arrival on the shore of the ocean to interior Brazil. Such travel across the continent must have taken a long time. We cannot even predict which ocean they crossed to arrive in Brazil. We are simply certain that this transfer occurred.

We can be certain that the archaeologically dated findings of plants and animals were not the record of the first arrival dates of these organisms, but just the ones that the researchers happened to find.

FAUNAL EVIDENCE

The European diet of dairy products (cows, sheep, goats and pigs), grains (wheat, barley, oats), as well as fruits (olives, figs, pomegranates, apricots, apples, peaches and grapes), derive from the domestication of these products by the Semites, Iranians, Phoenicians, North Africans, etc. Of that small list only the pig, peaches, and grapes made it to the Americas, apparently in ancient times. (Pig bones are still under review, but Polynesians always transported pigs, rats, and nets on their ocean craft across the entire Pacific wherever they sailed.) These foreign crops, pigs and rats, have been absorbed for use into Northwest European [now

U.S. also] culture with the passage of several centuries. So diffusion of foodstuffs both floral and faunal is not a new idea or practice.

What we have shown is that more representatives of fauna existed in both the old world (primarily Asia) and the new world prior to the arrival of Columbus. The fact that diffusion seems to have taken place in both directions, i.e. both from the New World to the old in the case of maize and various kinds of potatoes for example, and from the old to the new in the case of chickens, rats, and various pests and parasites.

The organisms we studied and wrote about here are those that would have been carried from their continent of origin across the oceans to the other locations on the world by the Southeast Asians (Indonesia), the Polynesians, the Chinese, The early civilizations of the Americas and other tropical mariners of the world. By definition, it was possible for sailors to carry and disperse whatever they wanted across the oceans in both directions 9,000 - 10,000 years ago on bamboo rafts that were completely seaworthy and safe to use. As a result, the similarities of these fauna in the Americas to those of the olds world are, of necessity, the result of diffusion, not independent evolution, on both sides of the ocean. Australian aborigines crossed open ocean some 60,000 or more years ago. If that is possible, and it is possible for modern scientists to realize and accept that, then it would seem these ancient paradigms can be shifted to the benefit of all concerned if people will just open their minds to it.

By the way, we have talked about sailors and sailing throughout this book instead of just mentioning drifting or paddling of seaworthy canoes or rafts, which did in fact exist, and we have done this because it is doubtful that Humans would have been able to paddle across the open seas and between the distant islands because, according to maritime experts such as Drs. Ed Doran and Mike Doran, in many locations the currents are simply too strong for this. There is hard evidence in South America for contact with the Old World that dates to between 7,000 and 8,000 years ago.

CULTURAL TRANSFERS IN GENERAL

When we look at cultural traits that may have transferred, it is helpful to understand a couple of things that researchers explore when deciding whether a trait was transferred or if the two cultures developed it independently due to similar necessities. If an object or trait has no survival function in one of the societies, then it is likely that they did not invent or develop the trait or object. There would be no reason for them to do so. If the trait or object seems to be referencing something that does not exist in one place but does in another place, then it is likely that it was transferred from the place where it was useful to the other location. For example, the ancient Egyptian calendar begins at the flooding of the Nile in February. This is a perfectly logical start for their calendar. The Mayan calendar, oddly enough, also starts in February and has certain other similar features to the Egyptian calendar. There is no special event that is known to happen at the time the Mayan calendar begins, so there is a possibility that the Egyptian calendar was transferred to the Americas and used by the Mayan peoples. In conjunction with the discovery of cocaine and tobacco in the mummies of Egyptian nobility, this also would be strong evidence for the cultural transfer between the Egyptians and the Mayans, and we definitely need to accept any dispersals suggested as valid as long as they are based on solid evidence.

ART ARTIFACTS AND ARCHITECTURE

In the case of the elephant images the evidence is significant, because there are so many sculptures, cultural artifacts and religious utilizations in rituals and iconography of the long nosed god, called the "god who brings rain" in India. In the New World we find that the rain-god, "Tlaloc" of the Aztecs, and "Chac" of the "Maya" (These words are translated by the Archaeological/Anthropological community as long-nosed god of the Aztecs and Maya) looks very much like the long nosed elephant rain-god of India, Egypt and Carthage. With all of this evidence it becomes difficult to imagine that the two images are not related and are in fact a 'diffused' religious and cultural trait. We can know without a doubt that knowledge of elephants and the elephant rain god had been introduced to the Mayan culture. For this reason, elephants are included, along with other animals that were "transported" across the oceans, in the lists of transported species in both our previous book and this one. Elephant images, or statuettes could have been carried in their sailing craft with ease.

The Amerinds obviously would have had to have been taught that this figure of an elephant head on top of a human body was a depiction of a god who could supply rain if they but prayed to him. They had most likely never seen an elephant, and so had no first- hand knowledge of how an elephant could spray water from its trunk, which seemed like rain, unless some of them had traveled on a trading vessel to India and witnessed it there. (This is probably not totally out of the question, as later several First Nation People from the British Colonies traveled to England to visit the King George.) This appearance of elephants in new world sculpture, religion and the language of the Nuatl and Maya speaking peoples creates a more than significant pool of credible evidence of pre- Columbian transoceanic travel and diffusion of ideas.

Given the abundance of statue and bas-relief evidence as well as the religious symbolism of the elephant to the natives of Southern Americas we must conclude that the Olmec and Mayan specifically had at least the idea of the existence of elephants in real life. Since the religious significance of these creatures in both the South Asia region and in the Olmec, Mayan, and Aztec cultures are nearly identical, it is difficult to continue to deny that there was regular contact between the tropical cultures on both hemispheres. This contact was likely through transoceanic voyaging, as these images do not appear in the northern American region with nearly as much frequency. Further, with the numerous bas-reliefs of plants of American origin in the temples of the Hoysala Dynasty in Southern India (950 C.E. – 1268 C.E.) we must conclude that there was regular and sustained interaction between the cultures in these regions long before Columbus sailed from Europe. We have to accept the fact that when depictions of plants show up in a Hindu or Jain or Mayan or Incan Temple, that the actual plants being depicted had to have arrived in that location hundreds of years earlier. The plant would have had to have been accepted into the culture and then added to the religious life before they were deemed worthy of inclusion on the walls of temples and sanctuaries, or in the practice of the religion.

Another way of looking at it, if some particular medical "cure" used in two distantly separated cultures does nothing to cure or alleviate the disease, then it is more likely that the two cultures shared the "cure" when they interacted than that they both independently decided that this ineffective treatment was useful.

ROCK AND MINERAL EVIDENCE

Further, there are certain other non-biotic substances with chemical signatures unique to where they originated, such as markers found in jade, obsidian, copper, and metal alloys that indicate dispersal in ancient times has occurred. The origin of a piece of Obsidian, for instance, is easily determined since samples coming from each and every volcano have a a different and distinctive chemical signature. Thus the specific eruption cycle and location of the sample can be ascertained. Therefore, obsidian samples in New Guinea that bear the chemical signature of obsidian originating in the Americas indicates that it had been brought there by sailors and mariners. In addition, if these samples happened to be found in strata that predates the 1400's, then the obsidian, jade, natural copper, or metal alloy would have had to have been transported prior to the European expansion.

MEDICINAL EVIDENCE - SHAMANS AND CURES

We have looked specifically at the way chickens were used medicinally especially with regard to psychosomatic illnesses which were treated and cured in a variety of ways without the use of drugs. Such a 'cure' simply would have had to have been observed first hand if not very carefully taught. These cures may not make any sense to a modern, medical doctor, but may have cured the patient in a way similar to how psychologists and psychiatrists sometimes cure people today. We are becoming more and more aware of the placebo effect and how powerful it can be in modern medical and research practices.

RATS, FLEAS AND PLAGUES

We took a really close look at what the plague is and how it is transferred from patient to patient with and without specific vectors such as the fleas from infected rats, etc. We decided that due to the make-up of the bacterial agent itself and the presence of various strains in different parts of the world we could ascertain its place of origin and probable course of dispersal around the world.

The evidence strongly suggests a Southeast Asian origin. From there it seems to have spread into China and South Asia and from there to Europe. Some have postulated that it also came across the land bridge to the Americas, but the actual strains involved indicate a more direct route from Southeast Asia to South America and then northward into Mesoamerica and eventually Europe and North America as well. This arrival of deadly viruses from the Old World on stowaway rats who carried the infected flea's, which in turn acted as agents or vectors, could very easily have infected and killed off the Mayas en masse and been the reason the Spanish found their cities vacant.

BLACK BONED/BLACK MEATED CHICKEN

On trips to China, South and Southeast Asia, Meso and South America we noted the presence of these very different species of chicken, namely the black boned and black meated chicken. This in and of itself did not seem to indicate anything of significance to our study of transoceanic diffusions, because, we thought, these chickens could have been transported from Asia to the New World by the explorers after Columbus. However, upon closer scrutiny we discovered that this would not have been possible as there was a ban on taking non Catholic persons and artifacts (religious symbols and objects) on board Spanish ships. We also discovered that these very special chickens were being used in both the Old and the New Worlds for rituals that purported to heal the sick and expel evil spirits.

It was with the discovery of the complexity of these rituals on both sides of the ocean and the fact that both the Americans and the Asians rituals were so similar that they could almost be considered to be identical that we realized that these practices had to have been copied, or diffused in some way in ancient times. In our travels and research, we documented the various illnesses and spiritual disturbances as well as the rituals used to cure them on both sides of the ocean. We created a chart (Table B) to show each of these practices and where they were used. The result is an astounding piece of evidence for cultural contact and diffusion of ideas and objects in Pre-Columbian times.

WEAVING

In the case of weaving we can see a definite practice where it would have been impossible for such a complicated and complex procedure to have developed independently in two distant parts of the world. The specific tying of thread for dyeing in order for it to result in a specific pattern once the threads were placed on a loom and woven into cloth is an unbelievably complex methodology. That it would be thought to have been invented by two different cultures simultaneously is beyond comprehension. It would seem to the inquisitive mind that such a difficult procedure would have to not only be handed down from generation to generation by way of careful instruction, but also passed to other interested cultures in the same way as say the idea of assembly lines in manufacturing was applied first to rifles and then later by Ford to automobiles. That idea then spread to the rest of the world and we believe that in the same way the idea of how to get a specific design in cloth by first tying and then dyeing and weaving according to a specific set of instructions was passed to the cultures of the Americas from those in Asia via personal contact and instruction. There is just no other feasible way for this to have happened, and therefore, this is yet another indicator of transoceanic contact prior to the voyages of Columbus and the European explorers.

BARKCLOTH

While China found the use of the Mulberry tree to be instrumental in the production of silk, other cultures in Asia used it in a decidedly different way to produce their own kind of cloth. They discovered that one could remove the inner layer of bark from the tree and soak it in water, then pound it using a special kind of beater (tool for beating) to create a very pliable cloth when a special glue is applied and the product is dried. This method of creating paper, clothe and other products is the same around the world. Again, the process is too specific to have been independently invented by so many varied peoples and cultures. It is one more feather in the cap of transoceanic diffusion prior to the time of Columbus.

BLOWGUNS

In the chapter on cultural diffusion we discussed the two types of blowguns found in the ancient world. There are those made from bamboo, and those made from regular wood. We showed that the process for making these weapons is similar wherever they are used. The idea of using poison to enhance their effectiveness is also known and used worldwide. Again the specific procedure of splitting, hollowing and reuniting the pieces of the tube is too similar to have been created independent of contact among cultures. This is especially true in the areas where the solid wood is used in place of bamboo. The idea of finding a straight piece of wood, then rounding it, splitting it in two and the hollowing it out and recombining the two pieces to create a tube for blowing darts involves too complex of a thought process to be an independent invention. While the idea of using a tube may have been transferred from areas where bamboo was plentiful to areas where it was not, the whole idea of using a straight piece of wood to achieve the same end does not seem to me to be the kind of idea that people everywhere would just happen upon. Again, it is too complex a procedure for a reasonable man to think it could have been developed independently.

MAHOUTS IN HONDURAS

In addition to the Ganesh and Chac religious symbolism that we found replicated in both India and the Americas, we found obvious depictions of Mahouts in Copan, Honduras, who were riding elephants complete with a saddle blanket and headgear that could only have come from India. As with the Ganesh there are multiple sculptures showing these men on the necks of elephants in Honduras. We compared the carvings of elephants in Sanchi, India and Copan and saw that they are so obviously similar that there would have to have been some sort of contact across the oceans.

Now it is possible that this came in the way of small artifacts, or carvings of elephants, that were brought to the Americas for trading, or simply because, like Bibles and other religious artifacts today, religious people tend to carry them with them wherever they go. There is another possibility that we have not discussed and that is that the Amerinds themselves might have traveled on the foreign craft to India and witnessed these creatures and their handlers first hand. Such trips would, of course, be total speculation as there is no record of such, but we did see the same kind of thing occurring in North America with Amerind Chiefs visiting King George in London. So the idea is not totally impossible. When things are left to human nature, if we hear of something exotic in a far off place we naturally want to see it ourselves. Often risk and time involved does not enter into the equation at all, take for example the plans to visit Mars and set up colonies there. Impossible and unheard of speculation just a decade ago, now a real possibility. Anyway, I'm just throwing this out there as food for thought.

What is real, however, is the presence of artifacts in the Americas that could only have gotten there by way of transoceanic contact between early peoples in both the Old World and the New. The exact nature of such contacts aside, we can deduce that it must have taken place by sea and especially along the corridors of least resistance to travel by sailing craft and those which would have been able to take advantage of the prevailing winds as discussed in the first chapter of this book. The Mahouts that we are discussing here become obvious inclusions on the stelae and carvings in Honduras when one is aware of how they look in their place of origin. Having visited both places and seen the Mahouts and their accouterments as regard the riding of elephants in India, when I saw the same men and the same accouterments on carvings in Honduras and elsewhere in the Americas I was astonished, but quickly made the connection. It then became simply a matter of connecting the dots and adding this to the already sizeable lot of evidence I had collected in my botanical and zoological studies which had led me to the realization that transoceanic travel had occurred prior to 1492 C.E.

The Mahouts under consideration here come complete (in Honduras) with saddle blankets, special whips and headgear for the elephants. These accouterments are easily visible on the carvings of the elephants at Copan and elsewhere. The elephantine noses (trunks) are easily visible on the carvings in figures 56 through 60 in this work and the Mahouts especially in figure 57 and others. As we noted earlier, the way the elephant raises his trunk is so distinctive that it is recognizable by just about anyone who has seen a parade, gone to the circus or visited areas where the elephant is a part of the culture as it is in India. The absurdity, in my opinion, is in thinking that these are representations of birds with large beaks. While macaws' and parrots' beaks do curve, they curve downward and never do they do a figure 'S' as in these representations. So once again we return to the idea that there is no other way that these representations of elephants could have gotten into the religious symbolism of the Americans unless there had been contact with other cultures in which the elephant played a central role in their everyday life.

BLOCKS AND PYRAMIDS

We saw in these chapters that the methods of construction of huge blocks used in walls and pyramids in ancient times were similar in all parts of the world. Again, it is unlikely that such similar methods could be devised independently of each other. Humans are very inventive and ingenious, and we see in most areas of technology that there is always more than one way to do something. Not everyone sees the solution to a problem in the same way. This explains why we have so many different kinds of cars and even silverware for example. I swear no two spoons in my kitchen drawer are alike. All of this would tend to indicate, I think, that it is unlikely that two very different cultures would arrive at the same or very similar ways of processing stone for the building of their structures, be they walls, buildings or pyramids. The use of wedges and dowel like inserts in cornerstones in various places around the world is one example of such a similarity. These kinds of evidence are bulwarks of our theory of Pre-Columbian transference of ideas across oceans.

In the case of the pyramids, we see a definite progression from the Ziggurats of Mesopotamia and the low slung pyramids in Peru to the step pyramids of early Egypt and Mesoamerica. We looked at the likely travel of the Mesopotamians to Peru taking their buildings and language with them as indicated by the similarity of the structures and the use of the exact same word for 'colorful bird.' It was easy to see the diffusion of the idea of pyramids from the Mid-East to China and from there to several Pacific Islands and to Mexico. All of which again could only have taken place if transoceanic travel was in vogue, which we have shown it was.

EVIDENCE OF DIFFUSION ACROSS THE SEAS

Many American academics have deprecated the hypothesis of the diffusion of cultural traits by insisting, "no significant traits diffused across the oceans before Columbus," and by then they were refusing to evaluate the new evidence on its merits. One can either deny all the evidence because of an existing prejudice for phenomena that could not have happened, or one can examine the data in relation to the possibility that it was transferred early and carried out in ways not supposed to have been possible, in order to learn what really happened. We maintain that the evidence for the transfer of large-sized maize, my favorite crop plant, to the Old World long before the Spaniards and Portuguese reached the New World is compelling. The evidence for about 130 additional organisms is also secure. The brown-skinned humans from the tropical world were sailing across seas and oceans more than 10,000 years ago on a relatively regular basis. The Ethnocentrism of north European and American academic scientists, who led the way in the early development of what has become modern science, is now handicapping these same scientists from applying the techniques they so carefully developed to a suitable and timely evaluation of evidence that shakes the foundations of their belief system. Nevertheless, science is showing that skin color, stature, body shape, and religion really have nothing to do with deterring the exploring and early colonizing activities that were occurring millennia ago.

One of the most essential goals of a teacher, at whatever level of education is to assist students to learn information that will not be shown to be false during the life of the students. I dislike the activity of this relearning process after giving erroneous information that should not have been taught originally. There is extant a hypothesis in the academic system at present, that no contact was made between the American continents and the Old World – so called because the kings in Europe and the powers in the religious organizations, apparently, thought Europe, Africa and Asia were known first and when the Americas were shown to be present by Columbus, the kings, queens, and religious potentates in Europe called these American continents the New World.

When we begin to find significant numbers of plants that were taken over seas from their continent of origin there is the need to remind us that a species of plants can only evolve or be selected from the wild origin on one hemisphere. The same species does not evolve in earth's biological history in more than one place. This biological phenomenon is well documented by the geneticists of Science, such as Steven J. Gould, among many others, and can be ruled a fact of science. The world's habitat is just too variable for evolution to have developed identical DNA over again especially if you do not have the wild plant of origin existent on the continent of development. The shifting continental Plates separated 50 millions of years ago before the flowering plants had evolved on Earth to any extent; so that hypothesis of similar wild plants on the earth's hemispheres is invalid as well.

The remainder of the story can be found in our book where the count of the 100 plants with a history of transfer across the ocean can be found in detail. Recognize that 84 of these were transported from Tropical America, mainly to the southwest to Asia and perhaps to the East as well. However, the book has also the story of the 28 diseases and micro-fauna.

The whole story of diffusions can be found in our book World Trade and Biological Exchanges Before 1492 C.E., Revised and Expanded Edition, where the count of the 100 plants with a history of transfer across the ocean can be found in detail. Recognize that 84 of these 100 plants were transported from Tropical America, mainly in a southwesterly direction ending up in SE Asia and Asia proper, but perhaps to the East and Europe as well. It should be noted that the book also includes the stories of the 28 diseases and micro-fauna which were taken across the seas via these routes as well. The most extreme of these is the Ascaris lumbricoides or giant roundworm parasite of the human intestine, which was found at an archaeological site in Central Brazil with an age of 9,800 years. Two genera of hookworm and the whipworm were also discovered, all four of which are dated to be over 7,300 years old in the middle of Brazil at the Pedro Furada Caves archaeological site. These parasites are absent in northern North America so they could not have come over the Bering Straits and we know that in order to transfer the parasites to another person their eggs have to have been deposited in human excrement in warm moist soil, which does not exist in the polar regions. Therefore, there are no parasites of this kind in the polar climes.

If you are not already caught in this search for the history of geography and the developing civilizations you will recognize that this first entry into America happened before the Polynesian Islands were known in detail, as far as academia is concerned. In fact, we have no way of determining whether the entry was after crossing the Atlantic or the Pacific. We recognize that the parasites left South East Asia at the start of the journey and were taken to America from somewhere on the route. The dates of record are even more extreme than immediately noticed in that they had to be distributed to the local inhabitants in South America and then they had to cross the Andes plus hundreds of miles of tropical jungle before they arrived at the location where they were found near Furada Caves in eastern Brazil.

CHAPTER 21: CHANGING THE PARADIGM OF EUROCENTRISM AND MORE

THE PREVIOUS PARADIGM

The prevailing paradigm in Cultural Geography and Anthropology has been that there had been no significant interaction between the tropical and subtropical cultures of the Old World and the Americas prior to the European voyages starting in the late 15th Century C.E. This idea has been maintained, in my opinion, because the authorities in archaeology and anthropology have not generally been willing to hire young Ph.D.'s who believed otherwise. This behavior tended to stifle research which would have created a different paradigm. There also seemed to have been a refusal to acknowledge any research that might indicate such a paradigm shift, by claiming that the data must simply be wrong because they "thought that is was." This stance was also taken, in my opinion, because to change would have meant that the textbooks and lecture notes would have to be rewritten, and no one seemed to want to do that. In addition, by accepting the idea that a lot of earlier interaction had taken place among the non- European cultures of the world, they would have had to re-examine the cultural bias inherent in how the history of human culture and civilization was viewed and taught. They would have had to acknowledge that many ideas and processes that had been traditionally accepted to be of European invention may well have been spread by diffusion from non-European cultural hearths perhaps by a method so simple as a sailor from one tropical culture showing someone across the ocean how to perform a given process. This is what we have purported to show has happened in this book, and in so doing, we hope we have created sufficient doubt about so called truths that have been held for centuries, that a major paradigm shift could begin to take place in academia.

PARADIGMS IN FLUX

Although the evidence for the discovery of the evolutionary process, first presented about one hundred and fifty years ago, has been rejected by segments of the world's population on religious grounds, today, nearly all scientists believe that evolution has occurred continuously in all living creatures. Personally, I know of no scientist who does not accept the idea that evolution is and has been an active process both historically and in the present. Once again, an earlier paradigm has been replaced. Unfortunately, in this instance, however, Doubt as to the efficacy of evolution, especially on religious and political grounds, is seemingly alive and well in our culture as evidenced recently in our political system particularly in some of the stump speeches we have heard coming out of the mouths of U.S. presidential candidates. Nevertheless, the paradigm has changed for all thinking and scientifically astute people.]

Another area where the paradigm has shifted is in the widespread acceptance now of scientific dating methods. Dating techniques using 14Carbon, 39Argon/40Argon, and other radioactive elements, for example, are now widely available to correlate the ages of archaeological sites with the geological strata in which they occur. This insures that the proper sequencing of cultural developments is known within limits and utilized. Such dating systems, together with computer modelling and satellite monitoring, allow scholars to better measure scientific data and to evaluate hypotheses more objectively. We now know enough about the history and development of cultures in many different environments to assert that the environment is not the major determinant of the characteristics of the cultures found in those habitats. In fact, looking at any element of the culture itself as well as how it may have come to be, its place of origin, or cultural hearth, might be a much more effective way of determining why it developed as it did, than would be, for example, looking at the climate or the landforms surrounding it. Yet, for the first half of the 20th century, "Environmental Determinism of Cultural Traits" was considered a valid hypothesis. Associated with this now-discarded hypothesis has been the entrenched and erroneous notion that diffusion of cultural traits and organisms could not possibly have occurred across the major oceans before the Europeans began travelling around the world looking for new routes to India and/or the locations of gold deposits, etc., in the historical era which we now erroneously call "The Period of Discovery.'

The first step in this process of changing a paradigm is to educate the targeted world and hope that the young-of-mind will assist by expanding the evidence that is presented. We have done that, hopefully with some success with our books, which were distributed among the educated elite. Now we think it is time for the entire world to be shown the data. Evolutionary biologists and bio-geographers state categorically that a plant, animal, parasite, or disease species can only evolve naturally, or be developed through domestication, in one place in the world, at least at the beginning of the process. A plant, for example, could not show up on another continent that is separated from its place of origin by the width of an ocean without some kind of contact having taken place between the cultures on those continents. We concur, and have shown that at least128 organisms show indisputable evidence of human transfer, intentionally or, in the cases of weeds and pests, unintentionally from one continent or land mass to another. John Sorenson has catalogued 5,000 cultural traits that he has identified as diffused traits and thus has strengthened the argument for regular and sustained contact between the tropical and subtropical civilizations across the oceans. This may even represent the discovery of the new "Science of Diffusion."

We understand, of course, that introducing this "Science of Diffusion" and expecting it to catch on and spread is kind of like trying to turn back a tidal wave. But we are idealists and believe that people are free thinking enough to perhaps attempt just such a thing if given sufficient supportive data. There is, after all, no scientific law that says free thinking people cannot come up with new ideas and seek to revolutionize, or at least somewhat alter things that are considered to be "truths." Who is going to try to turn back a tidal wave? As we have shown above, some people already have and perhaps, too, this new science will take root and change the ruling paradigm, which we find frightfully narrow minded.

We feel that the authorities of the former hypothesis cannot simply dictate that their hypothesis is true because they want it to be. This is especially true after someone shows it to be clearly incorrect. Granted it will not be a simple revolution, but change will occur and the truth will win out. In the face of threats to their lives and their freedom Copernicus and Galileo changed the very foundations upon which people saw the universe. They showed that the earth revolved around the sun, that earth was not the center of the universe. Our paradigm shift is as important to understanding history of our and other cultures as was their paradigm shifting discovery was to our realizing and understanding our place in the universe. We need to extend this knowledge and in the process change the Eurocentric thinking of the world. Even in non-European countries, especially ones dominated in the past by colonialism, the Eurocentric paradigm of cultural and species diffusion dominates the world's thinking in the areas of historical education and science Many of the ideas of earlier generations, such as Manifest Destiny, were grounded in the assumption of European superiority in all things. It would seem, therefore, that it is possible that there is still a subconscious religious bias against the hypothesized early contacts, and if that is the case, we need to root them out and eliminate these unfounded biases.

The great exploits, accomplishments and native intelligence of the ancestors of the Non-European majority of humans on the earth are shown to have allowed them to explore the World. This exploration began 100,000 years ago when the earliest mariners started their discoveries and colonization. According to a research team led by Dr. George Ferentinos, stone tools and other artifacts were found on the southern Ionian Islands of Kefallinia and Zakynthos in the Aegean Sea that were made by Neanderthals around 100,000 to 110,000 years ago. According to bathymetric data, these islands were insular during that period meaning that the Neanderthals living on the islands had to have been sea-faring. This research was published in the Journal of Archaeology in July of 2012.

When early diffusion is incorporated into the biased cultures, there will be less claim to superiority of intellect, bravery, economic acuity (trading propensity), and religious correctness. The scientific rationale for our proposal to accept early diffusion to alleviate stress related illnesses and diseases in humans can be shown by reports and books that are currently available and in the press that are initiating a re-evaluation of the older, incorrect beliefs of the totally independent development of cultural traits, languages, and civilizations across the oceans. The thousands of non-biotic cultural traits will be augmented because diffusion has now been shown to exist. That diffusion evidence has been rejected by the mind set of past social scientists, because they could not believe diffusion of people across the oceans had occurred. They were trained to disbelieve the diffusion process of these cultural traits by most of their mentors, but when they realize that their ancestors went sailing under relatively simple technological traditions and carried part of their civilization in the way of plants, animals and cultural traits with them, taking them to the far corners of the earth, carrying out major explorations, as we are now able to show by the discoveries of diffused organisms and traits that resulted. This knowledge should allow all dark-skinned peoples to finally feel that their history is important, too.

The great early civilizations of the Old World in Mesopotamia, Egypt, Indus R., Southeast Asia, China, and in the Americas by the Olmec, Maya, Inca and others all came from early world trade without the direct influence or assistance by the Northwestern Europeans. So now we have a problem of science or myth in the education promulgated in our current world's schools. The United States celebrates Columbus Day and never gives a thought that it is a myth that he was the first European to discover that sailing craft could cross oceans, that you need hollow ships to cross the oceans of the world, and that accurate long-distance sailing out of the sight of land is impossible without being able to measure longitude.

ELIMINATING THE BIAS IN THE U.S.

Early American cultures did not develop independently without any contact with Europe-Asia-Africa. We hope that this book will stimulate your search for careers of discovery in literature, geography, biology, anthropology, archaeology and history. You will find abundant new data if you look. Early findings came from dated, dried human bodies (and dried human scat) with infestations in their intestines that provided two species of hookworms of different genre in Brazil 7,350 years ago. The parasites had to have come from Southeast Asia by sailors for there are no records of hookworm in North America historically before European. This infection could not have come over the Arctic route to America. It is simply too cold for the infection to spread from defecation on snow.

We have found concrete evidence of the transport of ideas, art and cultural artifacts, including plant life and other organisms found in specific cultures across the seas as well as land masses in Pre- Columbian times. In order for us to accept evidence to include in our book as 'concrete' we have demanded that it be either a direct archaeologically dated discovery, or that there be at least two separate kinds, or pieces of evidence demonstrating early dispersal of the item in question. For plants and other living organisms, we have required and found two kinds of evidence from the following sources: dated art, painting, sculptures, linguistic information, epigraphy, descriptions in literature, chemical data, geographical information, or biological strictures on the distributions that indicate presence of the species on both hemispheres of the world. Eighty-four percent of the plants for which we have firm information came from the Americas to the "Old World" and the American aboriginal populations have to accept their role in improving the nutritional conditions of the world with their food crops. This data is new to modern science, although the publications from which the data originated are up to 150 years old. You have the chance to observe how collated science accepts a set of ideas that overturn beliefs in future years. With the increase in the speed with which information can travel with the modern tools of communication, you will probably experience this phenomenon.

Some change is already taking place. One can see evidence of this change in current political discussions happening around the United States. In 2014, both the cities of Seattle and Minneapolis ended the Columbus Day holiday celebration and replaced it with a holiday called "Indigenous Peoples Day." This change was done to recognize that Columbus in no way discovered America and to give credit to the indigenous people who did. The idea of discovery implies that no-one had been here before and no one knew of this continent's existence. Since the estimated population of the Americas at the time that Columbus landed was between 90 and 112 million people, according to the 1960's anthropologist William Dobyns (although other researchers, including me, feel that this estimate is still far too low), it is impossible to claim that no-one had been to the continent, or that no-one knew where it was. In fact, it can't even be said that Columbus was the first European to land in the Americas. Northwestern Europeans, especially the Norse, Basque, and Welch sailors did arrive in the Northeastern Americas in far greater numbers and influence than they have previously been given credit for by our traditional school system. Even the most conservative researchers have acknowledged that the Norse landed in Eastern Canada at least 600 years before Columbus landed in the Caribbean. Part of the impetus for my life's research was combating the Christian Eurocentric vision of history that has dominated education for five centuries.

The current dominant educational paradigm of the Social Scientists in the United States, however, and as a result, most of the school teachers and their students, is that dispersal across the open oceans did not occur before Columbus. , except for the peopling of the Polynesian Islands, All of the cultural similarities that Europeans had found (and are finding) in these new environments around the world after 1492 C.E. were said by western academics to have been distributed by European explorers, or created by the local inhabitants of the continent that they came to by crossing the land bridge. This was said to be possible because of the Psychic Unity of all human kind. The humor of this is that these tan-skinned Mariners, many of whom were from the islands in the Pacific Ocean, for example, and who were given credit for sailing abilities that would allow them to hit an island in the Middle of the Pacific Ocean (no small feat by the way), were not capable of finding two continents when some of the islands they had discovered were within eyesight of those same continents. I find this to be very humorous, indeed. Let me say that no evidence has been presented that would indicate that they would not or could not have traveled to the Americas.

The second thing in all of this that this author finds humorous is that the entire concept of 'Psychic Unity' among humans may have to be abandoned when objective, thinking scholars realize, or recognize that there really never was any evidence of any such thing going on among humans throughout our history of physical and cultural evolution and that that lack of evidence continues to this day. Given the historical evidence of evolution that we have, Carl Jung's theory just does not hold water. It is simply illogical to think that there was more than one track of evolution or that all humans everywhere would come up with the same ideas at the same time without any vector to facilitate the development.

There have been other modern researchers and thinkers who have contributed to our knowledge and research. Gavin Menzies (1421: When the Chinese Discovered the World; 1434: The Year a Magnificent Chinese Fleet

Sailed to Italy and Ignited the Renaissance; and Who Discovered America?) claims that Columbus had maps of the Americas in his cabin and knew where he was going because of Chinese maps that had been redrawn in Venice, before he left. The researcher Gunnar Thompson says that Columbus had been to Nova Scotia during an early voyage with other mariners from Scandinavia. The ruling elite were "playing their hand close to the chest". According to Menzies, very few people had seen the maps. He says he has the maps, now, and that all the major "Captains of European Discovery" had them! We "little people" were not privy to the extant knowledge of the time. Stephen Jett, editor of the journal Pre-Columbian, has proudly published scholarly research that explores the early diffusion evidence from many different scientific disciplines and deserves recognition.

Marshall Payne in the meeting of ISAC in Columbus, Georgia, USA, expounded on the processes that primitive sailors could have known and been able to approximate longitude from their own celestial observations. Recently, this rigid acceptance has begun to change as modern writers and historians, for the most part amateurs, have begun to bring to light evidence of earlier visits to the Americas by Old World civilizations as well as evidence of travels from the Americas to the Old World.

Archaeologist Dr. Betty Meggers' and Geographer Carl O. Sauer were two amazing visionaries, whose view that human cultures and civilizations had to have interacted across both oceans long before the 15th Century C.E.

Even the Minoan culture, great as it was, had little to do with Europeans. They recognized that none of the great civilizations were caused by North Europeans. None of the science of the historical world has been in support of any superiority for them. How could the paradigm of superiority arise? The idea of the diffusion of domestication of plants and animals around the world passed by Europe almost totally. They were not the origin of many food crops at all. Their food came from elsewhere around the world. The Whites of the world have no scientific basis for their superiority myth.

Frederick Douglass, in a speech in Canandaigua, New York, on August 3, 1857, said, "Power concedes nothing without a demand. It never did and it never will. Find out just what any people will quietly submit to and you have found out the exact measure of injustice and wrong which will be imposed upon them, and these will continue until they are resisted with either words or blows, or both. The limits of tyrants are prescribed by the endurance of those whom they oppress." (p. 204). It is time for the public and younger academics to demand a new and accurate paradigm be explored and taught. Progress towards a world that has overcome the crippling disease of Eurocentrism is the best path into the future and acceptance of the fact that all cultures in the world interacted regularly and made contributions to one another.

THE INFORMATION IS OUT THERE

This diffusion hypothesis has been rejected by the dominantly White Social Scientists of Europe and North America as a result of the belief that "no significant contact was made across the oceans before Columbus" (and the Norse) made the contact 500 (to 1000) years ago. The fact that this belief system has been incorrect now starting to be recognized and accepted by the anthropologists, archaeologists, historians, and geographers.

As with any scientific endeavor that spans so many different areas of science, there are actually quite a number of peer- reviewed articles already published that demonstrate evidence for a robust interaction between civilizations and cultures across the oceans long before the European Expansion beginning in the 15th Century C.E. These scientists recorded their observations of the world around them based on the evidence that they found in the field rather than what they had learned in the books. These observations contradicted the established 'truth'. These researchers included people like Carl O. Sauer, Thor Heyerdahl, David Kelley, Jim Parsons, Gunnar Thompson, John L. Sorenson, Steve Jett, Svetlana Balabanova, Alice Kehoe, and Bill Woods. The search has also included several notable amateur researchers such as Gavin Menzies, S. A. Wells, and Demetrio Charalambous.

Now, while our research presented here might be considered to be extensive, it was by no means exhaustive of all that is available. It is believed that at best we were only able to access about 20% of what is out there. This means that well over eighty percent of the historical literature on earth is still waiting to be mined for data which would show these kinds of movements. We have begun the search and now it will be up to someone else to continue it. Since there are peer-reviewed journals and magazine articles that have been and are being written in many other languages, we are sure that there is a wealth of information still to be found by anyone who would take up the cause. To this end, John and I included additional tables in the back of our book, listing some of the species that had some, but unfortunately inadequate proof of early presence. These tables, also listed in the back of this book will give future students a strong base from which to work when they start looking for other likely species. In addition, we also included tables of plants, animals, parasites and diseases that we encountered over the years while living in the tropics that did not show signs of transference, but which we figured will probably be found to have been brought across the oceans millennia ago.

The information is now gathered and available, it just needs recognized as useful then disseminated to all. Publication of these results and the gath-

ering of additional information will provide abundant research opportuni-
ties for future students around the world, wherever libraries exist and/or
observations can be made of the real world. As we have said, our research
has only begun the search for knowledge of these diffusions. For instance,
we have not researched fish poisoning plants as yet. It needs to be shown
that they, too, were moved around the world. The search for evidence of
the equality of contributions made to what we now know as modern culture, the recognition of the contributions of non- white cultures can begin
to instill feelings of equality among the peoples of the world and thus reduce stress and improve the health of the whole world. This, I think is a
much better answer to the need for improvement of health worldwide than
is operating out of the current paradigm which teaches the superiority of
the white races and therefore dependence upon them for everything.

CHAPTER 22: ERADICATING RACISM AND IM-PROVING THE WELL BEING OF THE WORLD'S PEOPLES

The reason why racial biases have been maintained over the last 500 years seems to come from several potential sources. It has been suggested that racism was created to allow the enslavement of Non-Europeans. Refusal to give them credit for diffusion was intended keep the slaves in their place, and, while making slaves feel bad about themselves, to help the owner of this this viewpoint maintain his status without feeling bad about it himself, even though his religion taught equality and fair treatment of all humans and simply flew in the face of the idea that slavery was good or necessary.

Another suggestion is that religious beliefs, writings and dogma were utilized to reinforce the need to expand control over non- European peoples of the Developing World to the benefit of the religious orders and royalty of Europe. The European colonizing powers were interested in exploiting the natural resources of the Developing World to benefit Europeans and bring about greater economic wealth by discounting the humanity of the colonized and/or enslaved peoples. They were considered to be a "subhuman" species. In this way, the colonial powers could extract wealth and demand subservience without loss of face, or feelings contrary to their "upright-standing" religious philosophies.

The value to be gained by changing the psychological mindset that follows on the heels of the feelings of white racial superiority embraced by the colonizers is tremendous, and would have implications for people of color who find themselves in prisons, hospitals or mental institutions of the United States, Canada, and Europe as well as in the Developing World both in the present and for the future. Members of ethnic minorities who find themselves in one of these institutions are generally treated as being inferior in intellect, with no real reason for it other than the self-fulfilling belief that 'simply are inferior,' We can change that with the presentation of new discoveries of the early dispersals of many plant and animal species, human DNA, social traits, etc. But in order for this to happen people will have to be taught to rely on facts, and to act rationally based on their new knowledge, and to discard the outmoded belief of "independent evolution" and/or "Independent cultural development,' which allows one culture to claim superiority over another.

If and when the ethno-centric feelings of European superiority are reduced, or eliminated, the attitudes toward non-white, non- European races will improve and violence against them will decrease. This current mental set of many Whites in the West permeates our legal, political and economic paradigms and underlies our treatment of all other races as inferior. The stresses that racism induces, from whatever cause, make for ill health.

Therefore, it is of paramount importance to world wellbeing to get the message out that the darker races of the world, not only are the most numerous, but also have been in the forefront of horticultural and cultural development and dispersal. Once they get the idea that they are important, the improvement we will see in mental health among those peoples will be significant and this will then necessarily lead to improvements in physical health as well.

It is time that we put forward the idea that the European cultures have touted their false superiority long enough. Even before Europeans experienced the Dark Ages and the Renaissance the dark-skinned peoples of the world were building great societies and civilizations in the rest of the world. It is only due to Europe's myopic view and extreme narcissism that they were not aware of it. Marco Polo made inroads on that ignorance, but it obviously was not enough for Europe to discover the greatness of the Chinese culture. They were still ensconced in their cultural centrism.

They were still touting their cultural superiority after the Age of Discovery while relegating the dark-skinned mariners of the world to obscurity and hence inferiority., when in fact the Northern Europeans made very few contributions to the wellbeing of the world during their period of establishing military dominance over the indigenous populations they found living on other continents, and this with the use of gunpowder, itself an Asian discovery and development. Now that we have been made aware of this it is incumbent upon us to spread the word.

These ideas need to be carried to all peoples and all languages, so that what has been considered an insoluble racial problem across the world can be addressed and remedied. The data is now available in sufficient quantity to totally shift the paradigm away from any innate racial superiority and back to the recognition of the worth of all people, as well as the ability of all peoples to discover, study, learn, write and publish. In my opinion, improving mental health, reducing stress, and creating livable habitats for all humans constitute the basic and underlying formula for the reduction of 80% of human ills. We have the power to reduce racism and gradually bring about improved conditions for all peoples. When the Western world's civilizations recognize that early diffusionists were Non- European, then feelings of superiority and racism will decrease.

What are the origins of a Eurocentric view of history? Of European feelings of superiority over all the people in the rest of the world? Are these feelings the result of, or the product of scientific inquiry and analysis that only looks at evidence as it applies to white man's history? Are the feelings that provide a product of a European self-image of superiority valid? The category of folk myth indicates that a sense of racial superiority is something any group of people can develop even though it is an untruth. If true science dominated the thinking vigor of the white populations in history, it would seem that it would have been the basis of a more rational paradigm, if it were accepted that is, than that of white supremacy.

There are many useful and well-documented books, ours among them, which have ample references and which should make it easier to attract students and youths to careers of discovery in this field. History can be marvelously stimulating and the re-writing of all the old social science textbooks will provide years of work for scholars in most fields. The results should provide a major revolution, the result of which will be that racism and feelings of racial superiority will be much more difficult to maintain for any thinking person.

The philosophical importance of the information presented in this book and associated other volumes published earlier is that the tropical people of the world can both learn and accept that their distant relatives were the first major explorers of the oceans rather than the Spanish, Portuguese, Dutch, British, or Danes (Norse). The non-white peoples had a major influence in the expansion of plants, animals, ideas, and cultural trait across the other early cultures. These early cultures are what modern-day culture grew out of. European culture owes a great debt to these early mariners. Tropical sailors should get credit for discovering all the continents. The feelings of superiority based on skin color or body shape has created terribly biased thinking in the modern world. The logic of racism, as defining the quality of intelligence, scientific prowess, and physical abilities of peoples simply does not exist in the written records or archaeological evidence from around the world.

It is my sincere hope that this book and the ensuing conversations which it causes, will assist in providing the values of equality, without racism, among all humans, by learning about the true origins of some of the U.S – European-Anglo history, which has been improperly claimed in the past five centuries, people will come to understand what has occurred in the rest of the world's early history. With the recognition of the early dispersal of plants, animals, medicines, and microorganisms demonstrated in this book, a truer understanding can develop about the development of cultures and their relationships that influence each other around the world. Again, it is my hope that through education, acceptance, and recognition of the facts presented here, all people of the world will accept the fact that the old beliefs of European superiority, and the general superiority of the white race are not valid, and never have been.

CHAPTER 23 - MOVING FORWARD – WHERE DO WE GO FROM HERE?

It is my hope, that with the publishing of this book, someone out there will take up the torch, so to speak, and continue the work that Carl Sauer, John Sorenson and others including myself, have begun. Believe me there is plenty to do to keep a person busy for the rest of his or her life.

One area where a lot of work is yet to be done, and as we have mentioned earlier in this work, is the area of plant transfers across the oceans prior to 1492 C.E. As discussed, we have found 128 organisms have been found on continents where they did not originate. Archaeologists who discovered and recorded these findings have carbon dated the botanical and zoological finds and all of them have returned dates that precede the arrival of Columbus in the New World. In addition, there are other artifacts such as sculptures, bas-reliefs, paintings, written documents, literature, and artwork that have been found in temples, in burial sites and other structures that show that these organisms, be they floral or faunal were present in a hemisphere other than their hemisphere of origin prior to 1492 C.E. The most likely explanation for this, and one which includes all the evidence we have put forth in this book, is that there was intentional and repeated contact between the various civilizations of the world, but especially those in the tropics, long before Columbus. We have deduced that those contacts must have been made by sailors, mariners and ocean going traders. There does not seem to be any other logical explanation for the occurrence of so many items in so many places where they did not originate. What we have not dealt with to any great extent here, are the many artifacts and flora and fauna that we have found on continents not of their origin, such as dye plants and fish poisoning, for which we do not have definitive proof (i.e. more than one piece of evidence or source) for their having been transferred, or even really existing in the newer place. These are the findings that need more work.

We feel, that using our methodology, the future researcher should have no problem expanding on our work and publishing even more definitive evidence than we have been able to come up with in our four decades of research and writing on this subject. Of course, a keen interest and adequate funding are always the main consideration, but we have found the methods we used to be more than adequate and generally accepted as defensible in the academic world. The methods we have used and would suggest for further research are the following.

- Visiting ancient sites and museums in search of artifacts that would indicate the presence of a particular organism or idea in a place other than its known place of origin, provided it's separated by an ocean from its cultural hearth.
- Gleaning information from ancient documents, or even modern research articles and books on the topics in question.
- Interviewing First Nation people to extract information pertaining to cultural habits, language, and practices, which may have been transferred from another hemisphere in ancient times.
- Studying religious and cultural rituals that seem to occur in disparate places.
- Following linguistic trails by studying ancient lexicons of various ancient languages, especially those where there seems to be an illogical connection that could be explained by transoceanic transference.

There are, of course, other ways to track these things down and I am sure the innovative researcher will find many new and perhaps better ways of getting his or her information, especially now with the widespread use of computers and internet search engines. These were not available to us until the latter stages of our work.

Some relatively new areas that need looking into would be, for example, Pre-Columbiana, which is a journal edited by Steve Jett. There are other journals which need further study as well, such as the New England Anthropological Research Association's journal (NEARA), or the Epigraphic Society's "Occasional Papers" (ESOPS), or the Midwestern Epigraphic Society's "Occasional Papers - Migrations and Diffusions." All of these explore and publish new discoveries about diffusion across the oceans prior to 1492 C.E. The first two look at research from around the world, and the last one focuses on the Americas.

We should not leave out the mainstream magazines such as National Geographic Magazine, The Smithsonian, The Atlantic, Ancient American Magazine and Scientific American, which have begun to publish these kinds of often previously rejected discoveries. The recent change in attitude about he old and broken paradigm allows these more popular and accepted scientific magazines to now be more accepting of papers resulting from research in this area. It also makes it easier for the general public to accept the ideas put forward in Professor Sorenson's any my book World Trade and Biological Exchanges before 1492 C.E. - Revised and Expanded Edition (2013), which uses biological evidence to show that such diffusions did occur. Up until the time of publishing that book, the evidence that we found, that showed that 128 species had definitely been diffused before Columbus, had been completely ignored by scientists who claimed that there was no proof of travel across the oceans by tropical or sub-tropical cultures.

Historical literature from the various civilizations and cultures has detailed descriptions of plants and animals present in these new locations. This literature includes religious texts, flora and fauna catalogs, literary texts and other writings of the time. Another valuable source of historical literary evidence would be official records kept by scribes, etc. and journals, notebooks, diaries, and letters written by the very first European explorers, priests and sea captains, etc. written after they made contact with the people of the new locations. Locations where the Europeans claimed they had not had contact prior to Columbus in 1492 C.E. in the Americas, or Vasco de Gama in 1498 C.E. in India.

In India, we found fifty plants, for example, that had originated in the Americas, present in that distant land. Research showed that these plants had already been assimilated into the religious practices and relics of India, a process that normally takes thousands of years. If the future researchers discussed here, were to familiarize himself with Sanskrit, an ancient religious language used by Hindu's, and which has not added a single word to its vocabulary for over one thousand years, he could begin to look through these ancient texts and there discover references to many more plants that had been transferred in antiquity. When found, due to Hinduism being a very conservative religion, the discovery of names for plants that was the same or very similar to the same plants in the Americas, would of necessity show that those names and the plants referred to were indeed ancient transfers. It would definitively place the transference as earlier than over 1000 years ago.

While on India, it should be mentioned that a search for names of plants, pests and animals in the common regional languages of the time (1000 B.P.) would likely turn up similar words as well. These names would also have been transmitted by the very early traders and explorers long before Columbus upon interaction with the receiving culture whenever that exchange occurred.

Another area where future focus is needed is the area of pilot's logs for ships crossing the seas to engage in trade. We still do not possess many actual pilot's log books even though it is well documented that most sea cap-

265

tains, or pilot's kept one, or more of these books, and so one must have existed for many of these journeys as well (rutters or books of rhumb charts, or charts and books showing the safe navigation routes between ports). We do not even have many of these charts from the post-1492 era of European sailing. We do know, however, that such charts and route maps were regarded as proprietary, or secret, to be seen by the eyes of a particular company's or country's pilot's and captains alone. This would explain why many of them have still not been located. They may have been destroyed, either purposefully as in the Mayan libraries by Cortez, or inadvertently as in the library at Alexandria, or they may have been put away in a safe locker in the Vatican or other religious depository or company vault. With diligent and persistent searching, however, we feel that many of them could be discovered and that they would probably yield tantalizing information regarding the origin of sea routes in use in antiquity as well as perhaps some evidence of items in transport (i.e. cargo) as well as what kinds of articles the ship's personnel may have taken with them on long journeys. From the dearth of information and lack of documents we can assume that the above described secrecy was an accepted practice and that it was carried out not only by European sailors, but also by those of previous civilizations such as Minoan, Greek, Arabic, Indian, Chinese, Polynesian, Incan and Mayan. For some of these we do have secondary sources from which we can conclude that such logs and journals did once exist and passages to trading partners anywhere in the world were carefully guarded secrets.

As we have mentioned earlier, there is an urgent need for someone to travel to the villages of South America in search of remnants of the ancient languages once spoken there. It may be too late already, but this information could lead to very specific and supportive, perhaps conclusive evidence of much earlier contacts there by peoples of the Old World. Some of the artifacts we have seen and some of the Shamanic incantations, or medical scripts, if you will, that I heard on my first trip there were definitely Chinese in origin. These bits of evidence still need to be sought out and recorded for posterity if not just to prove our theories correct.

Another thing which has not been done, but which needs to be done, is to research out and list all organisms where this theory, this new paradigm does not apply, so that future generations can see, 1.) that we have been objective in our research and have not overlooked other possibilities, and, 2.) so that certain possibilities can be eliminated out of hand and valuable time and resources not wasted on them. One such items would be the kangaroo and another, perhaps, Eucalyptus. Neither of them were transferred to the Americas prior to Columbus, and in the case of the kangaroo not even after Columbus except where they have been taken to zoological gardens for display. The Eucalyptus family of plants and trees, of course, probably originated in Australia, but there is some evidence of its existing in

266

New Zealand, Indonesia and even the Philippines. They, of course, seem to have made it to California after Columbus as well, but how they managed to find their way to the various island nations of the South Pacific is still something that needs to be more closely followed up. It may in fact, turn out to be one of those items that does not fit the hypothesis, but further research is required for definitive proof either way.

We mentioned pigs, bananas, sugar cane, rice, tea and coffee as well, but we did not go into the precise routes, places of origin and/or destinations of diffusion for these items. This is another group which needs to be fleshed out, so to speak, for admission into our group of definite Pre-Columbian transfers. Some work in this area has been done, but given the ancient paradigm of 'no-pre- 1492-transfer-across-oceans' has not been well defined or thought out. It is generally accepted that these things were diffused from their places of origin, but, since it was impossible that it was by ship prior to Columbus, it must have taken place later, right? So a lot of research similar to ours needs to be done on these products of culture as well.

There also needs to be follow up in the area of First Nation Cultures. The existing paradigm is that they brought nothing with them no matter how they arrived. It is, of course, of late being bandied about that they may have, or even that they had to have, come by routes other than the infamous 'land bridge.' Using the 'Land Bridge Theory' as a platform, however, linguists have tried to piece together just how the languages of the Amerinds, and there are over 200 of them, came to be where they are. Two such researchers and authors of several books on this topic are Dr. Merrit Ruhlen of Stanford, and Dr. Joseph Greenberg of Berkeley. Dr. Ruhlen's work is primarily comparative studies of the various languages showing connections where they exist. He works from the generally accepted families of Amerind and breaks them down into family groups. Dr. Greenberg's work has been more controversial as he claims there were three distinct waves of migration across the so called 'land bridge.' Those waves gave us the 'Eskimo-Aleut' family of languages, the 'Dene Family' and the 'Amerind.' He was the author of a similar model for Africa, which at first was not accepted as valid by anthropologists, but now is more widely accepted as the way it happened. Whether or not he is correct when it comes to the America's is yet to be seen. However, in keeping with what we are discussing here, more research in this area is definitely needed. We showed, for example, the use of the word for 'blowgun' as being fairly widespread throughout Southeast Asia and South America. The use of 'Uru' to mean 'colorful bird' is found in Peru, Greece and Iran as well as most Semitic languages. How these things came to be, or nailing down precisely how they came to be would be a most fascinating area of research. It is all work that needs to be done if we are to expand our knowledge of the past and how we fit into the march of mankind across history.

We feel that as we discover and accept that all peoples of the world had a hand in bringing us to where we are today, and not just the white folks in Europe, the better off we will be as a human race. Our aim here is to raise awareness of the fact that it is not Europeans alone who were responsible for improving the lot of mankind through trade and spread of cultures and civilizations, but all peoples of the world no matter the color of their skin, or the language the speak. English is the 'lingua Franca' of today for most of the world, but it was not always so. It once was Latin, before that perhaps Mesopotamian (Semitic). In some parts of Europe, it is presently German, in the Northwest of what is now the United States and Canada it was once Chinook Jargon and the Chinook Nation wrote the rules and the language for trade. Remember that only three cultures gave us the major cultural advances of modern man, the Chinese, the Mesopotamians, and the Maya. Each of those gave us writing and building technology. Each of them was on a different continental land mass and each of them had a darker skin color than did the Europeans. Each of these cultural inventions came about at about the same time, i.e. 4,000 B.C.E. and spread to their particular sphere of influence in the world and beyond. It is how they spread their influence over the oceans that we have written about here, and we have found that they most certainly did somehow manage to cross them on foot, but must indeed have sailed. The commercial intercourse of these civilizations long before Columbus gave us a diversity of languages, foods, building styles and religion that has in many cases been handed down to today. It is our contention that we owe them a debt of gratitude for their inventive ideas as well as their desire to take the good news to others.

The philosophical importance of the information presented in this book and other associated volumes published earlier, is that the tropical people of the world can both learn and accept that their distant relatives were the first major explorers of the oceans rather than the Spanish, Portuguese, Dutch, British or Norse. The non- white peoples had a major influence in the expansion of plants, animals, ideas and cultural traits across the oceans. These early cultures are what modern-day culture grew out of. European culture owes a great debt to these early mariners. Tropical sailors should get credit for discovering all the continents. The feelings of superiority based on skin color or body shape has created terribly biased thinking in the modern world. The logic of racism, as defining the quality of intelligence, scientific prowess, and physical abilities of people simply does not exist in the written records and archaeological evidence from around the world. This is the new paradigm that we propose. The paradigm that claims the equality of all peoples. The paradigm of open mindedness in the face of new ideas. With the help of future researchers and authors in this field we hope that those paradigms will come to rule the day in the world of the future.

APPENDIX

TRANSFERRED FLORA AND FAUNA OF THE WORLD

Table A1 - Plants for Which There is Decisive Evidence for Transoceanic Movement

Species	Common Name	Origin	Moved to	Moved by
Agave sp.	Agave	Americas	Mediterranean	300 B.C.E.
Agave americana	Agave	Americas	India	1000 C.E.
Agave angustifolia	Agave	Americas	India	1000 C.E.
Agave cantala	Agave	Americas	India	1000 C.E.
Ageratum co-nyzoides	goat weed	Americas	India, Marquesas?	1500 C.E.
Alternanthe ra philoxeroide s	Alligator weed	Americas	India	1000 C.E.
Amaranthu s caudatus	love-lies-bleeding	Americas	Asia	800 B.C.E.
Amaranthu s cruentus	Amaranth	Americas	Asia	1000 C.E.
Amaranthu s hypochondri acus	Amaranth	Americas	Asia	1000 C.E.
Amaranthu s spinosus	spiked amaranth	Americas	South Asia	800 B.C.E.
Anacardiu m occidentale	Cashew	Americas	India	100 B.C.E.
Ananas comosus	Pineapple	Americas	India, Polyne sia	600 B.C.E.
Annona cherimolia	large annona	Americas	India	1200 C.E.
Annona reticulata	custard apple	Americas	India	100 B.C.E.
Annona squamosa	Sweetsop	Americas	India, Timor	700 B.C.E.
Arachis hypogaea	Peanut	Americas	China, India	2800 B.C.E.
Argemone mexi-	Mexican	Americas	China, India	1100

Species	Common Name	Origin	Moved to	Moved by
cana	poppy			B.C.E.
Aristida subspicata		Americas	Polyne sia	1500 C.E.
Artemisia vulgaris	mugwort	E. Hemisphe re	Mexic o	1500 C.E.
Asclepias curassavica	milkweed	Americas	China, India	1000 C.E.
Aster divaricates	Heart-shaped aster	Americas	Hawaii	1500 C.E.
Bixa orellana	achiote, annatto	Americas	Ocean ia, Asia	1000 C.E.
Canavalia sp.	jackbean, swordbea n	Americas	Asia	1600 B.C.E.
Canna edulis	Indian shot	Americas	India, China	300 C.E.
Cannabis sativa	marijuana	E. Hemisphe re	Peru	100 C.E.
Capsicum annuum	chili pepper	Americas	India, Polyne sia	800 C.E.
Capsicum frutescens	chili pepper	Americas	India	800 C.E.
Carica papaya	papaya	Americas	Polyne sia	1500 C.E.
Ceiba pentandra	silk cotton tree, kapok	Americas	Asia	900 C.E.
Chenopodiu m ambrosioide s	Mexican tea, apazote	E. Hemisphe re	Mesoa merica	1000 C.E.
Cocos nucifera	coconut	E. Hemisphe re	Colom bia to Mexic o	400 C.E.
Couroupita guianensis	cannonbal l tree	Americas	India	1000 C.E.
Cucurbita ficifolia	chilacayot e	Americas	Asia	1500 C.E.
Cucurbita maxima	Hubbard squash	Americas	India, China	900 C.E.
Cucurbita moscha-ta	butternut squash	Americas	India, China	900 C.E.
Cucurbita pepo	pumpkin	Americas	India, China	500 C.E.
Curcuma longa		E.		1500

Species	Common Name	Origin	Moved to	Moved by
	turmeric	Hemisphe re	Andes	C.E.
Cyperus esculentus	sedge	Americas	Eurasi a	B.C.E.?
Cyperus vegetus	edible sedge	Americas	Easter Island, India	1000 C.E.
Datura metel	datura, jimsonwe ed	Americas	Eurasi a	B.C.E.
Datura stramoni-um	datura, thorn ap-ple	Americas	Eurasi a	B.C.E.
Diospyros ebenaster	black sapote	Americas	Eurasi a	1500 C.E.
Conyza canadensis (Erigeron canaden-sis)	Fleabane	Americas	India	1000 C.E.
Erythroxylo n novagranate nse	Coca	Americas	Egypt	1200 B.C.E.
Garcinia man-gostana	mangoste en	E. Hemisphe re	Peru	B.C.E.?
Gossypium arbore-tum	a cotton	E. Hemisphe re	South Ameri ca	3000? B.C.E.
Gossypium barba-dense	a cotton	Americas	Marqu esas Is-lands	1500 C.E.
Gossypium gossy-pioides	a cotton (genes)	Africa	Mexic o	1500 C.E.
Gossypium hirsu-tum	a cotton	Mexico	Africa, Polyne sia	1475 C.E.
Gossypium tomen-tosum	a cotton	Americas	Hawaii	1500 C.E.
Helianthus annuus	sunflower	Americas	India	200 B.C.E.
Heliconia bihai	Balisier	Americas	Ocean ia, Asia	1500 C.E.
Hibiscus tiliaceus	linden hi-biscus	Americas	Polyne sia	1500 C.E.
Ipomoea batatas	sweet pota-to	Americas	Polyne sia, Chi-na	300 C.E.
Lagenaria siceraria	bottle gourd	Americas	Easter n	1500 C.E.
			Polyne sia	

273

Species	Common Name	Origin	Moved to	Moved by
Luffa acutangula	ribbed gourd	Americas	India	B.C.E.?
Luffa cylindrica	vegetable gourd, loofa	Americas?	India, China	1200 B.C.E.
Lycium carolinianum	Christmas berry	Americas	Easter Island	1500 C.E.
Macroptilium lathyroides	phasey bean	Americas	India	1600 B.C.E.
Manihot sp.	manioc	Americas	Easter Island	1500 C.E.
Maranta arundinacea	arrowroot	Americas	Easter Island, India	1000 C.E.
Mimosa pudica	sensitive plant	Americas	India, China	B.C.E.?
Mirabilis jalapa	four-o'clock	Americas	India	B.C.E.?
Mollugo verticillata	carpetweed	E. Hemisphere	North America	B.C.E.?
Monstera deliciosa	a climbing aroid	Americas	India	1100 C.E.
Morus alba	mulberry tree	E. Hemisphere	Middle America	1500 C.E.
Mucuna pruriens	cowhage	Americas	India, Hawaii	B.C.E.?
Musa x paradisiaca	banana, plantain	E. Hemisphere	Tropical America	B.C.E.?
Myrica gale	bog myrtle	E. Hemisphere	North America	1000 C.E.
Nicotiana tabacum	tobacco	Americas	South China, Egypt	1200 B.C.E.
Ocimum basilicum	basil	Americas	India	1000 C.E.
Opuntia dillenii	prickly pear cactus	Americas	India	B.C.E.?
Osteomeles anthyllidifolia	'Ulei (Hawaiian Rose)	Americas	China, Oceania	1500 C.E.
Pachyrhizus erosus	jicama	Americas	Asia	1000 C.E.
			India, China,	

Species	Common Name	Origin	Moved to	Moved by
Pachyrhizus tuberosus	jicama, yam bean	Americas	Ocean ia	1500 C.E.
Pharbitis hederacea	ivy-leaf morning glory	Americas	India, China	1000 C.E.
Phaseolus lunatus	lima bean	Americas	India	1600 B.C.E.
Phaseolus vulgaris	kidney bean	Americas	India	1600 B.C.E.
Physalis lanceifolia	ground cherry	Americas	China	B.C.E.?
Physalis peruviana	husk tomato	Americas	East Polyne sia	1000 C.E.
Plumeria rubra	frangipani	Americas	South Asia	1000 C.E.
Polygonum acuminatum	a knotweed	Americas	Easter Island	1500 C.E.
Portulaca oleracea	purslane	Americas	Eurasi a	B.C.E.
Psidium guajava	guava	Americas	China, Polyne sia	B.C.E.?
Saccharum officinarum	sugarcane	Oceania	South Ameri ca	1500 C.E.
Sapindus saponaria	soapberry	Americas	East Polyne sia, India	B.C.E.?
Schoenoplect us californicus	totora reed, bulrush	Americas	Easter Island	1300 C.E.
Sisyrhynchi um angustifoliu m	blue-eyed 'grass'	Americas	Greenl and	1500 C.E.
Smilax sp.	sarsparilla	Central America	E. Hemis phere	B.C.E.
Solanum candidum/ S. lasiocarpum	naranjillo	Americas	Southe ast Asia, Ocean ia,	1500 C.E.
Solanum nigrum	black nightshad e	E. Hemisphe re?	Mesoa merica	B.C.E.?
Solanum repandum/ S. sessiliflorum	Pacific tomato / peach to-	Americas	Ocean ia	1500 C.E.

275

Species	Common Name	Origin	Moved to	Moved by
	mato			
Solanum tuberosum	potato	Americas	Easter Island	1500 C.E.
Sonchus oleraceus	sow thistle	Americas	China	1500 C.E.
Sophora toromiro	toromiro tree	Americas	Easter Island	1300 C.E.
Tagetes erecta	marigold	Americas	India, China	B.C.E.?
Tagetes patula	dwarf marigold	Americas	India, Persia	1000 C.E.
Zea mays	corn, maize	Americas	Eurasi a, Africa?	B.C.E.

Table A2 - Flora for Which Evidence is Significant but not Decisive

Species	Common Name	Old World	New World
Adenostemm avis-cosum	Boton, Tia juana	India	Origin
Amanita muscaria	fly agaric	Origin	Middle America
Chenopodium quinoa	Quinoa	Easter Island	Origin
Erigeron albidus	Horseweed	Hawaii	Origin
Gnaphalium purpureum	Purple Cudweed	Hawaii	Origin
Gossypium religiosum	a cotton	Hawaii	Mesoamerica
Indigofera tinctoria	Indigo	Polynesia, Asia?	Mexico, Peru
Ipomoea acetosaefolia		Hawaii	Origin
Lycopersicon esculentum	Tomato	India, Hawaii	Mexico, Middle America
Magnolia grandiflora	magnolia	India	Origin
Mangifera indica	Mango	Origin	Middle America
Musa coccinea	Chinese banana	China	South America
Polianthes tuberose	tuberose	Origin	South America
Salvia coccinea	scarlet salvia	India	Origin
Salvia occidentalis	a salvia	Marquesa s	Origin
Smilax sp.	sarsaparilla	Eurasia	Middle America
Tamarindus indicus	tamarind tree	South Asia	Tropical America
Triumfetta semitriloba	Sacremento bur-bark	Easter Island	South America
Verbesina encelioides	Golden crown-beard	Hawaii	Origin
Vitis vinifera	Grape	Eurasia	Mexico

Table A3 - Flora for Which Evidence Justifies Further Study

Species	Common Name	Species	Common Name
Acorus calamus	sweet flag	*Indigofera suffruticosa*	Indigo
Ageratum houstonianum	floss flower	*Lonchocarpus sericeus*	a fish poison
Alternanthera pungens	khakiweed	*Lupinus cruickshanksii*	field lupine
Alternanthera sessilis	Sessile joyweed	*Momordica balsamin*	Balsam apple
Alternanthera tonella		*Morus rubra*	Mulberry
Annona glabra	pond apple	*Nelumbo* sp	Lotus
Cajanus cajan	pigeon pea	*Nicotiana rustica*	wild tobacco
Cassia fistula	purging cassia	*Nymphaea* sp.	Lotus
Cinchona officinialis	quinine (bark)	*Ocimum americanum*	hoary basil
Colocasia esculenta	dry-land taro	*Paullinia* sp.	a fish poison
Cucumis sp.		*Phaseolus adenanthus*	a bean
Cyclanthera pedata	pepino hueco	*Sagittaria sagittifolia*	Wapatoo
Datura sanguinea	datura, Jimson weed	*Sesamum orientale*	Sesame
Derris sp.	a fish poison	*Sisyrhynchium acre*	a grass
Dioscorea alata	yam	*Spondias lutyea*	Hog plum
Dioscorea cayenensis	guinea yam	*Spondias purpurea*	hog plum
Dolichos lablab	a bean	*Synedrella nodiflora*	pantropic weed
Elaeis guineensis	guinea oil palm	*Tephrosia* spp.	a fish poison
Gossypium brasiliense	a cotton	*Trapa natans*	water chestnut
Gossypium drynarioides	a cotton	*Vigna sinensis*	Cow peas
Hibiscus youngianus	hibiscus		

Table A4 - Microfauna for Which There is Decisive Evidence

Species	Common Name or Caused Disease
Ancylostoma duodenale	a hookworm
Ascaris lumbricoides	roundworm
Bordetella pertussis	whooping cough bacterium
Borrelia recurrentis	relapsing fever spirochete
Entamoeba hystolytica	amoeba that causes dysentery
Enterobius vermicularis	pinworms
Human (alpha) herpes virus 3	cause of shingles, chicken pox, etc.
Human (gamma) herpes virus 4	cause of mononucleosis, etc.
Microsporum spp.	cause of ringworm of the body
Mycobacterium tuberculosis	bacterium causing tuberculosis
Necator americanus	a hookworm
Pediculus humanus capitis	the scalp louse
Pediculus humanus corporis	the body louse
Piedreaia hortai	a fungus that infests the hair
Rickettsia prowazekii	bacterium that causes typhus
Rickettsia rickettsii	bacterium that causes spotted fever
Rickettsia typhi	bacterium causing typhus murine
T celllymphotropic (retro) virus (HTLV-I)	lymphotropic virus
Treponema pallidum	Cause of syphilis, yaws, and pinta
Trichosporon ovoides	a fungus infesting hair of scalp or beard
Trichuris trichiura	whipworm
Yersinia pestis	the plague bacillus

Table A5 - Microfauna for Which Evidence Is less than Decisive

Species	Common Name or Caused Disease
Diplococcus pneumoniae	bacterium that causes pneumonia in humans and mice
Flavivirus spp.	organism causing yellow fever
Giardia lamblia	protozoan causing giardiasis
Influenza viruses	sources of influenza
Leishmania sp.	protozoan causing Leishmaniasis
Mycobacterium leprae	bacterium causing leprosy
Onchocerca volvulus	nematode causing onchocerciasis
Plasmodium falciparum	sporozoan causing malaria
Salmonella enterica serovar Typhi	typhoid bacillus
Schistosoma sp.	liver fluke
Shigella dysenteriae	cause of bacillary dysentery
Staphylococcus x aureus	bacillus causing impetigo, carbuncles
Streptococcus pneumoniae	a bacterial cause of pneumonia
Streptococcus pyogenes	cause of scarlet and rheumatic fever, etc.
Strongyloides sp.	threadworm nematode
Treponema pallidum	an organism causing yaws, pinta, and syphilis
Trichophyton concentricum	a funguscausing ringworm of the body
Trychostrongylus sp.	a helminthic parasite
Tunga penetrans	chigoe, chigger
Wuchereria bancrofti	a nematode causing filiariasis

280

Table A6 - Other Fauna for Which There is Decisive Evidence

Species	Common Name
Alphitobius diaperinus	lesser mealworm
Canis familiaris	edible dog
Gallus gallus	Chicken
Littorina littorea	a mollusk
Meleagris gallopavo	Turkey
Mya arenaria	American soft-shell clam
Stegobium paniceum	drugstore beetle

Table A7 - Other Fauna Needing Additional Study

Species	Common Name
Cairina moschata	Muscovy duck
Crax globicera	Curassow
Cicada sp.	Cicada
Dendrocygna bicolor	fulvous tree duck
Felis domestica	Cat
Lasioderma serricorne	tobacco or cigarette beetle
Mus musculus	Mouse
Rattus rattus	Rat
Oryctolagus cuniculus	a rabbit
Rhyzopertha dominica	lesser grain borer

Data from World Trade and Biological Exchanges
Before 1492, Revised and Expanded Edition
By John L. Sorenson and Carl L. Johannessen
Presented by Carl L. Johannessen (AAG 2013)
Find it on Amazon.com (Print or Kindle Editions)

Table A8 - Names of Strychnos Plants Around the World

Common Names	Scientific Name	Author of Name	Citation Page
Brucine		Modern Chemicals	Burkill, 2129
strychnine		Modern Chemicals	Burkill, 2129
Curarine		Modern Chemicals	Burkill, 2129
Curine		Modern Chemicals	Burkill, 2130
strychnacin e	*Strichnos, nux-vomica*	Modern Chemicals	Burkill, 2130
Ipoh krohi	*Strychnos*	Benua	Burkill, 2130
Ipoh tennik	*Strychnos*	Benua	Burkill, 2130
Ipoh kennik	*Strychnos*	Benua	Burkill, 2130
Ipoh mallaye	*Strychnos*	Benua	Burkill, 2130
Chey	*Strychnos*		Burkill, 2131
Ipoh akar	*Strychnos*	Jakun	Burkill, 2131
Chong ches	*S. tieute*	Pangan	Burkill, 2131
Belai (ipoh akar)	*Strychnos*	Generic name	Burkill, 2131
Bedara laut	*Strychnos. Ligustrina*	Timor	Burkill, 2131
Bedara hutan	*S.pubescens*	Timor	Burkill, 2131
Bedara laut hutan	*S. pubescens/S. ligustrina*	Timor	Burkill, 2132
Akar lada- lada	*Strychnos or Ervatamia*		Burkill, 2132
Semijo akar	*S. laurina*		Burkill, 2132
Semejan	*S. laurina*		Burkill, 2132
Ayer majan	*S. laurina*		Burkill, 2132
Ham	*Strychnos*		
Hoang nan	*S. malaccensis*	Indo-China	Burkill, 2132
Bedara laut	*S. ligustrina*	Java	Burkill, 2133
Belai hitam	*S. ovalifolia*	Malay	Burkill, 2135
Gria	*S. ovalifolia*	Pangan	Burkill, 2135
Umpas	*S. ovalifolia*	Mantera	Burkill, 2135
Umpas padi	*S. ovalifolia*	Mantera	Burkill, 2135
Gui-u-legop	*S. ovalifolia*	Perak	Burkill, 2136
Ipoh batang	*S. penicillata*	Malay	Burkill, 2136

283

Common Names	Scientific Name	Author of Name	Citation Page
Bedara utara	*S. penicillata*	Malay	Burkill, 2136
Akarlada- lada	*S. penicillata*	Malay	Burkill, 2136
Akar ipoh	*S. pubescens*	Malay	Burkill, 2136
Belai besar	*S. pubescens*	Malay	Burkill, 2136
Ipoh akar	*S. quadrangula ris*	Malay	Burkill, 2136
Belai besar	*S.scortechinii*	Perak	Burkill, 2137
Chètèk	*S. tieute*	Java	Burkill, 2137
lampong	*S. sp. No. 2*	Perak	Burkill, 2138
blay besar	*S. sp. No. 3*	Malacca	Burkill, 2138
Pougouly (ficus)		South America	Jett, 151
Pakuru- neara		American	Jett, 151
Ampi, Woorari, Woorara, Woora-li, Wourali, Wouralia, Ourare, Ourari, Urare, Urari, and Uirary.	*S. toxifera*	South America	Wiki
Poko ipoh		Malay	Jett, 151
Poko kayu		Malay	Jett, 151
Pokru		Sundanese	Jett, 151

Data taken from A Dictionary of the Economic Products ot the Malay Peninsula, Volum II (I- Z) By Isaac Henry Burkill, M.A., F.L.S. Published by the Ministry of Agriculture and Co-Operatives Kuala Lumpur, Malaysia 1931,1966

BIBLIOGRAPHY

lvarez, Ticul, and Aurelio Ocaña. 1999. Sinopsis de Restos Arqueozoológicos de Vertebrados Terrestres. Basada en Informes del Laboratorio de Paleozoología del INAH. (Colección Científica). México: Instituto Nacional de Antropología e Historia. 100-102.

lvarez, Ticul. 1976. "Restos óseos de las excavaciones de Tlatilco, Estado de México." in Apuntes para la arqueología, México: Instituto Nacional de Antropología e Historia, Departmento de Prehistoria.

mrhein, Laura M. 2003. An Iconographic and Historic Analysis of Terminal Classic Maya Phallic Imagery. http://www.famsi.org/reports/20001/

nonymous. (1978) "Fabulously Feathered Fowl: Another Name for Silkies." Western Farmer. Feb/Mar 1978. pp 10 – 11.

rbeit, Wendy. (1994). Tapa in Tonga. Honolulu, HI: Palm Frond Productions.

veni, Anthony F. (1983). Skywatchers of Ancient Mexico. Austin: University of Texas Press.

veni, Anthony F. (2000). Between the Lines: The Mystery of the Giant Drawings of Ancient Nasca Peru. Austin: University of Texas Press.

alabanova, S., F. Parsche, and W. Pirsig. 1992. First Identification of Drugs in Egyptian Mummies. Natur Wissenschaften 79/8: 358.

alfour, Edward G. (1871 – 1873) Cyclopedia of India, 2nd edition. 5 Volumes. Calcutta.

arnett, R. D. 1960. Assyrian Palace reliefs. London, Batchworth Press Limited.

ellwood, Peter. Man's Conquest of the Pacific: The Prehistory of Southeast Asia and Oceania. New York: Oxford University Press, 1979. Print.

ischof, Henning. "The Origins of Pottery in South America -- Recent Radiocarbon dates from Southwest Ecuador." 40th ICA 1:269-280. (1972)

ökönyi, Sándor, and Dénes Jánossy. 1959. "Adatok a pulyka kolumbusz ellötti Európai elöfordulás ához," Aquila: a Magyar Ornithologiai Központ Folyóirata 65: 265–9. (Budapest.)

orah, W. W. (1943). Silk raising in colonial Mexico. Berkeley and Los Angeles: University of California Press.

righam, Wilkliam T, (1911). Ka Hana Kapa: The Making of Bark-cloth in Hawaii. Honolulu, HI: Bishop Museum Press.

British Museum, Library Collection. 1890's Cd110.jpg. Stela B at Copan, Honduras (3/4 left angle front view) A.P. Maudslay.

British Museum, Library Collection. 1890's. Plate 35.jpg. Stela B at Copan, Honduras (3/4 right angle front view) A.P. Maudslay.

British Museum, Library Collection. Plate34.jpg. Stela B at Copan, Honduras (side view sketches of Stela B).

British Museum, Library Collection. Plate37.jpg. Stela B at Copan, Honduras (front view sketch of Stela B).

British Museum, Library Collection. 1890's. Cd119 lge.jpg. Stela B at Copan, Honduras (front view) A.P. Maudslay.

Buckland, P. C., and E. Panagiotakopulu. 2001. "Rameses II and the tobacco beetle," Antiquity 75: 549–56. 556.

Bussagli, Mario and Calembus Sivaramamurti. 5000 years of the Art of India. New York: Harry N. Abrams, Inc. 7-335.

Cardona M. (1970) "Magia y brujeria" Boln Inst. Folklore. 4: 245.

Carter, George F. 1971. "Pre-Columbian chickens in America," in Man across the Sea: Problems of Pre-Columbian Contacts, Carroll L. Riley, et al., eds., 7–22. Austin: University of Texas Press.

Castello, Salvador. (1924) "The Gallus inauris and the hen which lays blue eggs" In Second World's Poultry Congress and Exhibition, Books of the Congress and Description of the Exhibition. Barcelona: The Graphics Art Co, Ltd. pp. 113-118.

Chapman, J., R.B. Stewart, and R.A. Yarnell. "Archaeological Evidence for Precolumbian Introduction of Portulaca oleracea and Mollugo verticillata into Eastern North America," Economic Botany. (1974) p. 411-412.

Chen, Hsuan. (127) Commentaries and Annotations to Chou Li. This volume gives early Chinese rituals and rites. Chen was a commentator on the manuscript in 127 C.E. Translated for me by May Chen Fogg in 1980.

Clarke AC, Burtenshaw MK, McLenachan PA, Erickson DL, and Penny D. 2006. Reconstructing the Origins and Dispersal of the Polynesian Bottle Gourd (Lagenaria siceraria). Molecular Biology and Evolution 23(5):893- 900.

Codex Tro-Cortesianos (Codex Madrid)

Coe, Michael D. (1966) An Early Stone Pectoral from Southeastern Mexico. Studies in Pre-Colubiam Art and Archaeology, Number 1. Dumberton Oaks, Trustees for Harvard University.

de Groot, JJM, (1901) The religious system of China, its ancient forms, evolution, history and present aspect, manners, customs and social institutions connected therewith. Published with a subvention from the Dutch colonial government.

de la Fuentes, Beatriz, et al. 1996. Olmec art of Ancient Mexico, Washington D.C., National Gallery of Art.

Denham, Tim. 2013. Ancient dispersal of sweet potato in Oceania. Proceedings of the National Academy of Sciences: vol. 110 #6. pp. 1982-1983.

DNA Consultants. (2009). *Anomalous native american lineages now identified also among Micmac Indians*. Retrieved from: http://www.cherokee.dnaconsultants.com/_blog/DNA_Consultants_ B log/post/Acadian_Anomalies/#sthash.3nDr74o8.dpuf

Douglass, Frederick. [1857] (1985). "The Significance of Emancipation in the West Indies." Speech, Canandaigua, New York, August 3, 1857;

collected in pamphlet by author. In The Frederick Douglass Papers. Series One: Speeches, Debates, and Interviews. Volume 3: 1855-63. Edited by John W. Blassingame. New Haven: Yale University Press.

Dumont, H.J., Cocquyt, C., Fontugue, M., Arnold, M., Reyss, J.-L., Bloemendal, J., Oldfield, F., Steenbergen, C.L.M., Korthals, H.J., Zeeb, B.A. The end of moai quarrying and its effect on Lake Rano Raraku, Easter Island. Journal of Paleolimnology 20 (4), (1998) pp. 409-422.

Duncan NA, Pearsall DM, and Benfer J, Robert A. 2009. Gourd and squash artifacts yield starch grains of feasting foods from preceramic Peru. Proceedings of the National Academy of Sciences 106(32):13202-13206.

Erickson, D.L., Smith, B.D., Clarke, A.C., Sandweiss, D.H., & Tuross, N. (2005). An Asian origin for a 10,000-year-old domesticated plant in the Americas. *Proceedings of the National Academy of Sciences, 102*(51):18315–18320.

Errazuriz, Jaime. 2002. *Pacific Basin: 4,000 years of cultural contacts : Why do some scholars see macaws where the average man sees elephants?.* New WorldEditions,

Errazurriz, J., & Alvarado, C. (1993). An archaeologic bridge over the Pacific: transpacific currents and Tumaco-La Tolita transpacific crossing. *Audiovisual presentation, Tokyo, NHK (TV), July, 29.*

Evans, C. and Betty J. Meggers. (1966) "Transpacific origin of Valdivia phase potter on coastal Ecuador." Proceedings of the 36th International Congress of Americanists. Sevilla: Editorial Catholica Española. pp. 63-67.

Fenyvesi, Charles. 1996. "A tale of two cultures." U.S. News and World Report. Nov. 4, vol. 121, No. 18:46-48. (A report on Han Ping Chen, Shang Chinese Scholar from Beijing.)

Ferentinos, G., Gkioni, M., Geraga, M., & Paptheodorou, G. (2012). Early seafaring activity in the southern Ionian Islands, Mediterranean Sea. *Journal of Archaeological Science, 39*(7), 2167-2176.

Ferryn, Patrick. 1977. "Enquete sur les contacts transpacifiques" (part one). Kadath. Chroniques des Civilizations Disaparues, 23, May-June-July: 8-20.

Fiennes, Richard and Alice Fiennes. 1968. The Natural History of Dogs. London: Weidenfeld and Nicholson.

Finney, B. R. (1985). Anomalous westerlies, El Niño, and the colonization of Polynesia. *American Anthropologist, 87*(1), 9-26.

Finsterbusch, C. A. 1931. "The Araucano, the blue-egged fowl of Chile," The Feathered World 85 (2201):

Fraser, Douglas. 1965, Theoretical Issues in the Transpacific Diffusion Controversy, Social Research, 32(4):452-477.

Fuente, Beatriz de la., Los Hombres de Piedra. Mexico: Universidad Nacional Autonoma de Mexico.

Fuller DQ, Hosoya LA, Zheng Y, and Qin L. 2010. A Contribution to the

Prehistory of Domesticated Bottle Gourds in Asia: Rind Measurements from Jomon Japan and Neolithic Zhejiang, China. Economic Botany 64(3):260-265.

Gardini, Walter. (1974) "Asiatic Influences on pre-Columbian cultures." Diogenes. 87: p. 106.

Gould, Stephen Jay. 1994. In the Mind of the Beholder. Natural History 103: 14-23

Gupta, Shakti M. 1996. Plants in Indian Temple Art. B.R. Publishing Corporation (A division of D.K. Publishers Distribution Ltd). Delhi, India.

Guthrie, James L. (2011) "Tying it Together – The Transoceanic Contact Controversy Part III: Artifacts and Transmitted Techniques." NEARA Journal, New England Antiquities Research Association. 45:1 Summer 2011, pp. 23 – 28.

Guthrie, James L. (2011) "Tying it Together – The Transoceanic Contact Controversy Part IV: Old World Inscriptions In America." NEARA Journal, New England Antiquities Research Association. 45:2 Winter 2011, pp. 2 – 13.

Guthrie, James L. (2011) "Tying it Together – The Transoceanic Contact Controversy Part V: Transliteration of Inca Letters." NEARA Journal, New England Antiquities Research Association. 45:2 Winter 2011, pp. 14 – 22.

Hall, A. R., and H. K. Kenward. 1990. Environmental Evidence from the Colonia. London: Council for British Archaeology, for York Archaeological Trust. Archaeology of York 14/6.

Hamp, Eric P. 1971. "On Mayan-Araucanian Comparative Phonology." International Journal of American Linguistics. 37:3 pp. 156 – 159.

Hand, Wayland D. (1965) "The magical transference of disease." North Carolina Folklore, vol. 13 (1-2-) (Also Titled Folklore Studies in Honor of Arthur Palmer Hudson). Duke University Press, Durham, NC. pp. 83- 109.

Harms, H. 1922. "Uebersicht der bischer in altperuanischen graeben gefundenen Pflanzenreste," Festschrift Eduard Seler. Ed. W. Lehmann. Stuttgart: Strecker and Schroeder. pp. 157 – 188.

Harris, George L., et al. Iraq, its people, its society, its culture. New Haven, Hraf Press.

Hartman, Orar M. 1973. The Origin and Dispersal of the Domestic Fowl: A Study in Cultural Diffusion. Unpublished M.A. thesis, University of Oregon.

Heine-Geldern, R.V. & Ekholm, G.F. (1951) Significant Parallels in the Symbolic Arts of Southern Asia and Middle America. Sol Tax, ed. The Civilizations of Ancient America, Chicago. pp. 299-309.

Hennig, R. 1940. "Eine rätselhafte Tier—Darstellung im Dom von Schleswig," Natur und Volk, Ornithologische Monatsberichte, Band 70: 100–

1.

Heyerdahl, Thor. 1958. Aku Aku The Secret of Easter Island. New York:,Rand McNally & Company.

Heyerdahl, Thor. 1979. Early Man and the Ocean: A Search for the Beginnings of Navigation and Seaborne Civilization. Doubleday.

Hoffman letters: May 12, 1989—General discussion of origin and other matters, including routes to the Americas by sea.

Holdaway, R. N. 1996. "Arrival of Rats in New Zealand," Nature 384 (21 Nov.): 115-26.

Horrocks M, and Wozniak JA. 2008. Plant microfossil analysis reveals disturbed forest and a mixed-crop, dryland production system at Te Niu, Easter Island. Journal of Archaeological Science 35(1):126-142.

Horrocks M, Shane PA, Barber IG, D'Costa DM, and Nichol SL. 2004. Microbotanical remains reveal Polynesian agriculture and mixed cropping in early New Zealand. Review of Palaeobotany and Palynology 131:147-157.

Ifland, Peter. Taking the Stars: Celestial Navigation from Argonauts to Astronauts. Newsport News, Va: Mariners' Museum, 1998. Print.

James, K.E. (1988). Making Mats and Barkcloth in the Kingdom of Tonga. K.E. James, puiblisher.

Jeffreys, M. D. W. 1971. "Pre-Columbian maize in Asia." In Man across the sea: problems of Pre-Columbian contacts. ed. Riley, Carroll L. et al., Austin, University of Texas Press. Pp.376-400.

Jett, Stephen C. 1998, Pre-Columbian Transoceanic Contacts: What is the Evidence?, Journal of the West, 37(4):11-18.

Johannessen, Carl L. 1981. Folk Medicine Uses of Melanotic Asiatic Chickens as Evidence of Early Diffusion in the New World. Social Science and Medicine, 15D(4):427-34.

Johannessen, Carl L. 1982. Melanotic Chicken Use and Chinese Traits in Guatemala. Revista de Historia de America 93:73-89.

Johannessen, Carl L. 1986 "Distribution and Use of the Black-Boned and Black-Meated Chicken in Mexico and Guatemala," In Yearbook 1986, Conference of Latin Americanist Geographers, Vol. 12: 43-50.

Johannessen, Carl L. 1992."Distribution of Pre-Columbian maize and modern maize names." In Person, place and thing: interpretive and empirical essays in cultural geography, ed. Shue Tuck Wong, Geosciences and Man 31:313-333.

Johannessen, Carl L. 1997, Des epis de mais en Inde sur des sculptures des XII-XIIIeme siecles? Kadath: Chroniques des Civilisation Disparues, Fall/Winter:4-31.

Johannessen, Carl L. 1998, American Crop Plants in Asia before A.D. 1500. Pre-Columbiana: A Journal of Long Distance Contacts, 1(1&2):9-36.

Johannessen, Carl L. 1998a. Pre-Columbian American Sunflower and Maize

Images in Indian Temples: Evidence of Contact between Civilizations in India and America. New England Research Association Journal 32 (1):4- 18.

Johannessen, Carl L. 1998b. "Maize Diffused to India before Columbus Came to America". Across Before Columbus, Evidence for Transoceanic Contact with the Americas prior to 1492. Eds. Donald Y. Gilmore and Linda S. McElroy, Edgecomb ME: NEARA Publications, Printing at Worcester MA: Mercantile Printing Company, Inc. pp.111-124.

Johannessen, Carl L. 1998c. "Des E'pis de Mais en Inde sur des Sculptures des XII-XIII`emes Sie`cles?" Kadath, Croniques des Civilisations Disaparues, 89(Automne-Hiever1997):4-18.

Johannessen, Carl L. 1987. Domestication process: An hypothesis for its origin. Martin S. Kenzer (ed.) Carl O Sauer: A Tribute. Corvallis, OR: Oregon State University for the Association of Pacific Coast Geographers, 177-204.

Johannessen, Carl L. and Anne Z. Parker. 1989a. Maize Ears Sculpted in 12th and 13th Century A.D. India as Indicators of Pre-Columbian Diffusion. Economic Botany 43:164-80.

Johannessen, Carl L. and Anne Z. Parker. 1989b. American Crop Plants in Asia Prior to European Contact. Yearbook, Conference of Latin Americanist Geographers (CLAG) 1989. 14: 14-19.

Johannessen, Carl L. and Siming Wang. 1998. American Crop Plants in Asia before A.D. 1500. Pre-Columbiana, A Journal of Long-Distance Contacts. 1(1&2): 9-36.

Johannessen, Carl L. Gilmore and Linda McElroy, pp.111-24. Edgecomb, Me: New England Antiquities Research Association, NEARA Publications.

Johannessen, Carl L., & Fogg, May Chen. 1982. "Melanotic chickenuse and Chinese traits in Guatemala." Revista de Historia de Ame'rica, 93, 73-89.

Kearsley, Graeme R. 2003. "The Imperative of Migration by Land and Sea by Modern Humans from East Africa to the Pacific and to the Americas." http://www.world-mysteries.com/gw_kearsley/html.

Kelley, David H, and E F. Milone. Exploring Ancient Skies: A Survey of Ancient and Cultural Astronomy. New York: Springer, 2011. Print.

Kooijman, Simon. (1972). Tapa in Polynesia. Bernice P. Bishop Museum Bulletin 234. Honolulu, HI: Bishop Museum Press.

Kudo Y, and Sasaki Y. 2010. Characterization of Plant Remains on Jomon Potteries Excavated from the Shimo-yakebe Site, Tokyo, Japan. Bulletin of the National Museum of Japanese History 158:1-26. (in Japanese)

Latcham, Ricardo E. 1922. "Los animales domesticos de la America Pre-Columbiana." Publicaciones del Museo de Etnologia y Antropologia de Chile, tomo 3. (Santiago, Chile). pp 1 - 199 eles, D., Araújo, A., Ferreira, L. F., Vicente, A. C. P., & Iñiguez, A. M. (2008). Molecular paleoparasitological diagnosis of Ascaris sp. from coprolites: new scenery of ascariasis in pre-Colombian South America times. Memórias do Instituto Oswaldo Cruz, 103(1), 106-108.

ewer, S. H. 1912. Wright's Book of Poultry. New York: Cassel and Co. pp. 91 – 494.

i, Shih-Chen(1596) Pen T'sao Kang Mu [Bencao Gang Mu] Translated for me by May Chen Fogg in 1980.

Mair, Victor H. 1998. "Canine conundrums: Eurasian dog ancestor myths in historical and ethnic perspective," Sino-Platonic Papers 87. Philadelphia: University of Pennsylvania Department of Asian and Middle Eastern Studies.

Malmstrom, Vincent H. (1973). Origin of the Mesoamerican 260-Day Calendar. Science, New Series 181(4103): 939-41. Web. 26 July 2013.

Mangelsdorf, Paul 1974. Corn, its origin, evolution, and improvement. Cambridge, MA. Harvard University Press.

Marshack, Alexander. (1975). Olmec Mosaic Pendant. Archaeoastronomy in Precolumbian America, Austin: University of Texas Press, pp. 341-377.

Marti-Ibanez, Felix (1962) A Prelude to Medical History. New York: MD Publications. pp. 68-71.

Marti-Ibanez, Felix (1962) The Epic of Medicine. New York: Clarkson N. Potter, Inc. Publisher. pp.43-52.

Matisoo-Smith, E. and J. H. Robins. 2004. "Origins and dispersals of Pacific peoples: evidence from the mtDNA phylogenies of the Pacific rat," Proceedings of the National Academy of Sciences of the USA 101 (June 15): 9167-9172.

Matisoo-Smith, E., R. M. Roberts, G. J. Irwin, J. S. Allen, D. Penny, and D. M. Lambert. 1998. "Patterns of prehistoric human mobility in Polynesia indicated by mtDNA from the Pacific rat," Proceedings of the National Academy of Sciences of the USA 95 (Dec.): 15145-15150.

McNeil, William F. Visitors to Ancient America: The Evidence for European and Asian Presence in America Prior to Columbus. Jefferson, NC: McFarland and Company, Inc. Publishers. 2005.

Meggers, Betty J. 1963. "Cultural Development in Latin America: An Interpretive overview." Aboriginal Cultural Development in Latin America: An Interpretive Review, eds. Betty J. Meggers and Clifford Evans, Smithsonian Miscellaneous Collections, 146/1. (Smithsonian Institution: Washington. D.C.), 131-148.

Meggers, Betty J. 1997. "The Transpacific Origin of Mesoamerican Civilization: A Preliminary Review of the Evidence and its Theoretical Implications," New England Antiquities Research Association Journal, 31(1):64-71.

Meggers, Betty J. 2010. Prehistoric America: An Ecological Perspective, 3rd

Expanded Edition. New Brunswick, New Jersey. Aldine Transaction Press. (originally published in 1972)

Meggers, Betty J. and Clifford Evans. "A Transpacific Contact in 3,000 B.C." Scientific American, Vol. 214, No. 1: pp. 28 – 35.

Mendez, A., Barnhart, E.L., Powell, C., Karasik, C. (2005). Astronomical Observations from the Temple of the Sun. Archaeoastronomy 19.

Merrill, Elmer Drew 1954. "The botany of Cook's voyages." Chronica Botanica 14(5/6):164-384.

Merrill, William L., Robert J. Hard, Jonathan B. Mabry, Gayle J. Fritz, Karen R. Adams, John R. Roney, and A.C. MacWilliams. 2009. "The diffusion of maize to the southwestern United States and its impact." Proceedings of the National Academy of Sciences of the USA 106:50. 21019-21026.

Metropolitan Museum of Art. 1946. The great king, King of Assyria. Assyrian reliefs in the Metropolitan Museum of Art. New York, Metropolitan Museum of Art.

Neich, R. and Pendergrast M. (2001). Tapa of the Pacific. Aukland, NZ: David Bateman and Auckland War Memorial Museum.

Nordenskiöld, E. 1922. "Deductions Suggested by Geographical Distribution of Some Post Columbian Words Used by the Indians of South America." Comparative Ethnological Studies, Vol. 5. Gotheburg.

Olmstead, A.T. History of Assyria. New York, Charles Scribner's Sons. Olsen, Ronald D. 1964. "Mayan Affinities with Chipaya of Bolivia I: Correspondences." International Journal of American Linguistics. 30:4 pp. 313 – 324.

Panagiotakopulu, Eva. 2001. Archaeology and Entomology in the Eastern Mediterranean. Research into the History of Insect Synanthropy in Greece and Egypt. Oxford, UK: BAR International Series 836.

Pearsall DM. 2008. Plant domestication. In: Pearsall DM, editor. Encyclopedia of Archaeology. London: Elsevier Inc. p 1822-1842.

Petersen, K. S., K. L. Rasmussen, J. Heinemeier, and N. Rud. 1992. "Clams before Columbus?," Nature 359 (Oct. 22): 679.

Pokharia, A.K. and K.S. Saraswat. 1999. "Plant economy during Kushana Period (100 – 300 A.D.) at Sanghol, Punjab," Pragdhara [Journal of the Uttar Pradesh State Archaeology Department]. pp. 75-104.

Read, B. E. 1931 – 1939. Chinese Materia Medica, vol. 6 (4). Series No. 252 and 268. Peking Natural History Bulletin. Peiping.

Riddle, J. M., and J. M. Vreeland. 1982. "Identification of insects associated with Peruvian mummy bundles by using scanning electron microscopy," Paleopathology Newsletter 39.

Roys, Ralph L. 1957. Political geography of the Yucatan Maya. Washington D.C.: Carnegie Institution.

Roys, Ralph L. 1965 Ritual of the Bacabs. Norman: University of Oklahoma Press.

Russell, John Malcolm Senacherib's Palace without rival at Nineveh. Chicago, University of Chicago Press.

Saggs, H. W. F. 1962 & 1988. The greatness that was Babylon, A survey of the ancient civilization of the Tigris-Euphrates Valley. London, Sidgwick & Jackson.

Sauer, Carl O. 1952. Agricultural Origins and Dispersals. (Bowman Memorial Lectures). New York: American Geographical Society. 1952. (2nd edition. Cambridge: Massachusetts Institute of Technology Press. 1969.)

Sauer, Carl O. 1975. "Maize into Europe." in Seeds, spades, hearths & herds. the domestication of animals and foodstuffs. Cambridge, MA, The MIT press.

Schaffer AA, and Paris HS. 2003. Melons, squashes and gourds. In: Caballero B, editor. Encyclopedia of Food Sciences and Nutrition. second ed. London: Elsevier. p 3817-3826.

Schlereth, Hewitt. 2000. Celestial Navigation in a Nutshell. Dobbs Ferry, NY: Sheridan House. Print.

Schurtz, W. L. (1959). The manila galleon. New York: E. P. Dutton. Seligmann, Linda J. (1987) "The Chicken in Andean History and Myth: The Quechua Concept of Wallpa." Ethnohistory 34:2 American Society for Ethnohistory. pp. 139-170.

Simoons, Frederick J. 1961. Eat Not This Flesh: Food Avoidances in the Old World. Madison: University of Wisconsin Press.

Skottsberg, C. "Derivation of the flora and fauna of Juan Fernández and Easter Islands." In: The natural history of Juan Fernández and Easter Island. 2 Volumes. C. Skottsberg, editor. Uppsala, Sweden: Almqvist & Wiksells. (1956) Pages 193-439.

Skottsberg, C. "Derivation of the flora and fauna of Juan Fernández and Easter Islands." In: The natural history of Juan Fernández and Easter Island. 2 Volumes. C. Skottsberg, editor. Uppsala, Sweden: Almqvist & Wiksells. (1956) Pages 193-439.

Smith BD. 2005. Reassessing Coxcatlan Cave and the early history of domesticated plants in Mesoamerica. Proceedings of the National Academy of Sciences 102(27):9438-9445.

Smith, Grafton Elliot. 1924. Elephants and Ethnologists: Asiatic Origins of the Maya Ruins. London: Kegan Paul, Trench, Trubner.

Solheim, Wilhelm G. 1973. "An Earlier Agricultural Revolution." Scientific American. 226:24-41.

Sorenson, John and Carl L. Johannessen. 2006. "Biological Evidence for Pre-Columbian Transoceanic Voyages." In Contact and Exchange in the Ancient World. ed. Victor H. Mair. University of Hawaii Press. 238 - 297.

Sorenson, John L. 2009. A Complex of Ritual and Ideology Shared by Mesoamerica and the Ancient Near East. In Sino-Platonic Papers. Vol 195.

Sorenson, John L. and Carl L. Johannessen. 2005. Scientific Evidence for Pre-Columbian Transoceanic Voyages to and from the Americas. Sino-Platonic Papers, No. 133, April 2004

Sorenson, John L. and Carl L. Johannessen. 2009. World Trade and Biological Exchanges Before 1492. Bloomington, IN:iUniverse.

Sorenson, John L. and Carl L. Johannessen. 2013. World Trade and Biological Exchanges Before 1492, Revised and Expanded Edition. Seattle, WA: Create Space.

Sorenson, John L. and Martin H. Raish. 1996. Pre-Columbian Contact with the Americas across the Oceans, an annotated bibliography. Second Edition, Revised. 2 volumes. Research Press, Provo, Utah.

Spier, Robert F.G. (1973). Material Culture and Technology. Basic Concepts in Anthropology Series. Minneapolis, MN: Burgess Publishing Company.

Stierlin, Henri. 2001. The Maya, Palaces and Pyramids of the Rainforest, Taschen GmbH, Hohenzoliernring, Cologne.

Storey, Alice A., José Miguel Ramírez, Daniel Quiroz, David V. Burley, David J. Addison, Richard Walter, Atholl J. Anderson, Terry L. Hunt, J. Stephen Athens, Leon Huynen, and Elizabeth A. Matisoo-Smith, 2007. "Radiocarbon and DNA evidence for a pre-Columbian introduction of Polynesian chickens to Chile," Proceedings of National Academy of Science, (PNAS) 2007 104: 10335-10339.

Strasser, T. F., Runnels, C., Wegmann, K., Panagopoulou, E., Mccoy, F., Digregorio, C., Karkanas, P. and Thompson, N. (2011), Dating Palaeolithic sites in southwestern Crete, Greece. Journal of Quaternary Science, 26: 553–560. doi:10.1002/jqs.1482

Stresemann, Erwin. 1940. "Die 'vor-columbischen' Truthähne in Schleswig," Ornithologische Monatsberichte No. 5: 154–9. (Berlin.)

Stringer, C. (2000). Palaeoanthropology: coasting out of Africa. Nature, 405(6782), 24-27.

Teeter, Wendy G. 2004. "Animal utilization in a growing city: vertebrate exploitation at Caracol, Belize." Maya zooarchaeology: new directions in method and theory. Monograph 51. Ed. Kitty F. Emery, Los Angeles, Cotsen Institute of Archaeology, University of California, Los Angeles. pp. 177-191.

Thompson, J. Eric S. (1966) The Rise and Fall of Maya Civilization. University of Oklahoma Press, Norman.

Tozzer, Alfred M. Landa's relacion de las cosas de Yucatan: A Translation. Harvard University, Peabody Museum of American Archaeology and Ethnology, Papers, Volume 18. (1941)

Tozzer, Alfred M. Landa's relacion de las cosas de Yucatan: A Translation. Harvard University, Peabody Museum of American Archaeology and

Ethnology, Papers, Volume 18. (1941)

Turner, Christy G., II. 2002. "Teeth, needles, dogs, and Siberia: bioarchaeological evidence for the colonization of the New World," Memoirs of the California Academy of Sciences 27: 123–58.

Tzolk'in. Wikipedia 7/01/2013. http://en.wikipedia.org/wiki/Tzolk'in Accessed 26 July 2013.

Varshavsky, S. R. 1961. "Appearance of American turkeys in Europe before Columbus," New World Antiquity 8(8): 104–5.

Venzmer, Gerhard. (1972) Five Thousand Years of Medicine. Trans Marion Koenig. New York: Taplinger Publishing Company. pp. 43-57.

Wiford, John Noble. On Crete, New Evidence of Very Ancient Mariners. The New York Times. February 16, 2010.

Wilhelm, O.E. (1978) "The Pre-Columbian Araucanian chicken (Gullus inauris) of the Mapuche Indians. In Advances in Andean Archaeology. ed. Browland, David L. Mouton Rouge, The Hague. pp. 189 –196.

Winters, Clyde A. 1986 "The Migration routes of the Proto-Mande", The Mankind Quarterly 27 (1), 77-96.

Winters, Clyde A. 1997 The Decipherment of Olmec Writing. Paper presented at the 74th meeting of the Central States Anthropological Society, Milwaukee, Wis.

Wolf, Eric R. 1959. Sons of the Shaking Earth. Chicago: The University of Chicago Press. 302 pp.

Xu, H. Mike. 1996. Origin of the Olmec Civilization, Edmond, Oklahoma, University of Central Oklahoma Press

Xu, Mike. 1998. La Venta offering no. 4: A revelation of Olmec writing? Pre-Columbiana 1:131-4.

Yarnell, Richard A. "Paleo-ethnobotany in America," Science and Archaeology: A Survey of Progress and Research, revised and enlarged edition. D. Brothwell and E. Higgs editors. New York: Praeger. (1971) pp. 215-227.

Yarnell, Richard A. "Paleo-ethnobotany in America," Science and Archaeology: A Survey of Progress and Research, revised and enlarged edition. D. Brothwell and E. Higgs editors. New York: Praeger. (1971) pp. 215-227

Zeder MA, Emshwiller E, Smith BD, and Bradley DG. 2006. Documenting domestication: the intersection of genetics and archaeology. Trends in Genetics 22(3):139-155.

.